Great
Family Vacations

DATE DUE

MR 17'98	JA 2 9'13		
DEC 3 0'98	JY 2 4'13		
AG 2 1'99	JY 3 1'13		
MY 3 1'05			
AP 2 0'06			
AG 0 7'07			
FE 1 1'09			
NOV 2 4'09			
JA 1 2'13			

DEMCO

Cover photo background: Bill Backman/©1996 PhotoDisc, Inc.
Cover inset photographs: Lori Adamski Peek/©Tony Stone Images; Ken Fisher/©Tony Stone Images; Jess Stock/©Tony Stone Images
Cover design by Schwartzman Design

Library of Congress Cataloging-in-Publication Data is Available.
ISBN 0-7627-0058-0

Manufactured in the United States of America
First Edition/First Printing

To my favorite traveling companions
Alissa, Matt, and David

Acknowledgments

I want to thank my editors, Mace Lewis and Bruce Markot, for their patience and my agent, Carol Mann, for her assistance. I appreciate the hard work of Robert Moll, assistant editor, Deirdre Fernandes, editorial assistant, and Carol Eannarino. I also want to thank Dorothy Jordon and Christine Loomis for their companionship on trips and for their support.

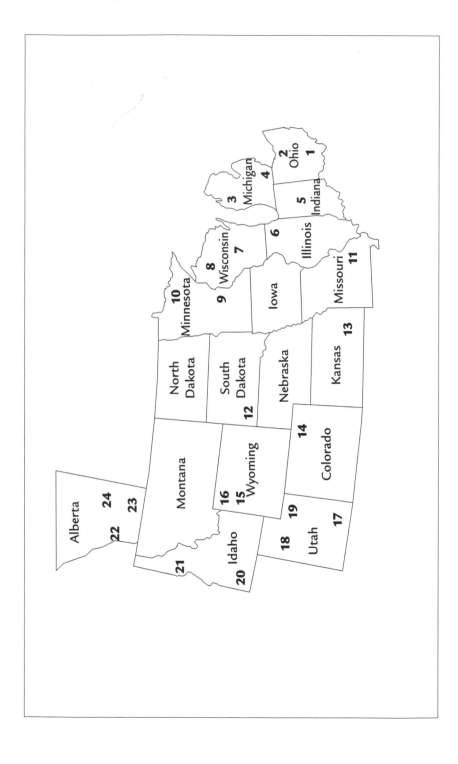

Contents

Introduction

There is a Chinese proverb that says the wise parent gives a child roots and wings. By traveling with your children you can bestow many gifts upon them: a strong sense of family bonds, memories that last a lifetime, and a joyful vision of the world.

Traveling with your children offers many bonuses for you and your family. These days no parent or child has an excessive amount of free time. Whether you work in the home or outside of it, your days are filled with meetings, deadlines, household errands, and carpool commitments. Your child most likely keeps equally busy with scouts, soccer, music lessons, computer clinics, basketball, and/or ballet. When your family stays home, your time together is likely to be limited to sharing quick dinners and overseeing homework. If there's a teen in your house, an age known for endless hours spent with friends, your encounters often shrink to swapping phone messages and car keys.

But take your child on the road with you, and both of you have plenty of time to talk and be together. Traveling together gives your family the luxury of becoming as expansive as the scenery. Over donuts in an airport lounge or dinner in a new hotel, you suddenly hear about that special science project or how it really felt to come in third in the swim meet. By sharing a drive along a country road or a visit to a city museum, your children get the space to view you as a person and not just as a parent.

Additionally, both you and your kids gain new perspectives on life. Children who spend time in a different locale, whether it's a national forest or a city new to them, expand their awareness. For you as a parent, traveling with your kids brings the added bonus of enabling you to see again with a child's eye. When you show a six-year-old a reconstructed Colonial village or share the stars in a Tennessee mountain night sky with a thirteen-year-old, you feel the world twinkle with as much possibility as when you first encountered these sites long ago.

Part of this excitement is a result of the exuberance kids bring, and part is from the instant friendships kids establish. Street vendors save their best deals for pre-schoolers, and, even on a crowded rush hour bus, a child by your side turns a fellow commuter from a stranger into a friend. Before your stop comes, you'll often be advised of the best toy shop in town and directed to a local cafe with a kid-pleasing menu at prices guaranteed to put a smile on your face.

New perspectives also come from the activities you participate in with your children. Most of these activities you would probably pass up when shuttling solo. Whether it's finding all the dogs in the paintings at the Metropolitan Museum of Art, going for a sleigh ride at a ski resort, or trying cross-country skiing in a park, you always learn more when you take your kids.

Surprisingly, traveling with your kids can also be cost-effective and practical. By combining or by extending a work-related trip into a vacation, you save money since your company picks up a good part of your expenses. Because tag-along tots on business trips are an increasing trend, several hotel chains have responded with a range of family-friendly amenities including children's programs, child-safe rooms, and milk and cookies at bedtime.

For all these reasons, traveling with your children presents many wonderful opportunities. It is a great adventure to be a parent, and it is made more wondrous when you travel with your children. You will not only take pleasure in each other's company, but you will return home with memories to savor for a lifetime.

Family Travel Tips

Great family vacations require careful planning and the cooperation of all family members. Before you go you need to think about such essentials as how to keep sibling fights to a minimum and how to be prepared for medical emergencies. While en route you want to be sure to make road trips and plane rides fun, even with a toddler. You want to be certain that the room that is awaiting your family is safe and that your family makes the most of being together. When visiting relatives, you want to eliminate friction by following the house rules. These tips, gathered from a host of families, go a long way toward making your trips good ones.

General Rules

1. Meet the needs of the youngest family member. Your raft trip won't be fun if you're constantly worried about your three-year-old being bumped overboard by the whitewater the tour operator failed to mention or if your first-grader gets bored with the day's itinerary of art museums.

2. Underplan. Your city adventure will dissolve in tears—yours and your toddler's—if you've scheduled too many sites and not enough time for the serendipitous. If your child delights in playing with the robots at the science museum, linger there and skip the afternoon's proposed visit to the history center.
3. Go for the green spaces. Seek out an area's parks. Pack a picnic lunch and take time to throw a Frisbee, play catch, or simply enjoy relaxing in the sun and people watching.
4. Enlist the cooperation of your kids by including them in the decision making. While family vacation voting is not quite a democracy, consider your kids' needs. Is there a way to combine your teen's desire to be near "the action" with your spouse's request for seclusion? Perhaps book a self-contained resort on a quiet beach that also features a nightspot.
5. Understand your rhythms of the road. Some families like traveling at night so that the kids sleep in the car or on the plane. Others avoid traveling during the evening cranky hours and prefer to leave early in the morning.
6. Plan to spend time alone with each of your children as well as with your spouse. Take a walk, write in a journal together, play ball, share ice cream in the snack shop, etc. Even the simplest of things done together create valuable family memories.

Don't Leave Home Without

1. *Emergency medical kit.* The first thing we always pack is the emergency medical kit, a bag I keep ready to go with all those things that suddenly become important at 3:00 A.M. This is no hour to be searching the streets for baby aspirin or Band-Aids. Make sure your kit includes items suitable for adults as well as children. Be sure to bring:
- aspirin or an aspirin substitute
- a thermometer
- cough syrup
- a decongestant
- medication to relieve diarrhea
- bandages and Band-Aids
- gauze pads
- antibiotic ointment and a physician-approved antibiotic

- a motion-sickness remedy
- sunscreen
- insect repellent
- ointments or spray to soothe sunburn, rashes, and poison ivy
- something to soothe insect stings
- any medications needed on a regular basis
- tweezers and a sterile needle to remove splinters

   Keep this kit with you in your carry-on luggage or on the front seat of your car.

2. *Snack food.* As soon as we land somewhere or pull up to a museum for a visit, my daughter wants food. Instead of arguing or wasting time and money on snacks, I carry granola bars with me. She munches on these reasonably nutritious snacks while we continue on schedule.

3. *Inflatable pillow and travel products.* Whether on the road or in a plane, these inflatable wonders help me and the kids sleep. For travel pillows plus an excellent variety of light yet durable travel products including hair dryers, luggage straps, alarms, adaptor plugs for electrical outlets, and clothing organizers, call Magellan's (800-962-4943). TravelSmith (800-950-1600) carries these items as well as clothing, mostly for teens and adults.

4. *Travel toys.* Kids don't have to be bored en route to your destination. Pack books, coloring games, and quiet toys. Some kids love story tapes on their personal cassette players. For innovative, custom-tailored travel kits full of magic pencil games, puzzles, and crafts for children three and a half or older, call Sealed With A Kiss (800-888-SWAK). The packages cost about $35. Surprise your kids with this once you are on the road. They'll be happy and so will you.

Flying with Tots

1. Book early for the seat you like. Whether you prefer the aisle, window, or bulkhead for extra legroom, reserve your seat well in advance of your departure date.

2. Call the airlines at least forty-eight hours ahead to order meals that you know your kids will eat: children's dinners, hamburger platters, salads, etc.

3. Bring food on board that you know your kids like even if you've ordered a special meal. If your kids won't eat what's served at meal

time, at least they won't be hungry if they munch on nutritious snacks.

4. Be sure to explain each step of the plane ride to little kids so that they will understand that the airplane's noises and shaking do not mean that a crash is imminent.

5. Stuff your carry-on with everything you might need (including medications, extra kids' clothes, diapers, baby food, formula, and bottles) to get you through a long flight and a delay of several hours . . . just in case.

6. Bring a child safety seat (a car seat) on board. Although presently the law allows children under two to fly free if they sit on a parent's lap, the Federal Aviation Administration and the Air Transport Association support legislation that would require all kids to be in child safety seats. In order to get a seat on board, the seat must have a visible label stating approval for air travel, and you must purchase a ticket for that seat. Without a ticket, you are not guaranteed a place to put this child safety seat in case the plane is full.

7. With a toddler or young child, wrap little surprises to give as "presents" throughout the flight. These work wonderfully well to keep a wee one's interest.

8. Before boarding, let your kids work off energy by walking around the airport lounge. Never let your child nap just before take-off—save the sleepy moments for the plane.

9. If you're traveling with a lot of luggage, check it curbside before parking your car. This eliminates the awkward trip from long-term parking loaded down with kids, luggage, car-seats, and strollers.

Road Rules

1. Use this time together to talk with your children. Tell them anecdotes about your childhood or create stories for the road together.

2. Put toys for each child in his or her own mesh bag. This way the toys are easily located and visible instead of being strewn all over the car.

3. Avoid long rides. Break the trip up by stopping every two or three hours for a snack or to find a rest room. This lets kids stretch their legs.

4. When driving for several days, plan to arrive at your destination each day by 4:00 or 5:00 P.M., so that the kids can enjoy a swim at the hotel/motel. This turns long hauls into easily realized goals that are fun.

At the Destination

1. When traveling with young children, do a safety check of the hotel room and the premises as soon as you arrive. Put matches, glasses, ashtrays, and small items out of reach. Note if stair and balcony railings are widely spaced or easily climbed by eager tots. Find out where the possible dangers are, and always keep track of your kids.

2. Schedule sightseeing for the morning, but plan to be back at the resort or hotel by early afternoon so that your child can enjoy the pool, the beach, miniature golf, or other kid-friendly facilities.

3. Plan to spend some time alone with each of your children every day. With pre-teens and teens, keep active by playing tennis or basketball, jogging, or doing something else to burn energy.

4. Establish an amount of money that your child can spend on souvenirs. Stick to this limit, but let your child decide what he or she wants to buy.

With Relatives

1. Find out the rules of your relatives' house before you arrive, and inform your kids of them. Let them know, for example, that food is allowed only in the kitchen or dining room so that they won't bring sandwiches into the guest bedroom or den.

2. Tell your relatives about your kids' eating preferences. Let the person doing the cooking know that fried chicken is fine, but that your kids won't touch liver even if it is prepared with the famous family recipe.

3. To lessen the extra work and expense for relatives and to help eliminate friction, bring along or offer to shop and pay for those special items that only your kids eat—a favorite brand of cereal, juice, frozen pizza, or microwave kids' meal.

4. Discuss meal hours. If you know, for example, that grandma and grandpa always dine at 7:00 P.M. but that your pre-schooler and first-grader can't wait that long, feed your kids earlier at their usual time, and enjoy an adult dinner with your relatives later.

5. Find something suitable for each generation that your kids and relatives will enjoy doing together. Look over old family albums, have teens tape record oral family histories, and have grade-schoolers take instant snapshots of the clan.

6. Find some way that your kids can help with the work of visiting. Even a nursery-school age child feels good about helping to clear a table or sweep the kitchen floor.

Family Travel Planners

These specialists can help you assess your family's needs and find the vacation that's best for you.

- *Family Travel Times.* This quarterly newsletter offers the latest information on hotels, resorts, city attractions, cruises, airlines, tours, and destinations. Contact Travel With Your Children, 40 Fifth Avenue, New York, NY 10011. For information call (212) 477-5524.

- **Rascals in Paradise.** Specializing in family and small-group tours to the Caribbean, Mexico, and the South Pacific, Rascals' tours sometimes include nannies for each family and an escort to organize activities for the kids. Call (800) U-RASCAL for more information.

- **Grandtravel.** This company offers a variety of domestic and international trips for grandparents and grandchildren 7 through 17. Call (800) 247-7651 for more information.

- **Grandvistas.** Depending upon bookings, this company offers a few trips to western locations. Call (800) 647-0800 for more information.

- **Families Welcome!** This agency offers travel packages for families in European cities and New York. Call (800) 326-0724 for more information.

- **Family Explorations.** Some of this company's departures feature Kids Counselors and special kids' activities. Trip destinations include Honduras, Costa Rica, Ecuador, and South Africa plus stateside getaways to Pennsylvania and Maine. For more information call (800) WE-GO-TOO.

The prices and rates listed in this guidebook were confirmed at press time. We recommend, however, that you call establishments before traveling to obtain current information.

 1 Ohio

COLUMBUS

Columbus will surprise you. The largest U.S. place named for the explorer, Columbus offers families a friendly and affordable urban destination within easy reach of the countryside. Among the finds are an impressive arts center, a high-technology, interactive children's science museum, and easy day trips that let you discover heartland history.

GETTING THERE

American, Continental, Delta, Midway, Trans World Airlines, and USAir offer international and domestic flights via Port Columbus International Airport; (614) 239-4000. Contact individual airlines for more information. **Port Express Shuttle,** 2509 Englewood Drive (614-476-3004 or 800-476-3994), transports visitors between Port Columbus International Airport and downtown Columbus.

Two major highways intersect in Columbus, making this city easy to reach. I-70 links the city with areas to the east and west. I-71 links Columbus with Cleveland the north and Cincinnati and other areas to the south. I-270 combines with I-670 to circle Columbus and its surrounding areas. The nearest **Amtrak** train (800-USA-RAIL) arrives in Cleveland. **Greyhound,** 111 East Town Street (614-221-5311 or 294-5100), provides bus service from Cleveland to Columbus.

GETTING AROUND

COTA (Central Ohio Transit Authority), 177 North High Street (614-228-1776), provides public bus transportation for the city. COTA offers normal and express fares, plus transfers for a minimal fee. Call ahead for information on routes, schedules, and hours of operation.

Columbus at a Glance

- Family friendly and affordable

- The German Village: historic houses, cobblestone streets, and parks for energetic kids

- A full-size replica of the *Santa Maria*

- Greater Columbus Convention and Visitors Bureau, (614) 221–CITY or (800) 345–4FUN

Several companies offer taxicab service, including the **Independent Taxicab Association of Columbus** (614–235–5551), the **Yellow Cab Company** (614–444–4444), and **Northway Taxicab Company** (614–299–1191).

WHAT TO SEE AND DO

Museums

Ohio's Center of Science & Industry, 280 East Broad Street; (614) 228–COSI. Called COSI for short, this first-rate, hands-on science museum is the place to take your young explorers. The adventure starts outdoors with the High Wire Cycle. When you ride this bicycle along wire suspended 20 feet above the ground, you not only feel like a circus performer, but you get a lesson in mass and balance.

The exhibit Toys and Games relates playthings to scientific principles. With the Kids Construction Company, learn how cranes and pulleys lift objects. At Catch the Wind test different sails for navigation, and at Roller Coaster find out why you experience the thrills without tumbling out. More not-to-miss highlights include Kidspace, a play area for preschoolers that features a computer whose touch-screen lets kids "fingerpaint," and a water area where the point is to get wet and wild with different toys.

At Familiespace the whole gang gets into the fun. Become an anchor and tape your own news show, make a music video, operate the toy trains, or simply be silly by trying on the dress-up costumes. Walk through the Old Time Street of Yesteryear, with its mock cobblestones, dry goods stores, and craftspeople, and be sure to browse the Cracker Jack Collection of more than 10,000 prizes. Yes, the prizes were really better then; it wasn't just that you were a wide-eyed kid happy at the thought of a plastic dinosaur, metal whistle, wooden top, or mini storybook.

Another nice touch: You can opt for valet parking. Instead of carrying tired kids back to the car, let the polite attendants bring your car to you, a welcome, small pleasure at the end of a busy touring day.

The Columbus Museum of Art, 480 East Broad Street; (614) 221-6801. The Sirak Collection, valued at $80 million, includes works of nineteenth- and twentieth-century European masters.

The museum is also known for its seventeenth-century Dutch and nineteenth-century French paintings and its collection of American art from 1850 through 1945. Don't miss the outdoor sculpture garden, an oasis with enough room for running. Kids like such works as *Streams,* a postmodern stainless-steel waterfall sculpture.

Allow time for the gift shop, which has the usual notecards and niceties, but also an interesting collection of jewelry by some local craftspeople.

Attractions

Columbus combines interestingly ethnic and all-American attractions. Columbus has The German Village—a restored area originally settled by German immigrants in the nineteenth century; it also has a major university and one of the largest state fairs in the country, held every August.

The German Village is a restored area of approximately 233 acres. It features brick homes built by German immigrants between 1840 and 1880 and offers cobblestone streets, boutiques, historic walks, and lots of bratwurst and beer. The sturdy, but small, houses, built by workers, often feature hand-carved lintels, clay chimney pots, wrought-iron fences, and small yards. Interestingly, the area is the largest privately funded restoration of its kind in the United States.

The Center of Science and Industry is a must-see when you visit Columbus.
(Courtesy Columbus Convention and Visitors Bureau)

Stop by the **Meeting Haus** of the German Village Society, 588 South Third Street (614-221-8888), for brochures on restaurants and bed and breakfast lodgings.

Another option is to buy a **Brick Tick,** which details a self-guided neighborhood tour that takes you by blocks of restored brick houses. If it's fall, plan on checking out the German Village's annual **Oktoberfest** (September); at Christmas there are tours of homes. June brings a **Haus Und Garten** tour, and August features a **Backyard Candelight Tour.**

For a time-out romp, stop by **Schiller Park,** bounded by Reinhard, City Park, Deshler, and Jaeger streets. It's a great green space in the heart of the village, perfect for the kids. In summer, come here for theater under the stars, usually two Shakespearean productions and one musical. Donations are requested.

In the **brewery district,** adjacent to the German Village, the former breweries are now beer gardens, offices, or shops. The **William Graystone Winery,** 544 South Fourth Street (614-228-2332), is housed in an 1875 brewery that's open for tastings, tours, and breakfast in the vault—a cozy space of limestone arched walls and wooden chairs. Even though your kids can't taste the wine, they'll like this winery. For a unique souvenir, take home the William Graystone wines; each bottle is graced with a scene or symbol of Columbus. For more information on the Brewery District, call (614) 241-2070.

Wexner Center for the Arts, the Ohio State University, North High Street at Fifteenth Avenue; (614) 292-0330 (building, offices, galleries) or 292-2354 (tickets). Part of the Ohio State University, the Wexner Center has four galleries, a film and video theater, two auditoriums, plus a smaller theater and fine arts library. Wexner's most active months are October through June. The center opens its galleries, performances, and screenings to the public. Traditionally, the galleries are closed on Mondays; call for operating hours and upcoming events. The center also features a good bookshop and a café

The **Ohio State University,** 30 West Fifteenth Avenue (614-292-0418), offers a free two-hour tour, which begins on the third floor of the Lincoln Tower, Monday–Friday 8:00 A.M.–5:00 P.M. Reservations are required for five or more.

Parks and Zoos

Battelle Riverfront Park and the Santa Maria. The Battelle Riverfront Park on the Scioto River waterfront near City Hall offers a pleasant bit of greenery. Its fountain, created especially for children, has a rim of stone slabs that are the perfect size for skipping along. This is a good place to bring a picnic lunch, rest, and enjoy the river view.

The area's main attraction is the *Santa Maria,* one of the more authentic, full-size replicas of Columbus's flagship. This one was built for the city's 1992 quincentennial celebration. On board you hear tales of a typical day at sea, find out why hot meals were rare (fear of fire) and where the crew slept (on deck), get a chance to ogle the signal cannons and touch the huge tiller, and find out why navigation was a shared responsibility (because there wasn't any way to see ahead and maneuver the tiller at the same time). Call (614) 645-8760.

Franklin Park Conservatory, in Franklin Park, 1777 East Broad Street; (614) 645-8733. At this indoor conservatory, stroll through acres of indoor gardens and several climate zones. Originally built in 1859, this facility was significantly enlarged for Ameriflora 92, the city's tribute to the Columbus quincentennial. The tiny and intricate bonsai plants, the tropical rain forest, and desert areas are kid favorites. Avoid strolling through the park, as this area has seen some crime.

The Columbus Zoo, 9990 Riverside Drive (614-645-3400), is actually located northwest of Columbus in Powell; it's off I-270 and Sawmill Road, exit 20. If your family loves animals, this is a worthwhile trip, especially in good weather. Consider combining this outing with a visit to Wyandot Lake Amusement Park. (See below.)

The Columbus Zoo, while offering a variety of animals plus a petting zoo for little ones, is a beautifully landscaped park known for its gorillas and cheetahs. Four generations of gorillas climb through the ropes of two adjacent yards. Sunshine, a muscular silverback gorilla, is a special crowd pleaser, especially when he shoves a head or two of lettuce into his mouth for lunch.

The walkway at the cheetah habitat literally gives you a unique perspective on these special cats. Peering down on them allows even preschoolers to get a good look at these sinewy animals stretched out on the grass. The Discovery Reef will eventually contain 300 to 400 species of fish and a wave machine to simulate the ocean's movements.

Hungry? Eat at **Wendy's,** one of the on-site restaurants. Columbus, after all, was the birthplace of this fast-food chain. One caution: The tram takes you around for an overview but doesn't let you get out to view the animals. For that, be prepared to walk. Strollers are available for rental.

The gift shop offers kids a good place to spend their allowance. Kids like the animal cards, T-shirts, books, and puzzles.

Wyandot Lake Amusement Park, 10101 Riverside Drive, is next to the Columbus Zoo; (614) 889-9283. Open May–September, your kids can cool off here with such wet thrills as a wave pool, water slides, and an inner-tube adventure that will take them through such "backcountry" scenery as a misty canyon, a waterfall, and a mill camp. Dry fun includes go-carts and miniature golf. There are locker and shower facilities.

Performing Arts

BalletMet, 322 Mt. Vernon Avenue (614-229-4860), performs a variety of classical to contemporary works, including a holiday favorite, *The Nutcracker.* **CAPA (Columbus Association of the Performing Arts),** 55 East State Street (614-469-0939), owns and operates the Ohio Theatre, 55 State Street, the Palace Theatre, 34 West Broad Street, and the Capitol Theater, 77 High Street, which traditionally attracts international jazz, pop, comedy, children's, folk, and classical entertainers. CAPA also offers a classic film series. Call (614) 469-1045 for information. **CATCO (Contemporary American Theater Company),** 512 North Park Street (614-461-0010), is a semiprofessional theater performing off-Broadway productions in an intimate 176-seat theater. The **Columbus Symphony Orchestra,** 55 East State Street, 5th Floor, (614-224-3291 for tickets or 224-5281), performs symphonic and pops concerts and has a series for children. **Opera/Columbus,** 50 West Broad Street (614-461-0022), is Columbus's opera company. Dress rehearsals, held on Tuesdays before opening night performances, are open to students and senior citizens at discounted admission. **The Wexner Center for the Arts,** Fifteenth and High streets (614-292-2354), presents a variety of contemporary groups and traditional concerts.

Ohio State, Capital, Otterbein, and **Ohio Wesleyan Universities** frequently hold theatrical, dance, and concert events. For information call OSU (614-292-2787), Capital (614-236-6801), Otterbein (614-898-1600), and Ohio Wesleyan (614-369-4431).

Ticketmaster (614-431-3600) has full-price tickets to theater, dance, concerts, and sporting events. Call for booth locations and hour of operation. For more information on the arts, contact the **Greater Columbus Arts Council** at (614) 224-2606.

SPECIAL EVENTS

Sports

Columbus Baseball Team, Inc., Columbus Clippers, 1155 West Mound Street; (614) 462-5250. The Clippers, the top farm club of the

New York Yankees, play AAA ball at Cooper Stadium, I-70 and Mound Street, from April through mid-September. **Columbus's Chill Hockey Team,** 1460 West Lane Road (614-488-4455), skates at the Fairgrounds Coliseum from November to March. **Columbus Crew,** a major league soccer team, plays at Ohio State University stadium. The city's professional women's basketball team, **Columbus Quest,** plays at the Greater Columbus Convention Center.

For golf enthusiasts, there's the **Memorial Tournament at Muirfield,** 5750 Memorial Drive, Dublin; (614) 889-6700. This Jack Nicklaus-designed course hosts the PGA for one stop of the tour during June. For college sports call the **Ohio State University Athletic Department,** 410 Woody Hayes Drive (614-292-2624), for information on all Buckeye sporting events.

Scioto Downs, 6000 High Street (614-491-2525), 2½ miles south of I-270, offers harness racing from May to September.

Festivals

Columbus's biggest festival is in August when the city goes "whole hog" for the **Ohio State Fair,** one of the city's most popular attractions and a tradition since 1848. This is a special treat for city kids, who may get their first chance to pet a cow, cheer at the pig races, ogle the huge butter sculptures, watch a tractor pull, and browse through buildings of agricultural exhibits. The midway, with its rides and games of chance and skill, may be unavoidable; to avoid nagging, set a limit ahead of time on how much money the kids can spend here.

The two-week fair also features nightly entertainment, free music concerts held twice a day, a free Kiddie Park, a quilt show, baking contests, crafts, a daily parade, and a petting zoo. For more information call the administrative offices; (614) 644-4000 or (800) BUCKEYE.

Additional festivals. **June:** The four-day Columbus Arts Festival features performances by the ballet and jazz groups, and the symphony. There's also a street fair with crafts and food. Especially for Kids offers two days of mime, music, puppets, and poets.

July: Celebrate the nation's birthday with food and festivities at Red, White and Boom! The Columbus Jazz and Rib Festival is an entire weekend of jazz music from the city, as well as the rest of the country, on three stages. Listen to the music while you enjoy the breeze from the riverfront.

August: Cruisin' on the Riverfront, a weekend of classic cars and food.

September: The German Village hosts its own Oktoberfest festival, which includes the Kinderplatz (Children's Place) with free kiddie rides and family entertainment. The **KidSpeak KidsFest** is a full day of free street performances, music and games at Franklin Park.

November: The Columbus International Festival, generally held at the Veteran's Memorial Hall, 300 West Broad Street, features the song, dance, arts, and food of more than fifty cultures, and usually special activities just for kids.

For more information, call (800) BUCKEYE.

WHERE TO STAY

Columbus offers a variety of lodging options in town and nearby. In town is **The Westin Hotel,** 310 South High Street (614–228–3800 or 800–328–2073), with a turn-of-the-century lobby and comfortable rooms. The **Hyatt on Capital Square,** 75 East State Street (614–228–1234 or 800–233–1234), is connected to the City Center and Ohio Theatre and is located across from the State Capitol. **Doubletree Guest Suites,** 50 South Front Street (614–228–4600), offers families extra space and in-room refrigerators. The **Crowne Plaza,** 33 Nationwide Boulevard (614–461–4100), is another family-friendly alternative.

Embassy Suites is near town at 2700 Corporate Exchange Drive (614–890–8600), located at I-270 and Cleveland Avenue. It offers suites, and indoor and outdoor pools. The **Worthington Inn,** 649 High Street, in nearby Worthington, began as a stagecoach stop in 1831 and now features twenty-six rooms decorated with Victorian furnishings, small inn hospitality, and full-service convenience. Not the least of the amenities at this four-star lodging is the regional American cuisine. The seared salmon wins acclaim as among the best in the city, as does the duck sausage. Try the sour apple tart for dessert. Rooms, which are oversized, include a continental breakfast.

Children are welcome. Kids twelve and under stay for free; (614) 885-2600.

WHERE TO EAT

Head for these restaurants in the German Village and in the Brewery District. **Schmidt's Sausage Haus und Restaurant,** 240 Kossuth Street; (614) 444-6808. Among the more famous eateries, this restaurant, open since 1886, offers steins of brew and an array of sausages. The place is noted for the Bahama Mama—a spicy sausage—plus good German potato salad, sauerkraut, and applesauce. If you're still hungry, try the huge cream puffs for dessert. Kids will like the accordion music and the festive air. Children are welcome at **Jeurgen's,** 525 South Fourth Street (614-224-6858), a German restaurant known for its excellent pastry and unusual varieties of pretzels. **The Engine House #5,** 121 East Thruman Avenue (614-443-4877), offers traditional seafood, pastas, and steaks, Your kids will like the ambience of the renovated firehouse. Come here to celebrate a birthday and watch the waiters slide down the firepole with a cake. Worth a visit if you have older children and teens, is **Handke's,** 520 South Front Street; (614) 621-2500. Noted chef Hartmut Handke offers such pleasing dishes as onion cream soup, grilled duck breast, and seared sea scallops.

Other Columbus eateries: **The Spaghetti Warehouse,** 397 West Broad Street (614-464-0143), serves pastas. **Morton's of Chicago,** 2 Nationwide Plaza, corner of Chestnut and High streets (614-464-4442), is more expensive but offers fine steaks and seafood; share your plate with the kids, as portions are large.

DAY TRIPS

Olentangy Indian Caverns and Ohio Frontier Land, 1779 Home Road, Delaware; (614) 548-7917. Only about one-half hour away, these caverns and a cave house museum are filled with Indian artifacts and geological displays. Open 9:30 A.M.–5:00 P.M. from April to October. Kids under seven are admitted for free.

Roscoe Village, 381 Hill Street, Coshocton; (614) 622-9310 or (800) 877-1830. The drive to Roscoe Village, about 90 miles from

Columbus, takes you through Coshocton County past farmland and fields. At the village, six restored nineteenth-century buildings are strung along two blocks and interspersed with nineteen shops, creating a sense of life circa 1830–1860, when the Ohio & Erie Canal brought goods, people, and prosperity to the area. Watch a blacksmith and a broom maker, tour the schoolhouse and the fashionable physician's residence, and browse the shops. Best bets include the duck carver, the basket maker, and the Johnson-Humrickhouse Museum, known for its collections of Oriental and Native American art.

Be sure to visit the **canal,** 2 miles away. From Memorial Day to Labor Day, barges pulled by draft horses take you along the canal as guides tell you anecdotes about the people and animals that made the trip. But in fall, allow time to walk the towpath. The brilliant foliage is a gift to the eye, and the soft peacefulness a welcome respite during any city tour.

Roscoe Village hosts a Gingerbread House Contest on the Fourth of July, a Gay 1890s Celebration in September, with banjo playing and barbershop quartets; and an Apple Butter Stirrin' Festival in October with demonstrations of rope making and chair caning, as well as hog-calling contests.

Roscoe Village has several bed and breakfasts, none of which welcome children, but the **Roscoe Village Inn** (614-622-2222 or 800-237-7397) welcomes children and has comfortable rooms and good food.

Hocking Valley Canoe Livery and Family Fun Center, 31251 Chieftain Drive, Logan; (614) 385–8685 or (800) 686–0386. Located about an hour outside of Columbus off U.S. 33 at Enterprise exit, this center offers canoe, kayak, raft, and go-cart rentals, miniature golf and a driving range, plus canoeing packages and tour of points of interest. Open April to October; reservations are required.

Sea World of Ohio, 1100 Sea World Drive, Aurora; (800) 63-SHAMU. It's two hours northeast of Columbus on Route 43, near I-271 and I-480 (Ohio Turnpike exit 13). Open mid-May–September, the center features ninety acres of marine life, entertainment, and a well-designed kids' play area—Shamu's Happy Harbor (named after one of Sea World's killer whales).

The Wilds, 14000 International Road; (614) 638–5030. This 10,000-acre preserve, a ninety-minute drive southeast of Columbus, is home to many endangered species from around the world.

FOR MORE INFORMATION

Ask for a copy of *Kids Connection* magazine, 572 City Park Avenue (614-224-3003), which lists items of interest to families. The magazine highlights hundreds of family-oriented programs. While some are geared to city residents, many are also of interest to visiting kids. **Ohio Council for International Visitors** (614-231-9610) offers translation services. **City of Columbus Construction Hotline;** (614-645-PAVE. For tourist information, contact the **Greater Columbus Convention and Visitors Bureau,** Monday–Friday 8:00 A.M.–5:00 P.M.; (614) 221-CITY or (800) 345-4FUN. When in town, stop by their Visitor Center on the second floor of the City Center shopping mall, 111 South Third Street. The hours are Monday–Saturday 10:00 A.M.–9:00 P.M., and Sunday noon–6:00 P.M. Visit the Ohio Internet site (http://www.travel.state.oh.us) or the Columbus website (http://www.columbuscvb.org).

Emergency Numbers
Ambulance, fire, police: 911
Children's Hospital, 700 Children's Drive; (614) 722-2000
Poison Control Center: (614) 228-1323
Police (nonemergency): (614) 645-4545
Twenty-four-hour pharmacy: Revco, 7660 Sawmill Road; (614) 889-5104

SANDUSKY AND THE LAKE ERIE ISLANDS

Often dubbed "Ohio's summer playground," Sandusky and the Lake Erie Islands offer lots of family finds. Sandusky has miles of lake shoreline for boating and bathing plus an old-fashioned amusement park with up-to-speed roller coasters. For island fun Great Lakes-style, visit the Lake Erie islands, especially Kelleys Island, and South Bass Island famed for Put-in-Bay. These islands gained significance in 1813 as the site of Commodore Perry's victory over the British in the War of 1812. But now the islands offer much more placid pleasures such as sunning, swimming, fishing, and bicycling, all at affordable prices.

GETTING THERE

The Cleveland-Hopkins International Airport (216–267–8282), about 65 miles from Sandusky, is the closest major airport to the area. Car rentals are available at the airport. **Amtrak** (800–USA–RAIL), arrives at Cleveland's main terminal, Ninth Street and Cleveland Memorial Shoreway. Amtrak also offers service to Sandusky. The schedule, however, is limited, and the station is not in a convenient area. Anyone taking a train directly to Sandusky should arrange for a ride beforehand. Also, there is no staff in the depot, so it is best to buy your return ticket before you leave; otherwise, you end up paying more for it on the train. **Greyhound/Trailways** (216–781–1400) offers daily bus service between Sandusky, 6513 Milan Road, and Cleveland, East Fifteenth Street and Chester Avenue.

Sandusky, Ohio, and the Lake Erie Islands at a Glance

- Sandy beaches and loads of water sports

- Prehistoric Indian mounds and petroglyphs

- Inland Seas Maritime Museum: nautical history of the Great Lakes

- Erie County Visitors and Convention Bureau, (419) 625-2984 or (800) 255-ERIE

To reach the Sandusky area by car, take the Ohio Turnpike, I-80, to exit 7 and follow U.S. 250 north to the Sandusky area. If you're heading to Port Clinton, take U.S. 250 and then follow Route 163 to the Port Clinton exit. Marblehead is off 269 east. To reach Catawba take Route 53 north from Route 2. Each of these towns has ferry service to the Lake Erie Islands. Catawba and Port Clinton have ferry service to South Bass Island. Marblehead serves Kelleys Island. (See Getting Around.)

GETTING AROUND

There are two things to remember when visiting the Lake Erie Islands: one, island hopping means living by the ferry schedule; two, don't think twice about leaving your car on the mainland. Getting around without an auto is easy and fun. Most of the islands offer bicycle and golf-cart rentals, and guided island tours. Walking is also great fun in good weather. Kelleys Island and Put-in-Bay also offer narrated tram services. If you're adamant about bringing your car, call ahead to reserve ferry space.

Miller Boat Line (410-285-2421) serves south Bass Island from Catawba Point. **Jet Express** (800-245-1JET) shuttles between South Bass (Put-In-Bay) and Port Clinton. **Sonny-S Ferry** (419-285-8774) serves Middle Bass from downtown Put-In-Bay with ferries departing on the hour. **Newman Boat Line** (419-798-5800 or 800-876-1907) and **Kelleys Island Ferry Boat Lines, Inc.** (419-798-9723 or 216-439-3555) both run boats between Kelleys Island and Marblehead. **Drawbridge Boatlines** (800-10-FERRY), which departs from Port Clinton, provides service to both islands.

If you're only in the Lake Erie Islands area for a day, take an island-hopping cruise aboard the *M/V City of Sandusky* (410-627-0198), which originates at the Jackson Street Pier in downtown Sandusky and stops at the Casino Docks in Kelleys Island, Put-In-Bay, Lonz Winery, and Middle Bass Island. **Emerald Island Express** offers seventeen different cruises weekly. They offer a variety of island-hopping, luncheon, and sunset-dinner cruises.

WHAT TO SEE AND DO

Sandusky Area

Combine two days in the Sandusky area with several days of island hopping for a sure-to-please, moderately priced family vacation that couples amusement park thrills with plenty of beach attractions.

Life's little ups and downs are lots of fun at **Cedar Point Amusement Park,** P.O. Box 5006, Sandusky (419-627-2350), situated on the 364-acre Lake Erie Peninsula. This 127-year-old amusement park, which debuted its first roller coaster in 1892, offers up-to-date excitement. Best known for its twelve roller coasters, the park bills itself as the largest ride park in the country, with 57 rides. (*Rides,* the promoters say, not *attractions* as in Disney World). Whether or not this phrase is a bit of hyperbole, the fact remains that there's lots to do here, and your kids won't be bored.

Thrill-seeker favorites include the Magnum XL200, one of the tallest and fastest coasters in the world, reaching heights of 205 feet and speeds of up to 72 miles per hour. The Mean Streak, a 161-foot-tall wooden wonder, has dips and drops calculated to make you shriek with delight. Snake River Falls, a log flume ride, rivals Disney World's Splash Mountain, hurtling passengers down a 50-degree, 80-foot slide at speeds close to 40 miles per hour.

Two of the newer rides in the park are the Ripcord and Mantis, a $12-million roller coaster. Ripcord combines the thrill of skydiving and bungee-jumping by launching riders from a 15-foot-tall tower. Tethered to a cable, the "flyers" free-fall to within 6 feet from the ground before swinging in a pendulum-like motion. Mantis features four upside-down inversions and one of the tallest vertical loops on any stand-up coaster. For some animal moments, drop by the Oceana Aquarium for dolphin and sea lion shows.

Importantly, this park also pleases preschoolers, especially tykes who love to listen to Berenstain Bears stories and tapes. This special bear family "lives" at Cedar Point's Berenstain Bear Country. Kids delight in sets taken from their favorite tales. Come inside the Bear Family Tree House, meet Papa, Mama, Sister, and Brother bear, play at the Berry Bush Island clubhouse, and sit at the desks the bears use in "Berenstain Bears Go To School." Your little ones will be charmed. Other pint-size attractions at the park include Kid Arthur's Court, KiddyKingdom, and the Gemini Children's area with its junior-size roller coaster.

Admission to Cedar Point goes by height. Persons over 54 inches tall pay adult fare.

You're not finished yet. The adjacent Challenge Park keeps kids busy with go-carts, miniature golf, and Soak City's ten water slides. There are four new ways to get wet at Soak City. The water park has added six and a half acres of pools—including a 500,000-gallon wave pool. There are three more slide for inner-tubers to enjoy, and a swim-up bar for adults. Tadpole Town and Choo-choo Lagoon are both great for younger children. Cedar Point's accommodations include the Hotel Breakers, a turn-of-the-century landmark property, as well as campsites. (See Where to Stay.) Details are available at the Cedar Point Internet site: http://www.cedarpoint.com.

If you can get your kids out of the water, and off the roller coasters, take them to **African Safari Wildlife Park,** 267 Lightner Road, Port Clinton; (419) 732–3606 or (800) 521–2660. At this drive-through safari, you see tropical birds and camels outside your window. Kids get close to the animals with camel and pony rides, and a Turtle Taxi service (bring the cameras). At the pig races, root for your favorite porker. Let the wee ones work off some energy at the Jungle Junction playground.

Were carousels a part of your childhood, and did calliope music always signal a good time? Share the pleasures with your kids at the

The whole family can take a spin on the Cadillac Cars at Ceader Point amusement park in Sundusky, Ohio. (Photo by Dan Fetcht/courtesy Ceader Point Image Library)

Merry-Go-Round Museum, corner of Jackson and Washington streets, Sandusky; (419) 626-6111. Take a spin on a merry-go-round and browse the carved animals, some caught in midprance. Check the schedule for carving demonstrations and hours.

The **Inland Seas Maritime Museum,** 480 Main Street, Vermillion (216-967-3467), details the nautical history of the Great Lakes. Step into the pilot house of a simulated 400-foot bulk-carrier ship, and view models, paintings, and photographs. Find out about some of the 10,000 vessels that were lost on the Great Lakes waters, from Sieur de la Salle's *Griffin,* which set sail in 1679 in search of furs, to the *Edmund Fitzgerald,* which sank nearly 300 years later.

The **Milan Historical Museum,** 210 Edison Drive, Milan; (419) 499-2968. This complex of six buildings takes you back to the nineteenth century. In the 1843 dwelling, once owned by Robert Sayles, see pressed glass, china, and doll collections. Other buildings to browse include a country store and blacksmith shop. It's open April through October.

Historic Lyme Village, Route 113, Bellevue (410–483–6052 or 419–483–4949), offers more nineteenth-century history. Tour restored homes, barns, shops, a post office, an 1880s mansion that serves as the village museum, a schoolhouse, and a general store. Call ahead for a listing of seasonal events, activities, and festivals. Guided tours of the village are available Tuesdays through Sundays June through August; and Sundays only May and September. The rest of the year tours are by appointment only.

Lake Erie Islands

For top walleye fishing and hours of sailing, visit **Kelleys Island and South Bass Island,** two of the most popular Lake Erie Islands.

Kelleys Island

Less than 5 miles from Ohio's Lake Erie shore, **Kelleys Island** offers beaches, natural areas, and interesting archaeological sites. Busy in summer, but not bustling, the island's year-round (winter) population hovers at about 200. To find out what's happening, pick up a copy of the *Kelleys Island Funfinder* when you arrive.

Summer vacationers began arriving at this 2,800-acre island, the largest American island in Lake Erie, by steamer in the 1830s, and guests have been coming ever since. On Kelleys combine a beach vacation with a bit of archaeological history. Take your kids to the prehistoric Indian mounds and petroglyphs, some of which date back to 12,000 B.C., while others portray Native American cultures. **Inscription Rock,** a large boulder on the south shore, is famous as having the most extensive and best-preserved prehistoric Indian pictographs in the United States. The animals, birds, and men that appear on **Inscription Rock** were created by Erie Indians between 300 and 400 years ago. The inscriptions, however, have not been well preserved and are difficult to see.

The Glacial Grooves State Memorial, on the north shore, offers another not-to-miss archaeological site. Among the finest glacial markings in the United States, this 400-foot-long trough, with its fossilized marine life, was pressed into Kelley's limestone during the Pleistocene Ice Age. **Kelleys Island State Park,** 661 acres, offers miles of hiking trails, relatively uncrowded beaches, campsites, and nature programs. Children may also enjoy searching for fossils throughout the island, especially along the trail that winds through an abandoned quarry.

The **Lake Erie Toy Museum;** (419) 746-2451, open Memorial Day through Labor Day, features more than 1,000 American and foreign toys dating from 1865 to 1980. Visitors can also stroll through the Butterfly Box, a garden where you can spot hundreds of butterfly varieties.

South Bass Island—Put-in-Bay

More developed than Kelleys Island, **Put-In-Bay,** on South Bass Island, features beaches, wineries, fish hatcheries, shopping, restaurants, and pubs. A bustling beach area, Put-In-Bay is famed for its tactical role in the Battle of Lake Erie, the War of 1812. On September 10, 1813, Commodore Oliver Hazard Perry and his troops sought much-needed shelter in Put-In-Bay. Here they rested before successfully battling the British. After winning, Perry sent his now famous message to General William Harrison: "We have met the enemy and they are ours." Today, the 352-foot **Perry's Victory and International Peace Memorial** stands in Put-In-Bay as a reminder of this historic event. The view from the top of the monument is one of the best in the area.

Near Perry's Memorial is a popular beach, called simply **Bathing Beach. Stone Beach,** part of **South Bass Island State Park** (419-285-2112), on the island's northwest, may be less crowded.

For some off-the-beach fun tour the **Heineman's Winery,** Catawba Avenue; (419) 285-2811. Afterward, taste the wine or sample nonalcoholic grape juice Even if your kids aren't excited by looking at crushers and storage tanks, they'll probably like the tour of **Crystal Cave,** included with admission to the winery. Inside, you see a giant geode discovered in 1897, whose largest crystal weighs about 300 pounds, and measures 2 feet in length and 1½ feet in width. The cave is open from mid-May through late September. For more cave sites go underground at **Perry's Cave,** 979 Catawba Avenue (419-285-2405), to see stalactites and stalagmites.

For above-ground tours little kids especially like a ride on the **Put-In-Bay Tour Train** (419-285-4855), whose one-hour narrated tour gives an island overview. What's also nice for families: for the same price, you can get on and off at different stops, which include all the island highlights—Heineman's Winery, Crystal Cafe, Perry's Cave, and Perry's Memorial. Beginning in late May, the tram runs all week during the summer months from 10:00 A.M. to 5:00 P.M. From September through October the tram will run on weekends only, 10:00–5:00. Children under six are free.

Another special ride is a spin on **Kimberly's Carousel,** Delaware Avenue, adjacent to the Carriage House, a children's clothing store. This restored 1917 carousel has thirty-six menagerie animals and a Wurlitzer organ. George Stoiber, a local businessman, bought the carousel in 1976, named it for his daughter, and spent eight years restoring this gem.

Shopping

On the mainland, near Sandusky, stop at the **Lake Erie Factory Outlet Center,** U.S. 250, ½ mile north of Ohio Turnpike exit 7 (419–499–2528). Scores of shops here advertise savings of 30–70 percent. As always with factory outlets, the quality and the price vary, but with a quick eye and some luck you could come away with bargains on brand-name clothing, housewares, and toys.

Performing Arts

On the Marblehead peninsula **Lakeside Associations,** 236 Walnut, Lakeside (419–798–4461), each summer organizes a series of summer performances in the well-preserved Victorian town of Lakeside. In the past these have included ballet, folk music, international puppetry groups, acrobats, the Lakeside Symphony, and Shakespearean productions. **The Huron Playhouse,** Ohio Street, Huron; (419) 433–4744. Ohio's oldest summer-stock theater offers performances Tuesdays through Saturdays, July through mid-August. Huron is a few miles east of Sandusky off U.S. 6. The **State Theatre,** 107 Columbus Avenue, Sandusky (419–626–3945), hosts concert pianists, ballet groups, drama, and popular musical groups. The **Playmakers Civic Theater,** Port Clinton (419–734–9089), also hosts plays.

SPECIAL EVENTS

From May throughout September **Port Clinton** hosts the Summer Jazz program every Sunday at the Mon Ami Restaurant and Winery. Call (800) 441–1271 to find out who will be performing.

April: Kelleys Island hosts a "Welcome Back" fish fry. Performance of a children's play at the Huron campus of Bowling Green State University.

May: Bed and Breakfast Tour of Kelleys Island. Port Clinton hosts its Walleye Festival at the Water Works Park.

June: Marblehead Lighthouse Tour, Marblehead. Tour of Homes and Bicycle Rally, Kelleys Island.

July: Fireworks at Lakeside, Port Clinton and Put-In-Bay. Also at Put-In-Bay is the Amish Quilt Festival. Kelleys Island Islandfest.

August: Clam Bake at Kelleys Island. Croquet Tournament, Kelleys Island.

September: Celebrate the Battle of Lake Erie during Put-In-Bay's historical weekend.

October: Oktoberfest, Put-In-Bay.

WHERE TO STAY

Sandusky Area

Adjacent to the Cedar Point Amusement Park are two lodgings. The **Sandcastle Suites Hotel,** Cedar Point, P.O. Box 5006 (419–627–2107), offers two-room suites. Take a breather from the park to play tennis or lounge on Sandcastle's beach on the shores of Lake Erie. Sandcastle Suites offers shuttle service between the park and the hotel. For those who like historic properties and grande-dame hotels, there's the **Hotel Breakers,** Cedar Point, P.O. Box 5006 (410–627–2106). This landmark property has 418 rooms, some stained-glass windows, lots of wicker, and dates to 1905. Impress your kids by telling them that former guests included Annie Oakley, Abbott and Costello, and John Philip Sousa. "Who?" they'll ask, but then you have something to talk about over lunch. The hotel has an ice-cream parlor, a swimming pool, and a beach, three kid-pleasing places.

Other possibilities include the **Holiday Inn, Sandusky,** 5313 Milan Road (419–626–6671 or 800–465–4329), which features an indoor pool and miniature golf. **The Econo Lodge,** U.S. 6, 1904 Cleveland Road (419–627–8000 or 800–424–4777), is a less-costly alternative and is across from the entrance to Cedar Point. **Camper Village,** also part of the Cedar Point complex, Cedar Point (419–627–2106), is a recreational vehicle campground with more than 400 sites. Each area has picnic tables, grills, electricity, water, showers, laundromat, and supply store.

Sawmill Creek Resort, off Route 13 North, Huron (419-433-3800), offers resort amenities within a reasonable drive of Cedar Point. With an eighteen-hole golf course, indoor and outdoor swimming pools, saunas, three restaurants, whirlpool, exercise room, tennis courts, gift shop, and marina docks, Sawmill has plenty to offer the family traveling with kids.

Kelleys Island

Kelleys Island has a number of bed and breakfast inns that more often than not prefer couples or families with older children. If you want to stay at a bed and breakfast, look in the *Kelleys Island Funfinder* for a list. Be candid about the ages of your children to be certain that your kids will feel comfortable at these properties.

More suitable family-friendly accommodations include **Sunrise Point,** P.O. Box 431 (419) 746-2543 or (419) 626-8779. They offer one-bedroom units and lakefront efficiencies, plus a play area for kids. **Chalet East Apartments,** P.O. Box 512 (419-746-2335 in summer or 813-624-3811) offers one- and two-bedroom suites with kitchens. A number of private homes are for rent as well. **Lake-Woods Edge** is on the lakefront. Contact the owner at 1036 Jeff Ryan Drive, Herndon, Virginia 22070; (703) 435-6635. For the most up-to-date listings, obtain a copy of *Kelleys Island Funfinder.*

Put-In-Bay

Accommodations in the Put-In-Bay area include motels, resorts, hotels, and cottages. **Saunder's Resort,** Catawba Avenue (419-285-3917), offers fully furnished cottages a mile from downtown. The complex includes a pool as well as tennis, badminton, and shuffleboard courts. The **Perry Holiday,** 99 Concord Avenue (419-285-2107), has thirty-three rooms, each with a private bathroom, air-conditioning, and color television. One block from downtown, their facilities include a pool, laundry, picnic tables, and grills. **East Point Cottages,** Massie Lane (419-285-2204) offers eight furnished cottages from May through October for rental. Each cottage has its own kitchen. Fishing licenses, tackle, and bait are available at the cottages.

For more accommodations information, contact the **Ottawa County Visitors Bureau,** 109 Madison, Port Clinton, Ohio 43452; (419) 734-4FUN or (800) 441-1271. Also contact the **Sandusky/Erie County Visitors & Convention Bureau,** P.O. Box 1639, Sandusky, Ohio; (419) 625-2984 or (800) 255-ERIE.

WHERE TO EAT

Your kids may even come away from a vacation at Sandusky and the islands liking fish. At least have them taste the local specialties of Lake Erie perch and walleye.

The Sandusky Area

In Port Clinton, try **Mon Ami Restaurant and Historic Winery,** 2845 East Wine Cellar Road; (419) 797-4445 or (800) 777-4266. Mon Ami serves perch, walleye, and Italian specialties. Just outside the Cedar Point Amusement Park, the **Breakwater Cafe,** Cedar Point, Sandusky (419-626-0830), is a casual restaurant serving up a range of good eats from walleye to fajitas. **Damon's** in Battery Park (419-627-2424), offers great food and a 360-degree view of Sandusky Bay and Cedar Point, including the roller-coaster skyline. Take your older children to the **Tea Rose Tearoom,** 218 East Washington Street (419-627-2773), for afternoon tea and a reading of the tea leaves.

Kelleys Island

Head to the **Village Pump,** Water Street; (419) 746-2281. Here, the locals recommend the roast beef sandwiches, the hand-dipped onion rings, and the Lake Erie perch. The **Casino,** on the lakeshore off Lakeshore Drive (419-746-2773), has weekend entertainment and is known for its barbecued ribs, perch, and clam chowder. Sample wines made from a hybrid of European varieties and an interesting selection of pasta and cheeses at the **Kelleys Island Wine Tasting Room and Gourmet Bistro;** (419) 746-2537. Close to the ferry docks and the downtown area, the bistro has a child's play area as well as an area for horseshoes and volleyball.

Put-In-Bay

The Boardwalk, downtown Put-In-Bay (419-285-3695), is the island's only waterfront restaurant. The food ranges from seafood to tacos to pizza. **The Village Bakery and Sandwich Shoppe,** at the Depot (419-285-5351), offers a variety of inexpensive choices and light meals. The **Bay Burger,** Village Center (419-285-6192), pleases kids with burgers and milk shakes. Try to get the tykes to try the walleye sandwiches. **The Snack House,** Delaware Avenue (419-285-4595), features homemade ice cream.

DAY TRIPS

For an interesting trip while visiting Lake Erie Area, consider **Maumee Bay State Park,** 1750 Park Road #2, off I-280, 10 miles east of downtown Toledo in Oregon, Ohio, a great spot for fishing on Lake Erie. Aside from fishing the park offers golf, swimming, hunting, cross-country skiing (seasonally), a nature center, and lodging. Call (419) 836-1466.

Also consider **Sea World of Ohio,** 1100 Sea World Drive, Aurora, Ohio (216-562-8101), which is thirty minutes southeast of Cleveland. See Shamu the killer whale in **Shamu's Happy Harbor,** a three-acre Caribbean-theme area, and thirteen "sea monsters and dinosaurs" at **Monster Marsh,** plus twenty geographically themed aquariums featuring a variety of sea life.

Teenagers and parents alike might be interested in the **Rock 'n' Roll Hall of Fame** in Cleveland.

Combine a visit to Sandusky and the Lake Erie Islands with a stay in Columbus, about 105 miles away (see the Columbus chapter) or Indianapolis, about 245 miles away (see the Indianapolis chapter).

FOR MORE INFORMATION

Contact the **Ottawa County Visitors Bureau** for information concerning the Port Clinton/Put-In-Bay area, 109 Madison Street, Suite E, Port Clinton, Ohio; (800) 441-1271; Internet: http://www.lakeerie.com. If you're looking for more information on the Sandusky/Kelleys Lake/ Bass Islands area, contact **Erie County Visitors and Convention**

Bureau, 231 West Washington Row, Sandusky, Ohio; (419) 625-2984 or (800) 255-ERIE; Internet: http://www.sanduskyohio.com. Or visit the state Internet site: http://www.travel.state.oh.us.

Emergency Numbers
Ambulance, fire, and police: 911

There are no hospitals on Kelleys or South Bass Islands. For hospitals with emergency facilities, try **Firelands Community Hospital,** 1101 Decatur Street, Sandusky (419-626-7400) or **Providence Hospital,** 1912 Hayes Avenue, Sandusky (419-621-7000). Port Clinton does have a hospital, the **Magruder Hospital,** 615 Fulton Street, Port Clinton; (419) 734-3131.

Poison Control: (419) 626-7423

Twenty-four pharmacy: Refer to the hospital emergency room facilities listed above. **Rite Aid Discount Pharmacy** has stores in Port Clinton and the Sandusky area, including one located at 220 Columbus Avenue, Sandusky; (419) 625-3801. Also located in Sandusky: **Discount Drug Mart,** 124 East Perkins Avenue; (419) 625-0733.

GRAND TRAVERSE AREA

Along with being the "Cherry Capital of the World," the Traverse City, Michigan, area is known as a "Great Lakes Paradise." This city of 17,000—the largest in Northwest Lower Michigan—is blessed by a superb location at the head of Grand Traverse Bay on Lake Michigan's northern shore. Grand Traverse County has a population of 70,000. (The bay is separated into east and west sections by the scenic Old Mission Peninsula.) Situated on the 45th parallel, halfway between the equator and the North Pole, the area has four distinct seasons. Summers offer miles of beaches, fabulous freshwater fishing, and countless recreational possibilities. Winter's bountiful snows bring cross-country and downhill skiing, snowmobiling, sledding, and skating. Add fall's spectacular foliage and abundant fruit harvests and spring's white and pink cherry blossoms, and you'll see why families come back season after season, year after year.

GETTING THERE

The area is easily accessible by car via state highways. Traverse City's Cherry Capital Airport (616-947-2250) is serviced by several national and regional carriers. Hertz and Avis car rental agencies are at the airport; others are in town.

Taxis and **BATA (Bay Area Transportation Authority)** bus service (616-941-2324) are also available. **Greyhound** buses (616-946-5180) link Traverse City to the Upper Peninsula and southern Michigan. There's no train service to this area.

GETTING AROUND

Although there are buses, taxicabs, and limousine services, it is quickest and easiest to have a car.

WHAT TO SEE AND DO

Museums and Zoos

Dennos Museum Center, 1701 East Front Street, Traverse City; (616) 922-1055. Located at the campus entrance of Northwestern Michigan College, this spacious museum's motto is Come Alive Inside. The Discovery Gallery's hands-on exhibits will tickle the fancy of any age. Among them: an antigravity mirror that gives you the illusion of floating, and Recollections II, a video experience that transforms a child's movements into delayed motion, multicolored images. Unique to the museum is Weiss Wall I (named after its creator, Detroit area artist and musician Ed Weiss), with multicolored wood panels that produce different sounds when touched: percussion, synthesizer, and even "rap." Older kids also like the museum's extensive collection of Inuit Eskimo Art, considered one of the country's most complete. The graceful *Dancing Bear* sculpture at the entrance is a charmer, and the *Enchanted Owl* print by a master artisan appeared on a Canadian postage stamp. There's also a sculpture court and galleries with traveling exhibitions. Open daily to 5:00 P.M. plus summer evenings.

The Music House, 7377 U.S. 31 North, Acme (about 6 miles east of Traverse City); (616) 938-9300. Automated instruments, including music boxes, nickelodeons, and a vintage hand-carved Belgian dance organ, are displayed in a nineteenth-century farm complex. Guided tours last about ninety minutes.

Clinch Park Zoo, Grandview Parkway at Cass, Traverse City; (616) 922-4906. Northern Michigan wildlife such as bear, otters, bison, and beavers; an aquarium with native game fish, including trout and perch; a beach; and a miniature steam-train ride make this stop a hit with kids.

Grand Traverse Lighthouse Museum, Leelanau State Park, CR-629, Northport; (616) 386-7553. This lighthouse, on the tip of the Leelanau Peninsula, is one of the oldest on the Great Lakes and has

---

Grand Traverse Area at a Glance

- Relaxed fun in the Cherry Capital of the World

- Beaches at Sleeping Bear Dunes National Lakeshore

- Wintertime sports galore

- Cruise on the tall ship *Malabar*

- Traverse City Convention and Visitors Bureau, (616) 947–1120 or (800) TRAVERS

---

recently been turned into a living-history museum. Relive nautical history by touring the tower that looks to Lake Michigan, and the museum where a Fourth Order Fresnel lens is displayed.

City Opera House, 112½ East Front Street, Traverse City; (616) 922–2070. If you're downtown and want to break from shopping, this 1891 Victorian opera house is quite impressive. Unfortunately, there is no tour, but visitors will still be able to appreciate the vaulted ceiling, gilded gold molding around the stage, and elaborate murals.

Listed on the National and State Registers of Historic Sites is the tall ship *Malabar,* 13390 West Bay Shore Drive; (800) 678–0383. Become an "old salt" for the day aboard this replica of an eighteenth-century topsail, gaft-rigged sailing vessel. Three two-hour cruises lap the bay daily.

More Attractions

Amon Orchards and Farm Market, U.S. 31 North, Acme; (616) 938–9160/(800) 937–1644. Orchard tours include a See It Made Kitchen, where goodies such as cherry butter are concocted. You can buy cherry mustard and pick your own fruit. Young children like the petting farm. Kids love it here! Closed November–April.

Candle Factory, Grandview Parkway, Traverse City; (616) 946–2280. This leading retailer features candle-making demonstrations at various times daily.

Pirates Cove/Adventure Golf, U.S. 31 North, Traverse City; (616) 938-9599. Sunken treasure and challenging minigolf.

River Country Funland, U.S. 31 North, Traverse City; (616) 946-6663. A kids' paradise, with miniature golf, go-carts, bumper boats, a water slide, and more.

Beaches and Parks

With 250 miles of Lake Michigan shoreline, beaches are the big summer attraction here. All have free public access, and the following particularly appeal to families. Take the kids beachcombing for Petroskey stones—gray hexagonal-patterned petrified coral. (If you don't find any, they're sold in local gift shops.)

East Bay: The majority of hotels and motels are located here, on a strip of beach called the Miracle Mile, or across the street.

West Bay: Bryant Park, at the foot of Garfield, is the area's best for families with young children; kids can safely wade in the shallow water. There's also a picnic area, large playground, and rest rooms. Clinch Park, on Grandview Parkway at Cass, (see previous zoo listing) is also popular, with more than 1,500 feet of sandy beach plus rest rooms and concessions. Because of the boats in the area, however, this is best for families with teens. Elmwood Township Park, off M-22, a mile north of the M-72 junction, is another family favorite, with playground and rest rooms.

Kids Kove, on the grounds of the Grand Traverse County Civic Center, is a guaranteed good time for younger kids. It's a 15,000-square-foot play structure designed by area school kids and includes mazes, a play lighthouse, swings, slides, and other traditional playground equipment. There's also a jogging track that loops around the Civic Center.

Sleeping Bear Dunes National Lakeshore: If you only have a short time in this area, start out early and spend the day at Sleeping Bear Dunes National Lakeshore, about 30 miles west, which includes 33 miles of Lake Michigan shoreline dotted with beaches. The one at North Bear Lake, central park area, reportedly has the warmest water. According to the Chippewa Indian legend that gave the park its name, a mother bear and her cubs swam across Lake Michigan to escape a forest fire. The mother waited on shore for her cubs, who lagged behind. It's said she still keeps watch in the form of a large, dark hill of sand, while her cubs became the North and South Manitou Islands.

The park boasts large dunes, deposits left by melting glaciers some 11,000 years ago, that rise more than 400 feet above Lake Michigan. If your kids are old—and adventurous—enough, you can try the Dune Climb, 5 miles north of Empire on M–109. The Platte River, on the southern end, and Crystal River, on the north, with adjacent lakes, provide ideal fishing and canoeing. Rentals are available from Crystal River Canoes; (616) 334–3090. Thirty-five miles of marked trails are set aside for hiking and cross-country skiing. At the Coast Guard's Historic Maritime Museum, 1 mile west of Glen Haven, displays relate the area's maritime history. The 7.1-mile Pierce Stocking Scenic Drive (open mid-May through early November) offers scenic views of the dunes, Lake Michigan, and the offshore Manitou Islands. (See Day Trips.) There are two campgrounds: one in Glen Arbor (616–334–4634), without showers; the other in Honor (616–325–5881), with them. The park is open in winter for cross-country skiing and snowshoeing. Stop at Philip Hart Visitor Center in Empire, at the center of the park, for brochures and slide shows; (616) 326–5134.

Ski Areas

These destination resorts close to Traverse City entice families with a variety of children's programs, affordable packages, and après-ski fun. Since most are open year-round, these resorts also make great warm-weather destinations, offering mountain biking, golf, tennis, and other summer recreation. Always inquire about packages when you call. In addition, the Traverse City Convention and Visitors Bureau lists public downhill and cross-country trails.

Crystal Mountain, M–115, Thompsonville; (616) 378–2000/ (800) 968–7686. This year-round resort, 28 miles southwest of Traverse City, offers summer and winter kids' programs, twenty-three slopes, and more than 16 miles of cross-country ski trails; plus mountain biking, tennis, golf, indoor/outdoor pools, and a fitness center. Stay in motel units, condos, or resort homes. During the winter there's a nursery for newborns to age three; nursery and skiing for potty-trained toddlers through age five; and a ski program for ages five to ten. Summers bring programs for ages three to ten or twelve, three days and evenings weekly, plus three weekly overnight camps for ages seven or eight through teens.

The Homestead, Wood Ridge Road, Glen Arbor; (616) 334–5000. In a scenic setting 25 miles west of Traverse City, this resort is open winter weekends and all summer. It offers downhill skiing from high above Lake Michigan, cross-country skiing into Sleeping Bear National Lakeshore, skating, and snowshoeing. You'll also find a game room, shops, and kids' programs, including child care for ages three to eight and ski instruction for ages three to five and five to twelve. Munchin' Movies are held Saturday evenings and holidays for ages three to twelve. The Homestead offers a wide variety of price ranges and packages for lodge rooms, suites, and condos.

Shanty Creek/Schuss Mountain Resort, Bellaire; (616) 533–8621/(800) 678–4111. Located 38 miles from Traverse City, this resort offers two ski areas, $3^1/2$ miles apart, but connected by a free shuttle. Summit Village is primarily for beginners and intermediates; Schuss Village, with a greater vertical drop, has terrain for beginner to expert. Snow Stars (ages three to five) and Kids Academy (ages five to eleven) teach youngsters the joy of skiing. Lodging at this all-season resort is in 600 rooms, suites, and condos. Ice skating, horse-drawn sleigh rides, indoor/outdoor pools, tennis, and a beach club round out the fun.

Sugar Loaf, Cedar Loaf; (616) 228–5461/(800 968–0574. This resort, 18 miles northwest of Traverse City, has slopes ranging from gentle beginners to steep terrain. Ski schools teach children age three and ages four to twelve. Look for midweek packages and special weeks where kids sleep, ski, and eat free. Slopeside lodging in hotel rooms, town houses, or condos. The resort opens in the summer when golf is the big attraction.

Golf

Traverse City is called "Michigan's Golf Coast," with dozens of courses throughout the area. The natural landscape of the area—the roll of the land, the dunes, the brooks, and water views—makes this an ideal area for golf courses. It has certainly brought pros—Jack Nicklaus, Arnold Palmer, Tom Doak, and Jerry Matthews—to Traverse City to design courses. Most of the architects have allowed the natural terrain to dictate the shape of the course.

Most of the courses are on resorts, but it is not necessary to be a guest to use their facilities. And for those just starting out, most of the following are some of the best courses in the area.

The Bear, 6300 U.S. 31 North, Grand Traverse Village; (616) 938-2100. Nicklaus designed this eighteen-hole championship course with elevated fairways and hummocks that recall golf's Scottish heritage. The Bear is the centerpiece of the Grand Traverse Resort and was rated in the top one hundred resort courses in the United States. The course winds through summer fruit orchards and is suited for the more advanced golfer.

The Shanty Creek Golf Course, One Shanty Creek Road, Bellaire; (616) 533-8621. One of three at the Shanty Creek Resort, this course was *Golf*'s Silver Medal winner in 1996 and is one of the more open-style courses in the area. Unlike the Bear, this course can accommodate all skill levels. The Schuss Mountain Golf Course, also part of the same resort, is one of the more popular public golf courses.

Sugar Loaf Resort Course, 4500 Sugar Loaf Mountain Road, Cedar; (616) 228-5461. The newest addition to Traverse City's golf culture opened in spring 1997. Designed by Arnold Palmer, Sugar Loaf Course is near the Leelanau Peninsula and offers views of Lake Michigan and Manitou Islands. For kids interested in joining their parents on the fairways, Sugar Loaf Resort Course offers a five-day instructional course for juniors held the first week of July.

High Pointe Golf Club, 555 Arnold Road, Williamsburg; (616) 267-9900. Rated as one of the "100 Greatest Public Courses in the United States" by *Golf Digest* (1995), this course offers an open-style front nine and a forested back nine, resulting in dramatic contrast.

Performing Arts

The Traverse City Players perform year-round at the **Old Town Playhouse** (616-947-2210), including kids-only productions, while the newly refurbished **State Theatre** on Front Street, downtown, hosts a professional touring productions, such as *Forever Plaid*. The **Dennos Museum Center's** winter series includes performances by the local jazz society, folk singers, and musicians. Classical music lovers can attend concerts by **The Traverse City Symphony** (616-947-2210) between October and April. The internationally known **Interlochen Center for the Arts,** 17 miles south of Traverse City on Route 137 (616-276-6230), presents free or nominally priced year-round concerts by the faculty, students, and renowned international performers.

There is always something special happening just for kids at Grand Traverse Resort.
(Courtesy Grand Traverse Resort)

Old Town Playhouse, 148 East Eighth Street, Traverse City; (616) 947–2210. Instead of the movies, take your kids to a play. It's more cultural and less expensive. Children's plays are performed here throughout the year, and kids get in for less than $3.00. Call for a schedule.

Shopping

Several shops in Old Town Traverse City cater to kids. **Children's World** offers toys, games, and dolls; **Horizon Books** stocks books, educational supplies, toys, and more; **Dandelion** has clothing and other items; **Hocus Pocus** is a magic and novelty shop; and there's **Grand Bay Kite.** The Cobblestone area has been voted the premier shopping district in Michigan for the past few consecutive years. Colorful awnings canopy the entrances to many of the coffee bars, specialty boutiques, restaurants, and bistros.

Popular malls include **Cherryland Mall,** South Airport Road (across the street from **Skateworld** roller rink), where there's a hobby shop, and a video-game arcade, plus **Grand Traverse Mall,** U.S. 31 and South Airport Road, with a carousel, food court, multiplex theater, and game arcade.

Bargains abound at **Horizon Outlet Center,** 3639 Marketplace Circle, an outdoor outlet mall with more than thirty stores, including Levi/Dockers and Eddie Bauer. A ten-screen cinema has recently opened here.

SPECIAL EVENTS

These calendar highlights include a sampling of area events.

January: Discover Michigan Skiing, special rates offered by all Traverse City area resorts.

February: Michigan Special Olympics at Sugar Loaf, winter sports competitions for handicapped children and adults. North America VASA Cross-Country Ski Race in Traverse City.

March: Spring Carnivals at Crystal Mountain and Shanty Creek and Sugar Loaf Resort.

June: Bay Day and Ribs, Bibs, Tall Ships & Kids is a weekend of tall-ship tours, food, and entertainment.

July: National Cherry Festival—eight days of fireworks, parades, concerts, competitions, ferris wheels, and lots of cherries! Traverse Bay Outdoor Art Fair.

August: Northwest Michigan Fair; Dunegrass & Blues Festival
Labor Day Weekend: Northport's Famous Fish Boil includes arts fair, entertainment, and tons of fish. Northport, on the tip of the Leelanau Peninsula, is about forty-five minutes from Traverse City.
Late September/Early October: Fall color season and winery tours.
Thanksgiving–Christmas: Hometown Holiday features a host of special gala activities and events plus affordable packages.

WHERE TO STAY

The area offers more than 4,700 hotel rooms in every price range. The Traverse City Convention and Visitors Bureau publishes lodging brochures. Always inquire about special packages. The bureau also operates a central reservations service; call (800) TRAVERS. In addition to the ski and summer resorts already mentioned, the following places in Traverse City have special family appeal.

In the East Bay Area

These lodgings are on or near the "Miracle Mile" beaches. **The Beach Condominiums,** 1995 U.S. 31 North, on East Bay, gives families a chance to stretch out in thirty units that sleep four and feature sundecks, whirlpool baths, kitchens, and cable TV. Outside there's a beach, heated pool, and hot tub. Call (616) 938-2228. **Driftwood Motel,** 1861 U.S. 31 North, on East Bay, boasts a beachfront and large indoor pool and recreation area with game room and whirlpool. Choose from poolside or economy rooms; most have refrigerators and cable TV. Free lift tickets at Mt. Holiday for each registered guest in your party. Call (616) 938-1600. **Sugar Beach Resort,** 1773 U.S. 31 North, Traverse City; (616) 938-0100/(800) 509-1995. Family suites are available. Continental breakfast is provided and there is an indoor pool.

Other Area Lodging

Grand Traverse Resort, 6300 U.S. 31 North, Acme, contains 750 rooms, suites, and condos, some with refrigerator, fireplace, and whirlpool; ten restaurants and lounges; shopping gallery; indoor-outdoor tennis; pools and whirlpools; weight room; aerobic studio; cross-country skiing; championship golf; and seasonal activities for kids. Call (616) 938-2100/(800) 748-0303/(800) 678-1308—in Canada.

Hampton Inn, 1000 U.S. 31 North, is across from State Park Beach, 3 miles from downtown, and adjacent to River Country Funland. The 127 units include complimentary continental breakfast, local phone calls, and airport transportation. There's also an indoor pool, whirlpool, and exercise room. Call (616) 946-8900/(800) HAMPTON.

Ranch Rudolf, 6841 Brown Bridge Road, a four-season resort, comprises sixteen motel units and twenty-five campsites in Pere Marquette State Forest. Located on the Boardman River, 12 miles southeast of Traverse City, the ranch features horseback riding, canoeing, and cross-country skiing. Call (616) 947-9529.

WHERE TO EAT

The Traverse City guide includes restaurant listings that feature everything from burgers to fresh seafood, such as Lake Michigan whitefish and rainbow trout. Morel mushrooms are a popular delicacy hunted in the local woods each spring. (Only do this if you know exactly what to look for.)

For in-between nibbles, try the famous cherry pecan muffins at **The Muffin Tin,** 115 Wellington at Front (616-929-7915), a country-style store that also sells other regional products; and the Traverse City Cherry Vanilla Fudge at **Kilwin's Chocolates,** 129 East Front Street; (616) 946-2403/(800) 433-0596. (Fudge is very big in this area.)

For the main course there are equally good options. On Friday and Saturday nights at **Dills Olde Town Saloon,** 423 South Union Street, kids (and adults) can sing family-style karaoke on stage to favorite tunes—including "Twinkle, Twinkle Little Star" for tots. Souvenir videos are available; ribs, steaks, seafood, and salads are on the menu; (616) 947-7534. At **Geppettos On the Bay,** 13641 West Bayshore Drive, dine on pasta specialties while enjoying the magnificent view; (616) 947-7079. **Cousin Jenny's Cornish Pasties,** 129 West Union Street, serves seven varieties, including the Breakfast Bobby; (616)

941-7821. **Mabel's,** 472 Munson Avenue, U.S. 31 North (two doors down from Days Inn), serves breakfast, lunch, or dinner anytime. Specialties include seven pastas, fresh steamed vegetables, Mabel's Original Vegetarian Nutburger, and "Just Enough Menus." Call (616) 947-0252. Don't be fooled by the name; the **Grand Traverse Dinner Train** serves lunch, too. Excursions wind through the north country on this restored 1950s railcar. It may not be appropriate for younger children. The menu lists such sophisticated dishes as smoked salmon and prime rib, and the prices reflect the menu selection. Call 93-DEPOT.

DAY TRIPS

There are eight wineries in the area; some open seasonally, others year-round. The closest is **Chateau Grand Traverse** on Old Mission Peninsula on M-37; (616) 223-7355.

Seaworthy older kids and teens might enjoy afternoon or sunset sailing adventures aboard the **Tall Ship Malabar,** on West Grand Traverse Bay. Picnic lunch or dinner is included. Call (616) 941-2000/(800) 968-8800.

The 8-square-mile **South Manitou Island** is worth a trip. It's part of the Sleeping Bear Dunes National Lakeshore (listed on page 29) and several miles offshore. Drive along the coast on scenic M-22 to the picturesque fishing village of Leland, where ferries (no cars allowed) leave daily; (616) 256-9061. Sights include the Valley of the Giants, consisting of 500-year-old light cedar trees, scenic dunes, a historic lighthouse, and a late 1800s cemetery. Kids can stand on the shoreline and see a real shipwreck (the Liberian freighter *Francisco Morazon*). There are guided jeep tours and overnight camping—but no food for sale and no visible bathrooms. The "wilder" North Manitou Island isn't recommended for families.

FOR MORE INFORMATION

Brochures and guides to the area are available from **Traverse City Convention and Visitors Bureau,** 101 West Grandview Parkway, Traverse City; (616) 947-1120/800-TRAVERS. Ask for their excellent *Traverse City* magazine, published seasonally.

Emergency Numbers

In Grand Traverse, Kalkaska, and Leelanau counties for **ambulance, fire, police, and medical emergencies:** 911

Emergency number in Antrim County: 533-8627

Emergency number in Benzie County: 882-4464

Munson MediCare, 550 Munson Avenue (359-9000), has a physician referral and health information service, 1:00 P.M. to 9:00 P.M. The hospital's Med-Care Walk-In Clinic is open twenty-four hours, seven days a week (922-8686). From the eastern part of town, this is most accessible in an emergency.

From the western part, head to the **Munson Medical Center,** 1105 Sixth Street (935-5000), for their Walk-In Emergency Service (935-8507, also the number for their physician referral service).

For the disabled, bus service within Traverse City is available from **Specialized On-Call Service** (SOS); (616) 947-0796.

Poison Control: (800) 632-2727

There is no twenty-four-hour pharmacy. The pharmacy at Meijer, 3955 U.S. 31 South (616-941-1793), is open 8:00 A.M.– 10:00 P.M. Monday through Saturday, and 9:00 A.M.–7:00 P.M. Sunday. After closing time either of the above hospitals can provide enough medicine to last until its pharmacy opens.

DEARBORN

Dearborn, Michigan, (about 12 miles west of Detroit) was founded by auto pioneer Henry Ford and welcomes two million tourists a year. They invariably head straight to the Henry Ford Museum and Greenfield Village, the most visited indoor/outdoor historical complex in North America. The museum alone is worth the trip, but you'll find other interesting and fun things to do with your family in this city of 90,000 and the surrounding area. You may want to avoid downtown Detroit, which can be rather bleak and busy and hot in summer.

GETTING THERE

Detroit Metropolitan Airport, about fifteen minutes west of the museum and village, is served by major commercial airlines (call individual carriers for information). Car rentals are available at the airport. **Commuter Transportation Company** (313–946–1000/800–351–5466) provides hourly coach service from the airport to major hotels in Dearborn from 6:45 A.M. to midnight. Taxis are plentiful. Detroit's City Airport (313–267–6400) is 30 miles east and serves commuter airlines.

Amtrak (800–USA–RAIL) runs trains to Dearborn's station, near Michigan Avenue and Greenfield. **Greyhound/Trailways** bus line serves Detroit's downtown terminal at 1000 West Lafayette Street. Call (313) 963–9840 for information about fares and schedules. Interstate highway systems provide easy access to Dearborn; take I–94 from the northeast and west, I–75 from the south.

GETTING AROUND

Taxis are available at hotels and on call. **SMART** (Southeast Michigan Area Rapid Transit) buses (313–256–8600) serve Dearborn's major arteries and also operate between Detroit and the Henry Ford Museum and Greenfield Village. The **Classic Trolley** is available for charter trips; (313) 945–6100.

WHAT TO SEE AND DO

Museums

Henry Ford Museum and Greenfield Village, 20900 Oakwood; (313) 271–1620/(800) 343–1929. Visitors arriving at the museum expecting to see endless displays of cars are pleasantly surprised to find there's so much more. One thing is for sure: You'll never hear the word "bor...ing" uttered by your kids while you're on the premises.

Be sure everyone wears very comfortable shoes; you will cover a lot of ground. (Although strollers are rented in Greenfield Village for a nominal fee, they aren't allowed in all the buildings.) The museum has twelve acres of exhibits; the adjacent outdoor Greenfield Village spreads out over eighty-one acres. Ideally, you should spend two days here, allowing one day per attraction. Admission is separate, but combination and two-day tickets are available.

At the entrance, there's a replica of Philadelphia's Independence Hall. Inside, fascinating exhibits show how technology changed life in America. Both kids and parents will enjoy the Automobile in American Life exhibit, which includes original landmarks such as an entire 1946 diner, a 1940s Texaco service station, a 1950s drive-in movie theater, and a 1960s Holiday Inn room, along with one hundred historically significant cars. All kids love trains, and yours will revel in the museum's enormous 600-ton Allegheny locomotive, used to haul huge coal trains. It's part of a transportation exhibit that also includes aircraft, horse-drawn vehicles, streetcars, an firefighting apparatus. Other museum highlights include the limousine in which President John F. Kennedy was shot and Robert Byrd's 1925 plane, the first to fly over the North Pole.

A must-see (and must-do) is the fun Innovation Station, a 3,200-square-foot interactive learning game on the main concourse that offers all ages a chance to find creative, new ways to solve problems. About thirty players team up at various activity stations to provide the manpower (pedaling bicycles, turning hand cranks, etc.) and brain-

---

Dearborn at a Glance

- Unlimited hands-on activities for kids of all ages

- The must-see Henry Ford Museum and Greenfield Village

- Cageless exhibits of animals at the Nature Center and the Zoological Park in Detroit

- Dearborn Chamber of Commerce, (313) 584–6100

---

power (sorting balls by color, etc.) to propel thousands of brightly colored balls through a network of tubes and sorting devices into bins. If a problem develops, everyone "brainstorms" to provide a solution. The game takes from twenty to thirty minutes.

The colorful Made in America multimedia exhibit uses hands-on activities, video and film presentations—even a troupe of cartoon characters—to show visitors of all ages how industry affects their lives. Kids will be fascinated by the overhead conveyer that carries a continuous flow of American-made products—including a kitchen sink. There's also a giant light bulb-making machine, a step-inside hydroelectric generator, and a touch-screen computer that lets visitors feel what it's like to run an electrical power plant. Another treat is the Motown Sound, a multimedia exhibit that tells the story of rock 'n' roll with music.

The adjacent **Greenfield Village** features more than eighty homes, workplaces, and community buildings from different periods and locations, each displaying the day-to-day processes that helped build this nation. Some are homes of famous people: the Wright Brothers' model Ohio home (their Cycle Shop is elsewhere in the Village); the city home of Noah Webster, author of America's first dictionary; the farm where Henry Ford was born and raised; and tire magnate Harvey S. Firestone's 1880s farm, where costumed interpreters perform daily tasks. Other residences reveal the struggles and adversities faced by less famous people: the 1850 slave homes from a Georgia plantation, for instance, and the wilderness home of an eighteenth-century Connecticut family.

Thomas Edison's Menlo Park Laboratory is restored to its 1880 state and includes more than 400 inventions created here, including the phonograph and incandescent light. (Who knows how many future inventors will be inspired by what they see?) Nearby, the Sarah Jordan Boarding House, one of the first residences wired for electric light, housed several of Edison's assistants.

Your kids can take part in the day's lessons at **Scotch Settlement School,** which Henry Ford attended, or enjoy hands-on activities and old-fashioned games on The Green. Demonstrations in glassblowing, pottery, and other crafts are also fascinating for kids, and you can buy many of the products created in the museum gift shop.

Learn about the innovators of the automotive industry at the relocated **Automotive Hall of Fame,** which is scheduled to reopen in the fall of 1997. Located conveniently next to the Henry Ford Museum, you can learn about speed demons like Wilbur Shaw, the first driver to win consecutive Indy 500 titles. There are also exhibits about business leaders, like former Chrysler chairman Lee Iacocca.

Suwanee Park will delight the entire family with 1913 carousel rides. Stop for a soda at the old-fashioned 1870 ice-cream parlor. For an extra fee you can ride a paddle-wheel boat or steam-powered locomotive around the village perimeter. Narrated carriage tours (sleigh tours in the winter, weather permitting) and 1931 bus rides are also available for an additional charge.

From early January to mid-March, there is a single admission fee to both museums, although visitors to Greenfield Village may view building exteriors only.

Henry Ford Estate, Fair Lane, the campus of University of Michigan Dearborn, off Evergreen and U.S. 12: (313) 593-5590. If your museum visit whets your family's interest in Henry Ford, stop by his mansion, 1 mile away. You can tour the house with its self-contained power plant, which is connected to the mansion by a tunnel, or stroll along the gardens and trails on the grounds. In the summer, follow a self-guided forty-five-minute walking tour that includes a treehouse,

Learning about cars is just one of the many activities you can participate in at the Henry Ford Museum and Greenfield Village complex.
(Courtesy Henry Ford Museum and Greenfield Museum, Dearborn, Michigan)

bathhouse, boathouse, and scenic views. Christmastime brings Santa's Workshop, breakfast with Santa, a floral tour of the estate, and special holiday luncheons and events.

For those interested in Arab Culture, the **Arab Folk Museum,** 2651 Saulino Court (313-842-7010), has exhibits on Arab cultures and archives on Michigan's Arab community.

Parks and Zoos

Belle Isle is reached via a toll-free bridge at East Jefferson Avenue and East Grand Boulevard, Detroit; (313) 267-7115. About 15 miles from Dearborn, it's the nation's largest urban island park, with 1,000 acres of wooded paths and drives, including one that goes along the shore. Recreational possibilities abound here: golf, tennis, and swimming (at a sandy beach with lifeguards). Signs point the way to the various attractions.

Younger kids will love the terrific playground where they can climb up and down nets and over wooden structures, crawl through tunnels, and slide down poles. **The Nature Center** (313-267-7157) has wooded trails where you can view plants, animals, and changing exhibits (donations requested). Allow about an hour for the thirteen-acre zoo where, for a fee, you can stroll the winding elevated walkway and view uncaged animals in natural settings. **Dossin Great Lakes Museum** (313-267-6440) is worth a visit with older kids who may appreciate the restored smoking lounge taken from the 1912 steamer *City of Detroit III*, complete with walls of hand-carved oak work. There's also a 40-foot hydroplane (*The Miss Pepsi*), observation deck, periscope, and ship-to-shore radio messages (donations). If your family is lucky enough to be around during one of the six seasonal flower shows at the **Whitcomb Conservatory** (313-267-7134), you're in for a fragrant visual treat. There are permanent displays of palms, ferns, and cacti, as well as one of the country's largest orchid collections, and it's all free. Another no-cost attraction is the **Aquarium,** one of the country's oldest, where you can see various freshwater fish from the Great Lakes and beyond.

The Detroit area has another zoo. The **Detroit Zoological Park,** Woodward Avenue and Ten Mile Road (I-696), Royal Oak (a northern suburb of Detroit, about 12 miles from Dearborn); (313) 398-0900. This zoo is one of the country's largest and most modern. It has 125 acres of landscaped grounds with cageless exhibits grouped according to continent, simulating the animals' natural habitats. Don't miss the four-acre chimpanzee exhibit. There's also a miniature railroad ride around the park. You can buy food, or bring your own and picnic. Allow about four hours for a visit here.

History buffs will enjoy the **Dearborn History Museum,** 95 Brady Street. The museum comprises three historic buildings. The commandant's quarters, a four-bedroom Victorian decorated with period furnishings, is the only surviving building from the Michigan arsenal. The Roff House is a Federal-style home with rotating exhibits and a resource-room upstairs, enabling visitors to trace their genealogy. The Richard Gardner House is an 1831 farmhouse. The museum hosts a historical-theme weekend twice each year; Rendez-vous in Rouge, a French-Indian War reenactment in mid-June; and a Civil War reenactment during the first week of October.

Performing Arts

The Greenfield Village Theatre Company performs time-honored plays (*Father of the Bride* was a recent selection) suitable for family viewing at the Henry Ford Museum Theater throughout the year. Although season subscriptions are sold, individual tickets and dinner/theater tickets also are available. Call (313) 271-1620 for information.

Shopping

Fairlane Town Center, between Hubbard Drive, Evergreen Road, Southfield Expressway (M-39), and Michigan Avenue (U.S. 12), is one of the state's largest indoor malls with The Disney Store and two toy stores of special interest to kids. The information center on the lower level is the place to stop for bus schedules, tips on lodging, and the answers to other questions. The mall is open every day; call (313) 593-3330 for more information.

SPECIAL EVENTS

Sporting events

Sporting enthusiasts may want to take in a Detroit Tigers baseball game at Tiger Stadium or Lions football at Pontiac Silverdome. The Detroit Pistons play basketball at the Palace of Auburn Hills, while Red Wings hockey games are played in the Joe Louis Sports arena, part of the city's downtown riverfront Civic Center. Games are frequently sold out; you can order tickets in advance of your visit from Ticketmaster (313-645-6666) or call the Detroit Visitor's Hotline (see For More Information) for specifics.

Fairs and Festivals

Call the Detroit Visitor's Hotline for more information on sporting events as well as other goings-on. The Dearborn Chamber of Commerce also publishes a calendar of events. There are three notable area fairs and festivals.

March: Maple Syrup Festival, Cranbrook Institute of Science, Bloomfield Hills, first three weekends.

Late June–early July: International Freedom Festival, a celebration shared by Detroit and Windsor, Ontario, with fireworks, parades, craft shows, and entertainment. Ford Senior Players Championship Tournament, Players Club, Dearborn (313-441-0300), which is kicked off by the Dearborn Ford Festival.

Late August–early September: Ten-day Michigan State Fair, Michigan Exposition and State Fairgrounds, Detroit.

WHERE TO STAY

Some Dearborn hotels offer packages that include tickets to the Henry Ford Museum and Greenfield Village. Request a list from the Dearborn Chamber of Commerce (see For More Information). Three of these are also on the Classic Trolley circuit, making them especially convenient.

The Dearborn Inn, 20301 Oakwood Boulevard, a Marriott hotel, is a recently renovated landmark building with three separate wings: Main Inn, Colonial Lodge, or Famous Americans Colonial Homes suites. It's a good choice for families. Call (313) 271-2700/(800) 228-2900.

Hyatt Regency Dearborn, Fairlane Town Center, offers a shopping mall at your doorstep, plus an indoor pool, restaurants, a fitness center, and more. Your family won't have to worry about how to pass the time here. Call (313) 593-1234/(800) 233-1234.

Quality Inn—Fairlane, 21430 Michigan Avenue, is one-half mile from the Henry Ford Museum and Greenfield Village and features an outdoor pool, on-site picnic grounds, complimentary breakfast, VCRs, movie rentals, and refrigerators. Call (313) 565-0800/(800) 228-5151. Also on the site is the Dearborn Historical Museum, which you might not bother visiting unless you're a guest at the inn or an avid history buff. Exhibits show the development of Dearborn in two historical buildings: one, part of an original arsenal; the other, the original powder magazine, which stored ammunition as early as 1839. Call (313) 565-3000 for museum information.

Two more family-friendly choices are the **Hampton Inn of Dearborn,** 20061 Michigan Avenue, Dearborn (313-436-9600/800-HAMPTON) and **The Courtyard by Marriott,** 5200 Mercury Drive, Dearborn (313-271-1400).

Bed and breakfast homes recommended for families include the **Dearborn Bed and Breakfast,** 22331 Morley, Dearborn (313-563-2200), and the **York House,** 1141 North York, Dearborn (313-561-2432).

Also worthy of note: For the big splurge, there's the **Ritz-Carlton Dearborn,** Fairlane Plaza; (313) 441-2000/(800) 241-3333.

WHERE TO EAT

The Dearborn Chamber of Commerce offers a helpful restaurant guide that includes maps and general price ranges. East Dearborn is home to the largest Middle Eastern population in the United States, and if you like that style of cooking, locals say you can't go wrong at any of their restaurants. **LaShish,** 12918 Michigan, is a casual family restaurant serving authentic Middle Eastern dishes and fresh juices; call (313) 584-4477. Some other styles of cooking: **Bill Knapp's of Dearborn,** 3500 Greenfield, serves affordable American food and has a children's menu; (313) 271-7166. No matter when your family's appetite kicks in, **Andoni's Family Dining,** 1620 North Telegraph, open twenty-four hours, can whip up a satisfying meal; (313) 582-2024. **Dimitri's,** 2424 South Telegraph, Dearborn (313-565-7066), offers a wide selection at moderate prices.

DAY TRIPS

If your kids have never been to Canada, you can take a quick trip some 15 miles south of the border to the pleasant town of **Windsor, Ontario.** That's right—south. Look at a map, and you'll see that Dearborn and Detroit are actually north of Windsor, Ontario, where you can grab a bit to eat and stroll around town. Access is via bridge or tunnel. If you're in town during the **International Freedom Festival** (see Special Events), you'll find plenty to do during the week-long celebration of Canada Day and Independence Day.

Cranbrook is the former estate of George Booth, publisher of *The Detroit News.* It's now a well-known cultural and educational center 18 miles away from Dearborn, in Bloomfield Hills. Surrounding Booth's home are forty acres of public gardens, woods, pine walks, and two lakes. Also on the property: an art museum, which exhibits both contemporary art and artwork by students at Cranbrook schools; a natural history museum with a large mineral collection; a planetarium with weekend shows; and a nature center. Call (313) 645-3000 for information.

FOR MORE INFORMATION

Dearborn Chamber of Commerce, 15544 Michigan Avenue, has helpful pamphlets and brochures; (313) 584-6100. Call the Metro-Detroit Convention & Visitor's Bureau; (313) 259-4333 or (800) 338-7648. Internet: http://www.visitdetroit.com.

Emergency Numbers

Police and fire: 911

Henry Ford Hospital at Fairlane Center: (313) 593-8100

Oakwood Hospital, 18101 Oakwood Boulevard: (313) 593-7000

Poison Control: (313) 745-5711

Twenty-four-hour pharmacy: Rite Aid, Shaefer at Ford Road; (313) 581-3280

INDIANAPOLIS

The movers and shakers of this heartland USA town made a concerted effort to establish Indianapolis as a sports center. After they built the arenas and stadiums, numerous athletic organizations came, bringing with them top sporting events. These results are great facilities—many of which are available for public use—and a city known as the Sports Capital of the United States.

Besides watching world-class competitions, visitors to Indianapolis enjoy two surprises: the world's largest children's museum and, nearby, Conner Prairie, a re-created pioneer town.

GETTING THERE

Indianapolis International Airport (317-487-9594) is 8 miles, about fifteen minutes, from downtown. The airport services **Air Ontario, America West, America West Express, American, American Eagle, American Trans Air, Comair, Continental, Continental Express, Delta, Midway Connection, Northwest, Skyway, TWA, United, USAir, USAir Express,** and **ValuJet.** Call the individual airlines for flight information and reservations. Affordable Limousine (317-264-8485) and Indy Connection (317-241-2522, ext. 205) offer van service to downtown.

Amtrak pulls into Union Station, 350 South Illinois Street (800-USA-RAIL), and buses arrive at the **Greyhound/Trailways** station, 127 North Capitol Avenue (317-635-4501).

Three major U.S. highways—I-69, I-70, and I-65—lead directly to Indianapolis, and I-74 leads traffic into the bypass route, I-465.

GETTING AROUND

The public bus system, the METRO (317-632-1900), is equipped to serve physically challenged riders; call (317) 635-3344 for schedules.

There are several cab companies, including Yellow Cab (317–637–5421). Car rental companies include Budget Rent A Car, 7050 West Washington Street (317–248–1100); Hertz Rent A Car, 2621 South High School Road (317–243–9321), National Car Rental, 7111 West Washington Street (317–243–1177; and Avis Rent-A-Car, 6315 West Washington Street (800–486–3913).

WHAT TO SEE AND DO

Museums

The Children's Museum of Indianapolis, 300 North Meridian Street (314–924–5431), is the world's largest. As its motto indicates, it "is a place where children grow up, and adults don't have to." This museum appeals to kids of all ages. The What If gallery aims at ages six to ten by presenting three exhibits requested by more than 1,000 children: a dinosaur den, an underwater coral reef, and an Egyptian mummy. Kids dig for fossils, peer at a coral reef, and put together a mummy puzzle. Playscape lets preschoolers ages two and up experiment with water, shapes, and sand. Teens aren't forgotten either. At the Center for Exploration, visitors get to vote on such controversial issues as capital punishment and gun control.

An IWERKS CineDome movie theater, as well as the Science Works gallery, are the museum's latest attractions. The 67-foot domed theater hosts hourly, nature-themed films. If your kids are feeling antsy after the film, they can climb the walls—literally—in the 12,000-foot Science Works gallery. The gallery has a 22-foot limestone wall with three different degrees of difficulty (safety harnesses are provided). Kids can also dig for fossils, use a pedal-operated dump truck at the construction-site exhibit, or crawl through one of two tunnels to observe twelve different animals.

This is the place to give in to the child within. Be sure to ride the Victorian carousel, browse the antique-doll collection, and view the extensive array of model trains, among the largest train exhibits anywhere. For special kid's events, call the Kidsline at (317) 924–KIDS.

Eiteljorg Museum of American Indian and Western Art, 500 West Washington Street; (317) 636–WEST. The Eiteljorg holds one of the most extensive collections of American Western art and Native

---

Indianapolis at a Glance

- Indianapolis Motor Speedway, and a whole lot more

- World-class sports facilities for your family to use

- The world's largest children's museum

- Conner Prairie, a re-created pioneer town

- Indianapolis City Center visitor's center, (317) 237-5206 or (800) 468-INDY

American art and artifacts. Situated next to an old grain elevator, the Eiteljorg looks both incongruous and intriguing. Cleverly designed to resemble the adobe architecture of the Taos Pueblo, the museum houses a first-rate collection of western paintings, including one by Georgia O'Keeffe, as well as Native American art and artifacts. The first-floor galleries capture the faces and forms of the West, from the dignity and power of Indian chiefs and warriors painted in the nineteenth and early twentieth century to contemporary and whimsical mixed-media works that depict cowboys with hip slouches, and toy guns.

Upstairs, Spirited Hands: Continuing Traditions in Native American Art displays an eye-catching array of everyday artifacts decorated with beadwork. Ask your kids to compare the varying cradle boards (carriers used to transport infants) fashioned by the different tribes.

Before you leave the museum, be sure to browse the gift shop. Kids will love spending their allowance on drums, posters, cards, charms, and some great T-shirts.

Indianapolis Museum of Art, 1200 West Thirty-eighth Street (317-923-1331), is not only an art museum with European, American, contemporary, Asian, and African art on permanent display; the facility also features a 152-acre park, a botanical garden, a theater, a concert terrace, and a restaurant. In this museum, the seventh largest art museum in the United States, be sure to see the Eiteljorg Collection of African Art. The masks, carvings, and jewelry appeal to kids. A special touch: The videos near the displays show the masks in motion being worn in ceremonial dances. Other highlights include the largest collection of J.W.M. Turner works outside the United Kingdom, a comprehensive collection of Oriental art, and the famous *Love* sculpture by Robert Indiana (remember the Love stamp?) out on the lawn. Allow time to stroll the botanical gardens and browse the gift shop.

Sports Museums

Serious about sports, Indianapolis boasts several museums dedicated to the subject.

Indianapolis Motor Speedway Hall of Fame Museum, 4790 West Sixteenth Street; (317) 481-8500. If your kids collect model racing cars and root for their favorite speed demon, they will love it here. Crammed into the two large galleries of this hall are the sleek, shiny, and select cars—more than thirty of them—from the world of racing. Admire the 1914 Duesenberg driven by Eddie Rickenbacker (the first car to reach the amazing speed of 79 miles per hour), A.J. Foyt's four winning cars, and recent Indy champions. The walls feature photographs of racing's Hall of Fame.

Do your kids want to brag they rode the Indy? Then, board the bus for a narrated trip around the track and a close-up view of the stands, work pits, and famous finish line.

National Art Museum of Sport, University Place Conference Center and Hotel; (317) 274-3627. Although small, consisting of several galleries and a second-floor office hallway, this museum is the only one in the United States devoted exclusively to sporting art. The general collections and special exhibitions rotate. You might see oils, prints, and sculpture on boxing, baseball, basketball, horse racing, or hockey. A visit here could be a good way to interest your sports enthusiast in art.

Several other sports museums are worth a browse. **The RCA Dome,** One Hoosier Dome; (317) 237-5200. Go inside the stadium and look at the VIP suites and the locker rooms as part of a tour of the 60,500-seat slice of history. The site has hosted the NCAA Final Four basketball games, and, of course, it is the home of the Indianapolis Colts. The tour includes an eight-minute multimedia show. Guests on the tour can also inspect the Astroturf and tour the owner's suite. For more information, call (317) 237-DOME.

The Children's Museum of Indianapolis is, as its motto professes, "a place where children grow up and adults don't have to." (Courtesy Indianapolis Project)

Victory Field Baseball Park opened in July 1996. The open-air, 13,500-seat stadium is home to the Indianapolis Indians, a Triple-A farm team for the Cincinnati Reds.

Located in New Castle, the **Indiana Basketball Hall of Fame,** One Hall of Fame Court, New Castle (317-529-1891), pays homage to Indiana's love of hoops. Interactive exhibits take you onto the playing floor, and into the locker rooms.

Additional Attractions

President Benjamin Harrison Home, 1230 North Delaware Street (317-631-1898), is a National Historic Landmark. This Victorian home features many original family pieces plus rotating exhibits about the twenty-third President of the United States. **Hook's 1890 Drug Store,** 1202 East Thirty-eighth Street (317-924-1503), is outfitted like a Victorian soda parlor; grab an ice-cream cone along with turn-of-the-century ambience. **The Indiana War Memorial,** 431 North Meridian Street (317-232-7615), is dedicated to soldiers killed in the two world wars and the Korean and Vietnam wars. It displays military weapons, uniforms, a jeep, and a helicopter. **The Murat Centre,** 510 North New Jersey Street (317-635-2433), modeled after an Islamic mosque, is the largest shrine temple in the world. Check out its stained-glass windows, theater, mosaic mural, and the Egyptian room constructed like Tutankhamen's burial chamber. If you have kids older than fourteen (or if you're still a bit of a child yourself), then go to the **Stephen Johansson Karting Center,** 3549 Lafayette Road; (317) 297-KART. You can zoom around a track for fifteen minutes at about 30 miles per hour at the first indoor cart-racing center in the home of the most famous car race. Younger kids are not allowed to drive or be passengers because drivers must wear special suits that don't come in small sizes. The center underwent $11 million of renovations in 1996, including the addition of 700 seats to the theater and a new sound system. It will host about 170 concerts and other events this year. **Holcomb Observatory and Planetarium at Butler University,** 4600 Sunset Avenue (317-283-9333), operates a 38-inch reflecting telescope that is available to the public. Call ahead for hours.

Sports Amateur Facilities Open to the Public

As the Sports Capital of the United States, the city offers visitors world-class facilities not just for watching, but for doing. Simply show your hotel-room key to take advantage of the inexpensive entry fees and the top-rated facilities, which are open to the public when not hosting major events. Always call first to check availability and to find out about any age restrictions.

Indiana University Natatorium, 901 West New York Street; (317) 274-3517. Bring your own towel and a lock for the lockers, and swim, swim, swim in this first-class pool. Doing laps here, your teens will feel like Matt Biondi, Summer Sanders, or Rowdy Gains. Work out at the aerobics classes and in the weight room.

Indiana University Track & Field Stadium, 901 West New York Street; (317) 374-6780. Located in the same complex as the natatorium, the check-in for the track-and-field facility is at the east entrance of the natatorium. Jog on the 400-meter, outdoor, rubber lanes or join in the free fun runs every Wednesday at 6:00 P.M. Registration is at 5:30 P.M.

Practice your tennis at the indoor and outdoor courts at the **Indianapolis Tennis Center,** 815 West New York Street, (317) 278-2100. While it's better to bring your own racquet, a limited number are available for use at no charge. Lessons are available, too.

National Institute for Fitness and Sport, 250 North University Boulevard; (317) 274-3432. Parents and teens especially appreciate working out on the Olympic-quality training equipment and running on the 200-meter indoor track. Admission fee is reduced when a hotel key is presented.

Your clan can cut quite a figure when skating together at the indoor **Indiana World Skating Academy,** Pan American Plaza, 201 South Capitol Avenue; (317) 237-5565. For more skating September through April, try the **Perry Ice Rink,** 451 East Stop 11 Road; (317) 888-0070.

Cyclists aren't forgotten, either. Pedal around the top-notch track at the **Major Taylor Velodrome & BMX Tracks,** 3649 Cold Spring Road (317-926-8356), the site of many national competitions. Riders must be at least eight years old and wear helmets. Next door the BMX Track offers more training possibilities. Enjoy rowing and paddling at the **Regatta Course at Eagle Creek,** 7840 West Fifty-sixth Street; (317-327-7110.

Parks and Zoos

Indianapolis Zoo, 1200 West Washington Street (317-630-2001), close to downtown Indianapolis, is worth a trip. Known for its large whale and dolphin pavilions (check the times for the daily shows), this sixty-four-acre "cageless" zoo exhibits animals in waters, deserts, forests, and plains. The Waters building, always a favorite, features penguins, reef fish, turtles, and seals. Living Deserts of the World, an enclosed conservatory filled with cacti and other desert plants, takes you by free-roaming lizards, turtles, and hummingbirds.

In addition, young kids covet the camel, pony, and elephant rides, as well as a stint on the free trolley—a good way to get around and avoid aching feet. A stroll through this beautiful zoo is a delight, especially in spring when beds of black-eyed Susans, day lilies, and lilacs bloom.

In May, attend the Zoopolis 500, a humorous take-off on the famed Indy race. In this race two tortoises—A.J. and J.R.—vie for the championship. On Thursday nights in summer, stay after hours for Animals and All That Jazz performances by local groups.

Eagle Creek Park, 7840 West Fifty-sixth Street (317-203-4827), is run by the Indianapolis Department of Parks and Recreation and stretches for more than 3,000 acres. One of the largest municipal parks in the country, the fun here includes swimming, sailing, and canoeing in the 1,300-acre reservoir.

White River State Park, 801 West Washington Street (317-634-4567), is located on 250 acres downtown. It includes the Indianapolis Zoo, the National Institute for Fitness and Sport, and the Eiteljorg Museum of American Indians and Western Art. The park has a six-story, 450-seat IMAX theater.

Thunder Island Water and Recreation Park, 19830 U.S. 31 North, Westfield (317-896-5172), has water slides, kiddie and adult pools, miniature golf, go-carts, tubing, bumper boats, and softball batting cages.

Shopping

For shopping and even some entertainment, head to the **Circle Centre,** 49 West Maryland Street; (317) 630-5483. This entertainment and retail complex, opened in September 1995, features more than one hundred specialty shops, department stores such as Nordstrom and

Parisian, restaurants and nightclubs, a nine-screen movie theater, and a virtual-reality theme park, United Artists Starport. Circle Centre also contains the Indianapolis Artsgarden, a space for the local arts community's performances and exhibitions.

Special Tours

If young children get cranky during the early evening hours, take a soothing horse-drawn carriage ride around the city. Stately Percherons pull the carriages of **Colonial Carriages,** 435 South Senate Avenue (317-637-2002), and **Yellow Carriages,** 327 North Capitol Avenue (317-634-3400), which pick people up in front of the Holiday Inn, Union Station. On this half-hour tour, you can sit back and enjoy Indianapolis lit up at night. The horses take you around the landmark **Soldiers and Sailors Monument,** in the center of Monument Circle past the **State Capitol Building,** Capitol Avenue and Washington Street (317-232-8687), by the famed **RCA Dome,** 100 South Capitol (317-262-3452), and to **Union Station,** Georgia Street between Meridian Street and Capitol Avenue. Besides falling in love with the horses, your kids will enjoy the leisurely pace and the Cinderella ambience.

Carriage tours are available year-round, weather permitting, Monday through Friday from 6:30 P.M. to midnight, and Saturday and Sunday from 3:30 P.M. to 1:00 A.M. While you can hail a coach most evenings, reservations are strongly suggested for Saturday night.

Performing Arts

Deer Creek Music Center, 12880 East 146th Street; (317) 776-3337 (box office), (317) 841-8900 (main office). This outdoor covered amphitheater seats 18,000 and hosts musical performances in summer. The **Indiana Repertory Theatre,** 140 West Washington Street (317-635-5277), has three stages and a variety of performances. **Indianapolis Ballet Theatre,** 502-B North Capitol Avenue (317-637-8979), performs full-length and contemporary ballets. **Indianapolis Civic Theatre,** 1200 West Thirty-eighth Street, Indianapolis Museum of Art (box office 317-923-4597, main office 317-924-6770), uses volunteers and professionals. This is the home of the Kid Connection, an adult acting group that tours Medwestern elementary schools. **Indianapolis Opera,** 250 East Thirty-eighth Street (box office 317-921-6444, main office

317-283-3531), performs at Clowes Memorial Hall, Butler University. **Indianapolis Symphony Orchestra,** 45 Monument Circle (box office 317-639-4300, main office 317-262-1100), performs classical and popular music each season at the Circle Theatre. In summer there are performances under the stars at Conner Prairie (see Day Trips). **The Phoenix Theater,** 749 North Park Avenue (317-635-PLAY), performs off-Broadway and contemporary plays. Nationally known stars lead this resident professional company as they perform musicals in the summer at Hilton University's Brown Theatre. **Beef and Boards Dinner Theatre,** 9301 North Michigan Road (317-872-9664), is an Equity troupe that serves up Broadway shows in dinner-theater format.

For performing arts schedules at local universities, contact **Clowes Memorial Hall,** Butler University, 4600 Sunset Avenue; (317) 283-9696.

For tickets, call the individual box offices listed above, or try these agencies: **TicketMaster,** (317-239-5151) and **Tickets Up Front and Travel,** 1009 North Meridian Street, Suite 150 (317-633-6400).

Sports

The **Indiana Pacers,** a National Basketball Association team, play at the Market Square Arena, 300 East Market Street (main office 317-263-2100, tickets 317-239-5151). Catch the **Indianapolis Colts,** a National Football League team, at the RCA Dome, 100 South Capitol Avenue, P.O. Box 535000; (317) 297-7000. The **Indianapolis Indians,** the farm-league team of the Cincinnati Reds baseball team, plays from April to November at Bush Stadium, 1501 West Sixteenth Street; (317) 269-3545.

The **Little League Baseball Central Region Headquarters,** 4360 North Mitthoeffer Road (317-897-6127), hosts the Central Region Little League Baseball Championship each August, the winner goes on to the World Series. Find out about the summer camps held at this thirty-acre facility.

SPECIAL EVENTS

Festivals and Sporting Events

March: Biennial National Piano Fellowship Auditions and Finals. NCAA Men's and Women's Division I Indoor Track Championships.

NCAA Men's Division I Basketball Championship. Indiana High School Athletic Association (IHSAA) Boy's Basketball Finals.

April: Children's Folk Dance Festival, Indiana Convention Center (317–636–4556).

May: The Indianapolis 500 is held Memorial Day weekend each year. The city celebrates with a month of events that include a mini-marathon, parade, and the 500 Festival Kids' Day—the largest festival for children in the city. The fun includes splashing paint on old cars, racing Big Wheel bikes, and creating arts and crafts. The fair is generally held around Monument Circle. Although overshadowed by the Indianapolis 500, the A.J. Foyt's Hulman Hundred may be more fun to watch with kids. More than thirty cars compete on the dirt track of the Indiana State Fairgrounds, 1202 East Thirty-eighth Street (317–927–2869).

June: Savor more than six tons of Indiana strawberries at the Strawberry Festival. Indy Jazz Fest, Massachusetts Avenue (317–262–5161), Midsummer Fest, Monument Circle (317–637–4574).

July–August: 4th Fest, Indiana Black Expo, Hoosier State Games, Kroeger Circle Fest.

August: Indiana State Fair and the Indiana Avenue Jazz Festival.

September: National Hot Rod Association (NHRA) U.S. Nationals, Indiana Raceway Park. The Hoosier Storytelling Festival at the Indianapolis Arts Center hosts storytellers from around the country who share their personal stories, fairy tales, folktales, and literature to an audience of roughly 3,000.

October: ZooBoo at the Indianapolis Zoo; Oktoberfest.

November: Butcherin', Stuffin', and Smokin' demonstrations at Conner Prairie; Heartland Film Festival.

December: Conner Prairie by Candlelight, a holiday candlelight tour. Christmas at the Zoo; Celebration of Lights.

WHERE TO STAY

Embassy Suites Hotel—Downtown, 110 West Washington Street: (317) 236–1800 or (800) EMBASSY. Situated just blocks from the Indiana Convention Center and RCA Dome, this all-suite hotel offers families extra space and the conveniences of a microwave, refrigerator, coffee maker, and fold-out sofa bed. The property also has an indoor pool.

Crowne Plaza Union Station, 123 West Louisiana Street; (800) 2-CROWNE. Located across from the RCA Dome, this hotel has 276 rooms, twenty-six of which are authentic Pullman-car suites permanently parked on tracks off the hotel's main floors. Named for famous personalities of the twenties and thirties such as Diamond Jim Brady and Greta Garbo, these cars are furnished with period pieces and reproductions; many have pull-out sofas, and all add fun to an overnight stay. Lurking near the trains are white fiberglass statues of soldiers, sailors, and people of the era. Called the "ghosts" of Union Station, they add charm. The hotel also has an indoor pool. Be sure when requesting rooms you are not near the pool or central atrium, which can be noisy.

Hyatt Regency Indianapolis, One South Capitol Avenue; (317) 632-1234 or (800) 233-1234. Located directly across from the Indiana Convention Center and RCA Dome, this hotel features a twenty-story atrium, and a 20-foot waterfall in the lobby, and an indoor pool.

The **Westin Hotel Indianapolis,** 50 South Capitol Avenue; (317) 262-8100/(800) 228-3000. Located in downtown's business district, the hotel has a restaurant and lounge, indoor pool, and exercise facilities. For less pricey lodging try the **Comfort Inn** at 5040 South East Street (317-783-6711 or 800-221-2222), located ten minutes from downtown.

WHERE TO EAT

Capitol Food Court, 25 Market Street (317-634-4148), houses Ed and Marge's Cafeteria and a variety of fast-food restaurants: Long John Silver's Wendy's, Arby's, Pizza Hut. **Charlie and Barney's Bar and Grill,** Merchants Plaza (317-636-3101) and 225 East Ohio Street (317-637-5851), serves award-winning chili, gourmet burgers, fresh soups and salads, and specialty sandwiches. **Noble Roman's Pizza,** 136 North Delaware Street (317-637-9997), offers four styles of pizza: pan, deep-dish Sicilián, hand-tossed round, and super thin; sandwiches and salads are also on the menu. **Union Station,** 39 West Jackson Place (317-267-0701), is a century-old, refurbished station that now includes shops and restaurants (including inexpensive eateries), as well as trains. Kids like the "ghosts," those white statues of Victorian-era train riders.

The Indianapolis Convention and Visitors Association offers a visitor's guide that lists many family-friendly restaurants throughout the city.

DAY TRIPS

Conner Prairie, 13400 Allisonville Road, Noblesville; (317) 776-6000. This 250-acre living-history museum with about forty buildings is definitely worth a trip. Just fifty minutes from Indianapolis, the facility transports you to 1836. History is anything but boring here. Kids will be intrigued by the costumed interpreters who make the frontier come alive. The doctor's wife tells you how her piano had an easier trip from the East than she did, and the carpenter shows you how to fashion a chair leg. At the Golden Eagle Tavern, Martha Zimmermann bakes cookies and warns you about the dangers of women traveling alone. It's hands-on fun at the Pioneer Adventure area, where kids try their skill at weaving, grinding corn, and walking on stilts, a popular pioneer pastime.

The seasonal events are fun as well. In June be a guest at a wedding. On July 4th kick up your heels at a traditional village celebration. During August the Indianapolis Symphony Orchestra performs evening concerts in the museum's outdoor amphitheater. Bring a picnic supper and blanket for the lawn. Special fall events include demonstrations of hog butchering—the real thing—and smoking meats pioneer style.

Zionsville, a northern suburb of Indianapolis, features nineteenth-century architecture. Lincoln stopped here in 1861 to speak while en route to Washington, D.C., for his inauguration. A monument dedicated to the speech stands near the train station. Guided walking tours are available. Annual events include Country Market Arts Fair in May and a Fall Festival in September. For a brochure write to Zionsville Chamber of Commerce, 125 South Elm Street, or phone (317) 873-3836 from Tuesday to Friday, 10:00 A.M. to 4:30 P.M.

Indiana Dunes National Lakeshore. The lakeshore, in Indiana's northwestern corner, covers 13,000 acres along the southern shores of Lake Michigan. In season enjoy swimming, fishing, hiking, and cross-country skiing. Dunes, of course, are big here. See the view from the top of Mount Baldy, the lakeshore's tallest dune. As the area is located on a north-south migratory route, seasonal bird watching is great here. The visitor's center at Kermil Road and U.S. 12 has information, pamphlets, and maps. Call or write to Indiana Dunes National Lakeshore, 1100 North Mineral Springs Road, Porter, Indiana 46304; (219) 926-7561.

The French Lick Springs Resort, 8670 State Road 56, French Lick, Indiana 46432 (800-457-4042 or 812-936-9300), caters to children by offering summertime family programs including Mysterious Monday, for amateur detectives; the Pluto Club, for ages five through twelve; and Chuckwagon Cookouts every night of the week. Ask about reduced rates for children.

FOR MORE INFORMATION

Begin your visit with a stop at the visitor's center in the **Indianapolis City Center,** 201 South Capitol Avenue; (800) 468-INDY or (317) 237-5206. Browse the more than 300 brochures, examine the model of the city, and watch the eight-minute slide show, a fast-paced pastiche of city images. The hours are Monday to Saturday, 10:00 A.M. to 9:00 P.M., and Sunday, noon to 6:00 P.M. Call for information about weekend packages and special events. Internet: http://www.indy.org.

Emergency Numbers
Ambulance, fire, and police: 911
Poison Control: (317) 929-2323
Riley Hospital for Children, at Indiana University Medical Center, 702 Barnhill Drive; (317) 274-5000
Twenty-four-hour pharmacy: Revco, 1744 North Illinois; (317) 923-1491

6 🏠 Illinois

CHICAGO

Chicago, one of the Midwest's most popular destinations, offers great architecture and art, world-class museums, a top-notch aquarium, and miles of lakefront and bicycle paths. Stroll through the parks and the zoo, pedal by the lake, take a boat ride, and play ball on the beach. In this exciting city you and your kids won't be bored. Take your family on weekends when hotels are discounted, or be sure to bring the kids along on a business trip so that all of you can savor this dynamic city.

GETTING THERE

O'Hare International Airport (312-686-2200), 17 miles from the Loop, is served by most major airlines. The **Chicago Transit Authority** (CTA-312-686-7000) offers train transportation between Chicago and O'Hare. Train service originates at O'Hare Terminal #4 and in Chicago at the Dearborn Subway station. Midway Airport (312-767-0500), 15 minutes from the Loop at 5700 South Cicero Avenue, is the second most traveled airport in Chicago. A one-hundred-year-old plan will come to completion with the Northerly Island Park. Formerly the site of Meigs Field, a landing strip for private planes, the park will feature a botanic garden, ball fields, marinas, and a wildlife refuge.

Amtrak (800-USA-RAIL) stops at Chicago's Union Station, 210 South Canal Street; (312) 558-1075. **Continental Bus Airport Service** (312-454-7800) shuttles to and from Chicago's main airports. **Greyhound/Trailways** buses (312-781-2900) stop at Chicago station, 630 West Harrison Street.

The main highways to Chicago are I-90, which cuts across Chicago's northwest axis and becomes the Chicago Skyway south of the Loop; I-94 (the Dan Ryan Expressway), which runs north-south. From the south, take I-55 (Stevenson Expressway) and I-57. From the west, take I-294 west of Chicago and I-88.

GETTING AROUND

The key to Chicago's streets is to know where you are in relation to Lake Michigan, due east of the city, which looms like an inland ocean. Chicago's north-south axis is Madison Avenue, and its east-west axis is State Street. As you move away from these streets, addresses increase 100 for each block. The city is in a grid pattern, so it is easy to find your way around.

Chicago's elevated train system, fondly called the "El," operates six routes throughout the city and suburbs. For information contact RTA Travel Information Center at (312) 836-7000 or (800) 972-7000, or the CTA office on the 7th floor of the Merchandise Mart. Fares can be paid in cash or in tokens, which are offered, among other places, at Jewel and Dominick's grocery stores.

CTA buses (312-836-7000) travel along Chicago's major streets. For both bus and the El, senior citizens, the physically challenged, and children seven to eleven receive discounted fares and transfers. Kids under seven ride for free. For a **PACE** bus (312-836-7000), which provides additional service, wait at the blue-and-white PACE signs. PACE transfer tickets are valid for El trains. The hearing impaired can get transportation information by dialing **TDD** (312) 836-4949.

METRA offers train service from the suburbs into the city, with eleven commuter routes transporting riders from 225 outlying stations to four Chicago stations. Call (312) 322-6777 weekdays from 8:00 A.M. to 5:00 P.M., (312) 836-7000 evenings and weekends.

Sometimes the easiest and quickest way to get somewhere is by boat. **Wendella Commuter Boats,** Michigan Avenue Bridge at the Wrigley Building (312-337-1446), offers boat taxi service on the Chicago River at prices competitive with CTA transit. Boats leave every ten minutes from a commuter dock north of Madison Avenue, or from the Wendella dock south of Michigan Avenue below the Wrigley Building. Besides its seven-minute Madison-Wrigley Building route, the company offers extended trips into Lake Michigan, as well as two-hour, ninety-minute, and one-hour guided tours. Senior citizens and kids under eleven receive discounted tickets.

WHAT TO SEE AND DO

Must-See Museums

At the **Museum of Science and Industry,** Fifty-seventh Street and Lake Shore Drive (312-684-1414; TDD 312-986-2302), the diverse exhibits take you on a fun tour of fact and fantasy. A walk through a U-505 German submarine captured in 1944 makes the hard-to-envision world of undersea gauges, gizmos, and cramped quarters real. Browse silent-screen-star Colleen Moore's elaborate Fantasy Castle. With its tapestries, and more than 1,000 miniature pieces, this dollhouse delights the child within and the one by your side. Explore the human body by walking through a 16-foot pulsating heart and by looking at fetuses floating in bottles.

Train buffs won't want to leave the model train exhibit with its eight railroads that run through reconstructed sets of the Midwest, the Great Plains, the Grand Canyon, and California, and there is a new train exhibit in the underground parking lot. Two more top picks are the OMNIMAX theater, with its five-story-high screen, and, for kids ages seven to twelve, the Kids Stairway, a Path to Self-Discovery. This interactive exhibit is designed to build children's self-esteem, help them discover feelings, and teach them about alcohol and substance abuse. A visit here serves as a start to important discussions you and your children continue later.

For another, less intense take-home "item," visit the gift shop, where your kids can bring home a bit of science fun with a physics game, a rocket model kit, an anatomical coloring book, stickers, and puzzles.

Marine science is the thing at the **John G. Shedd Aquarium and Oceanarium,** 1200 South Lake Shore Drive; (312) 939-2438. Billed as one of the world's largest indoor marine mammal habitats, kids fall in love with this undersea world of brightly colored fish, coral reefs, turtles, sea otters, dolphins, and whales.

Time your visit for 11:00 A.M. to 2:00 P.M., and watch the action in the 900,000-gallon Coral Reef tank as divers feed the sharks, sea turtles, and scores of tropical fish. Each of several galleries serves up tankfuls of colorful critters. In the Indo-Pacific gallery, admire such

---

Chicago at a Glance

- Sophisticated city attractions surrounded by plentiful outdoor activities

- Lakefront parks, beaches, and zoo

- Science centers and museums for everyone

- Tours of buildings by Frank Lloyd Wright and other noted architects

- Chicago Office of Tourism, (312) 744-2400

---

brightly marked wrigglers as the yellow longsnout butterfly fish or the white-and-brown spotted clown triggerfish. Other galleries feature anemones swaying gently in the water, neon-colored starfish, and purple sea urchins.

The spectacular **Oceanarium,** with its sweeping view of Lake Michigan, re-creates a Pacific Northwest coastal environment. The view alone is worth the admission, but the wildlife is great, too. Follow the "trails" through a mini-rain forest, accompanied by chirping birds and crickets, and the rush of a waterfall; then admire the sea otters in tidal pools, the beluga whale, and the colony of penguins. Fall asleep to the soothing images of fish peacefully swimming in beautiful pools of water during special Sleeping with the Fishes weekends. The museum occasionally offers family sleepovers.

But the big attraction is the dolphin show, held five times daily in the amphitheater. Learn why these graceful behemoths lobtail (slap their tails on the water), breach, porpoise (leap out of the water and enter again), and tail walk (move backwards on their tails). These are just some of the animal behaviors explained and delightfully demonstrated.

Across the street from the Shedd Aquarium, the **Field Museum of Natural History,** Roosevelt Road, Lake Shore Drive (312-922-9410; TDD-312-341-9299), is an amazing place of a different sort. It's housed in a large, 1921 marble building claiming to be the largest

The interactive exhibits at Chicago's Field Museum of Science will intrigue adults and kids alike. (Photo by Ron Schramm/courtesy Chicago Tourism Council)

marble structure in the United States. Although the collection celebrated its centennial in 1993–1994, the exhibits are anything but old-fashioned and stodgy. Interactive, visually exciting, and interesting, these exhibits intrigue kids. There's too much here even for one visit. So let your kids hit the highlights, pausing at what intrigues them.

Don't miss Inside Ancient Egypt, a well-done exhibit that demystifies and explains the ancient burial rites. Walk into a re-created Egyptian tomb, with its passageways, and learn about mummies, hieroglyphics, and embalming. See your face transformed with "Egyptian" features, and find out the symbolism of the pyramid.

Traveling the Pacific brings you to a world of outrigger canoes, intricately carved masks, and a re-created Tahitian market. Into the Wild takes you through habitats as diverse as prairies, wetlands, lakes, and cliffs to learn about birds and other critters.

If you liked this place during the day, try it out on a special family overnight. Ever wonder what it would be like to roam through a museum after-hours when the crowds have left, and it's only you, the elephant bones, and the sound of your footsteps echoing on the linoleum? This Chicago museum gives you the chance to sleep with the dinosaurs, the Polynesian spear throwers, or the gigantic mounted elephants. On overnights, families select two workshops from possibilities as diverse as how to read Egyptian hieroglyphics, recognize dinosaur footprints, or identify owl calls. After a snack the evening offers such fun as a storyteller who relates Eskimo or African legends, or an educational scavenger hunt. When the lights go out, join a group of adventurers for a flashlight tour of the Egyptian tomb, or walk into the prairies, oceans, and forests of Into the Wild, alive with birdcalls and insect noises. Then, cuddle up in your sleeping bag, maybe next to a bushman, the gorilla, or among the thousands of mounted birds. This is a night you'll remember. A family overnight occurs each month. Fees are charged, and you must book well in advance. Call (312) 322-8854.

Explore the skies at the **Adler Planetarium,** 300 South Lake Shore Drive; (312) 322-0304 or TDD (312) 322-0995. The planetarium's multimedia Sky Show shuttles visitors through our solar system and off into distant galaxies. Before Sky Show ends it transports you back in time fifteen million years to revisit the origins of the universe. As part of the Evening Sky Shows, which occur each Friday night, the planetarium gives close-up looks at the moon, planets, and galaxies via the planetarium's 20-inch telescope, which is hooked up with a large-screen closed-circuit monitor. For children under six, who are not admitted to the regular sky show, reserve a spot in the Children's Sky Show, Saturdays and Sundays. Allow time to browse the exhibits on the solar system, the stars, telescopes, and astronomy.

Heavenly is what you're likely to call the art at the **Art Institute of Chicago,** Michigan Avenue at Adams Street; (312) 443-3600 or TDD (312) 443-3890. Spanning more than forty centuries from Mayan to modern, this place is a visual treat. Among the highlights are the prized collection of French Impressionist and Postimpressionist paintings by Degas, Monet, and Renoir; the collection of American and European painting 1900–1950; the sixty-eight Thorne Miniature Rooms, and Marc Chagall's stained-glass work *American Windows.*

Drop by the Kraft General Foods Education Center, a just-for-kids-and-families place that has changing exhibitions, a computer, story-telling, and often hands-on workshops. Tuesdays are free admission days at the Art Institute.

If the Art Institute piqued your interest in the arts, then head to the **Museum of Contemporary Art,** 220 East Chicago Avenue; (312) 280-2660). Under construction since 1986, the museum opened a new building and a sculpture garden in July 1996. The 125,000-square-foot addition increases the exhibition space by seven times. The museum's holdings include works by Franz Kline, Jeff Koons, and Andy Warhol. Kids may prefer the bright colors of modern art rather than the more traditional styles of art. From October 1997 to January 1998, there is a major exhibition called Hall of Mirrors: Art and Film Since 1945. Some kids might enjoy viewing older movies and comparing them to present-day films.

The city's history comes alive at the **Chicago Historical Society,** Clark Street at North Avenue; (312) 642-4600. Learn about pioneer life in the Land of Lincoln—often crafts demonstrations are held—climb aboard the *Pioneer,* the first twelve-ton locomotive to steam through this railroad town, and find out what Mrs. O'Leary's cow did or didn't do in the Great Chicago Fire, October 1870.

Visiting with a child ages five to nine? Then check out History Quest. Kids paint, listen to tales, make crafts, and do a variety of other projects. At the Hands-on History Gallery, little fingers touch some real city legends by feeling a beaver skin, perusing old Sears' Catalogues, and listening to tapes of "Fibber McGee and Molly."

More Attractions and Views

Watch the art of the deal at Chicago's big three exchanges. From visitor's galleries look at the bustling floor frenzy at the **Chicago Board of Trade,** 141 West Jackson Boulevard (312-435-3590), open 8:00 A.M.–2:00 P.M. It's the oldest and largest futures exchange. The **Chicago Mercantile Exchange,** 30 South Wacker Drive (312-930-8249), is open 7:30 A.M. to 3:15 P.M.; and you can visit the **Chicago Board Options Exchange** at 400 South LaSalle Street (312-786-5600), from 8:30 A.M. to 3:15 P.M.

A Chicago institution of another sort is Frank Lloyd Wright. At the **Frank Lloyd Wright Historic District Visitors Center,** 158 North Forest Avenue, Oak Park, Illinois 60301 (708-848-1500), take a guided tour of this architect's home and studio, and see the birthplace of the Prairie School of architecture. Wright's vision and others made this midwest city famous for its buildings.

From the **Sears Tower Skydeck,** Jackson Boulevard between Franklin Street and Wacker Drive (312-875-9696); or from the **John Hancock Center Observatory,** 875 North Michigan Avenue (312-751-3681), enjoy a panoramic view of Chicago, which on a clear day can include a glimpse of Michigan, Indiana, and maybe even Wisconsin.

For some great skyline views, visit **Navy Pier,** 600 East Grand Avenue (312-791-7437) and **North Pier,** 435 East Illinois Street (312-836-4300). In summer Navy Pier hosts many free public programs both indoors and outdoors. North Pier also has a shopping mall, the Chicago Children's Museum, and the Chicago Academy of Science. Relatively small, the **Chicago Children's Museum,** at Navy Pier, 600 East Grand Avenue (312-527-1000), offers a playful place where kids can dress up as a CTA driver, slip into a body bubble, pretend in a log cabin, and crawl through a tunnel of textures. A separate walled-in area for toddlers and tots eighteen months and younger has boxes of safe goodies, balls, and mirrors. Find out when crafts workshops are held so that your kids can create their own special Chicago souvenir.

Chicago Academy of Science, 465 East Illinois (312-836-4343), at North Pier, offers hands-on exhibits.

Chicago also boasts world-class street art that's worth a look. Among the best is the **Picasso Sculpture,** Washington and Dearborn streets at the Daley Center. The artist dedicated this 50-foot-tall structure to the people of Chicago.

If you happen to be stuck with kids at O'Hare International Airport, the world's busiest airport, then drop by the **Kids on the Fly Children's Museum.** There is an air-traffic-control tower that has an actual air-traffic-control recording, as well as an exhibit where kids can pass layover time by building skyscrapers with Duplo blocks. Kids can pretend to be pilots in a cargo plane that has a special treasure in it. While your kids play, you can check on the status of your flight at the museum's information center. The interactive museum is located in Terminal 2.

Another city staple is **Wrigley Field,** 1060 West Addison; (312) 404–CUBS. One of the oldest baseball stadiums, it has ivy-covered fences and home runs that catch the wind and fly out of the park onto Waveland Avenue. Check the schedule for Cubs' games.

Green Spaces and Lakefront

Parks along the lakefront were part of Chicago's design. These include **Lincoln Park, Grant Park, Burnham Park, Jackson Park,** and **Washington Park.** All have playing fields and usually host a festival or two throughout the year. Grant Park hosts the Taste of Chicago Festival in July, the Blues Fest in May, and a Jazz Fest in September. An 18-mile bike path cuts through these parks and offers scenic views of both the lake and Chicago's skyline; for more information on the park's bike path, call (312) 744–8092.

Gardens and Zoos

Brookfield Zoo, First Avenue and Thirty-first Street, Brookfield, Illinois 60513; (708) 485–0263. Located 14 miles west of downtown, this naturalistic habitat zoo covers 204 acres and displays more than 2,000 animals. Visit Tropic World and The Fragile Kingdom for Brookfield Zoo's most extravagant attempts at re-creating nature. Tropic World portrays life in the three great rain forests: Africa, Asia, and South America. The exhibit features a mixture of fauna, free-roaming small animals, exotic birds, and three daily thunderstorms. The Fragile

Kingdom highlights desert, rain-forest, and mountainous regions. The Seven Seas Panorama displays bottle-nose dolphins, and the Children's Zoo has tame creatures to pet. And don't miss the zoo's newest exhibit, Habitat Africa! Save your feet and take a Motor Safari tour. During the winter the tram offers heated tours of the zoo aboard the Snowball Express. The zoo can be accessed by I-55 and I-290 (Stevenson and Eisenhower expressways) as well as I-294 (Tri-State Tollway).

Chicago Botanic Garden, Lake Cook Road, a half-mile east of I-90-94 (Edens Expressway), Glencor, Illinois; (708) 835-5440. This blooming, three-hundred-acre wonder contains a sensory garden for the visually impaired, a nine-acre prairie and nature trail, and a three-island authentic Japanese Garden. Be sure to visit the greenhouses, gift shop, and the Museum of Floral Arts.

Minutes north of downtown, the **Lincoln Park Zoo,** 2200 North Cannon Drive (312-294-4600), is the place to bring your kids for a city safari. Take a close look at a swimming polar bear, elephants, rhinos, giraffes, gorillas, orangutans, and chimpanzees. To entertain wee ones, head for the petting zoo at the Pritzker Children's Zoo.

Tours

For **Architecture/Walking** tours of the city contact the following: **Chicago Architecture Foundation,** 224 South Michigan Avenue (312-922-3432); **Charnley-Persky House Tours,** 1354 North Astor Street (312-573-1365); **Chicago Cultural Center Architectural Tours,** Chicago Cultural Center, 78 East Washington Street (312-346-3278); **Oak Park Tour Center/Frank Lloyd Wright Tour,** 951 Chicago Avenue, Oak Park, Illinois (708-848-1500); and **Pullman Historic District,** 11111 South Forrestville Avenue (312-785-8181).

Boat Tours. **Chicago's First Lady,** southwest corner and lower level of the Michigan Avenue bridge and Wacker Drive (708-358-1330), offers lunch, brunch, and dinner tours of Chicago sailing aboard the *Chicago's First Lady* 1920s-style luxury cruiser. **Mercury, Chicago's Skyline Cruiseline,** southwest corner and lower level of the Michigan Avenue Bridge (312-332-1353), offers daily one-hour, ninety-minute, or two-hour cruises and skyline tours during the morning, afternoon, and evening from May 1 through October 1 (ask about the

Pirate Cruise for Kids). **Chicago from the Lake,** North Pier Terminal, 455 East Illinois Street (312-527-1977 and 527-2002), offers a ninety-minute tour of the Chicago River or the Chicago skyline; both tours are led by a member of the Chicago Architecture Foundation.

Bus Tours. **Gray Line of Chicago Sightseeing Tours,** originating at the Palmer House, 33 East Monroe Street (312-427-3107), offers daily comprehensive tours. **London Motor Coach** departs from Pearson and Michigan Avenue (312-226-2870) on its one-hour narrated double-decker bus tour of the city. Day Long Transfer passes are available for getting on and off the bus at designated points of interest, including the Wrigley Building, Art Institute, Sears Tower, Shedd Aquarium, the Field Museum, Adler Planetarium, Water Tower, and the Magnificent Mile.

Other Tours. **Untouchable Tour's Chicago's Original Gangster Tour** takes you back to Chicago's gangster days. Visit Al Capone's, John Dillinger's, and Bugs Moran's notorious hangouts and hit spots. For reservations call (312) 881-1195.

For a slow-paced, sweet, horse-drawn tour in a buggy, see the **Chicago Horse and Carriage Company,** southeast corner of Pearson Street and Michigan Avenue (312-94-HORSE); or try the **Noble Horse,** available at the southwest corner of Pearson and Michigan (312-266-7878).

Shopping

Hit the Magnificent Mile's shops along Michigan Avenue, from the Chicago River north to Oak Street. If you have time for just one stop, you might visit **Water Tower Place,** 835 North Michigan Avenue (312-440-3165), which has department stores such as Marshall Field's and Lord & Taylor, as well as specialty shops such as Benetton, Laura Ashley, a Disney Store, Beauty and the Beast, F.A.O. Schwarz, and, for snacks, Aunt Diana's Old Fashioned Fudge, Mrs. Field's Cookies, and California Pizza Kitchen.

State Street shopping includes Chicago's own Marshall Field's and Carson Pirie Scott. For the budget-minded the famous street also includes TJ Maxx and Filene's Basement. Kids can play in Toys "R" Us and the Sharper Image. Restaurants in the area offer everything from infamous Chicago-style pizza to Chinese and Thai food. The street was renovated in November 1996. The new and improved location includes tours and a theater district.

Performing Arts

Chicago offers cutting-edge theater, good comedy, and well-done plays. Home to some of the best are the **Steppenwolf Theatre,** 2851 North Halstead (312-472-4141), **Second City,** 1616 North Wells (312-337-3992); and **Second City Children's Theater.** Around Christmas, the **Goodman Theater,** 125 East Monroe Avenue (312-855-1524), puts on *A Christmas Carol;* and the **Arie Crown Theater,** McCornick Place (312-791-6000), hosts *The Nutcracker* ballet.

Some children's theaters include the **Animart Puppet Theater,** 3901 North Kedzie Avenue (312-267-1209); **The Children's Theatre Fantasy Orchard** (Chicago Historical Society), 1629 North Clark Street (312-539-4211); and **DePaul Merle Reskin Theatre,** 60 East Balbo Drive (312-362-8455). **Hystopolis Puppet Theater,** 441 West North Avenue (312-787-7387) offers sophisticated puppet plays, and the **Stage Left Theater,** 3244 North Clark Street (312-883-8830), offers plays about social issues aimed at kids. Check local listings or call the **Theater Information Line** at (312) 977-1755.

The **Chicago Symphony Orchestra,** as well as other orchestras and singers, perform at the **Civic Opera House** (312-346-0270) an the **Lyric Opera House** (312-332-2244), both located at 20 North Wacker Drive.

Looking for art galleries? Head to Chicago's "Su-Hu" district, located aptly enough at the intersection of Superior and Huron streets.

What child wouldn't enjoy a performance of *The Nutcracker* or *Swan Lake?* Now you can see the famous Joffrey Ballet of New York, which moved to Chicago in the spring of 1996.

More Useful Numbers. **Hot Tix** booths are at 24 South State Street, Chicago; 1020 Lake, Oak Park, Illinois; and 1616 Sherman Avenue, Evanston, Illinois. They offer half-price day-of-performance and full-price advance tickets for theater, music, dance, and all Ticketmaster events. Call (312) 977-1755 for hours and additional booth locations. **Ticketmaster** (312-559-8989 or 559-1212) offers full-price tickets for theater, dance, and musical events.

SPECIAL EVENTS

Sporting Events

Chicago Bears Football, Soldiers Field Stadium, 425 East Mcfetridge Drive; (312) 663-5100.

Chicago Blackhawks Hockey, United Center, 1901 West Madison Street; (312) 733-5300.

Chicago Bulls Basketball, United Center, 1901 West Madison Street; (312) 559-1212.

Chicago Cubs Baseball, Wrigley Field, 1060 West Addison; (312) 404-CUBS.

Chicago White Sox Baseball, Comiskey Park, 333 West Thirty-fifth Street; (312) 924-1000.

Festivals

The big crowds come to Grant Park in May, usually Memorial Day weekend, for **Chicago's Blues Festival** and in June for the annual **Gospel Festival. Ravinia Festival** in north suburban Highland Park, Illinois, draws large crowds during the summer months for its schedule of outdoor jazz, blues, classical, and fold concert.

January: University of Chicago Folk Festival.

February: African-American History Month.

March: St. Patrick's Day Festival, where parents can drink green beer and see the Chicago River dyed green.

April: Chicago Cubs and White Sox Baseball season opens. Chicago Park District Public Golf Courses open. Spring Festival of Dance. Spring Flower Show (free). International Kennel Club Spring Dog Show Weekend

May: Chicago Blues Festival. Chicago Day.

June: Chicago Neighborhood Festivals (free). Chicago Gospel Festival (free). International Children's Festival. Lincoln Central Association Dickens Street Summerfest. Taste of Chicago begins (free admission).

July: Taste of Chicago continues. Independence Eve Concert and Fireworks Show (free). Chicago Neighborhood Festivals (free). Grant Park Music Festival (free).

All summer long: Ravinia Outdoor Music Festival. Swimming at Chicago Park District lakefront beaches and outdoor pools (free). Grant Park Music Festival (free).

August: Chicago Park District Air and Water Show (free).

September: Chicago Jazz Festival (free). "Viva! Chicago" Latin Music Festival (free). Chicago Bears Football season begins. Chicago Symphony Orchestra season begins. Chicago Neighborhood Festivals (free).

October: Columbus Day Parade (free). Chicago International Film Festival. Children's Film Festival. Chicago Blackhawks Hockey season begins. Lincoln Park Zoo's Spooky Zoo Spectacular. International Kennel Club Fall Dog Show.

November: American Indian Center Powwow. Chrysanthemum Show. *A Christmas Carol* at the Goodman Theatre. City of Chicago Christmas Tree Lighting Ceremony (free). Christmas Around the World Festival at Museum of Science and Industry, Christmas Parade (free). Chicago Bulls Basketball season begins. Holiday Lights Festival (free). Skate on State (free outdoor ice skating).

December. *The Nutcracker* ballet at Arie Crown Theater. Caroling to the Animals at Lincoln Park Zoo. Christmas Eve Flower Show (free). Holiday Lights Festival (free).

WHERE TO STAY

Embassy Suites Hotel, 600 North State Street (312-943-7629), offers suites and a hot breakfast, as does the **Guest Quarters Suite Hotel,** 198 East Delaware Place (312-664-1100 or 800-424-2900). **The Hyatt Regency Chicago,** 151 East Wacker Drive (312-565-1234 or 800-233-1234), offers big-hotel amenities, plus the Camp Hyatt kid's menus, and a 50-percent discount on a second room for the kids. They do not usually offer children's activities.

The Four Seasons Hotel, 120 East Delaware Place (312-280-8800) comes with large rooms and special turndown of milk and cookies for the kids (ask). The **Holiday Inn-Mart Plaza,** 350 North Orleans Street (312-836-5000), the **Sheraton Plaza,** 160 East Huron Street (312-787-2900 or 800-325-3535); and the **Days Inn-Lake Shore Drive,** Lake Michigan and the Navy Pier (312-943-9200), are less costly options.

Marriott's Lincolnshire Resort, 10 Marriott Drive; (800) 228-9290 or (708) 634-0100, is located forty-five minutes from downtown. The Children's Activity House has plenty of activities that will amuse kids including swimming, relay races, crafts, movies, and outdoor games.

Since the summer of 1993, the resort has sponsored these supervised activities in one-hour blocks on Saturdays. Different age groups participate at different times: ages four to six from 9:00 to 10:00 A.M. and from 2:00 to 3:00 P.M.; ages seven to ten from 10:00 to 11:00 A.M. and from 2:00 to 3:00 P.M. Be sure to confirm these times, as they may be extended. There is a theater on the premises that features occasional children's productions as well as standard movie fare.

WHERE TO EAT

The Berghoff, 17 West Adams Street (312-427-3170), is famous for its bratwurst, sausage, schnitzel, and strawberry short cake. **Carson's For Ribs,** 612 North Wells Street (312-280-9200), offers barbecued ribs, chicken, and children's menus. **Claim Company,** 900 North Michigan Avenue (312-787-5757), serves chicken, ribs, burgers, and has kid's menus and crayons for paper-covered tabletops. **Ed Debevic's Short Orders Deluxe,** 640 North Wells Street (312-664-1707), open for lunch and dinner, is a fifties-style diner with prizes for kids and a nostalgic atmosphere and inexpensive diner fare for parents, including five-way chili, roast turkey, chicken fried steak, burgers and fries, meatloaf, cherry cokes, and chocolate shakes.

You can't visit Chicago without sampling the deep-dish pizza. **Giordano's,** 747 North Rush (312-951-0747), serves up the traditional thick, Chicago-style pizza. **Pizzeria Uno,** 29 East Ohio (312-321-1000), is the birthplace of Chicago-style deep-dish pizza. Uno also serves generous portions of soup, sandwiches, salads, and gourmet appetizers. **Pizzeria Due,** 619 North Wabash (312-943-2400), Uno's sister restaurant, serves the same, tasty, Chicago-style deep-dish pizza. **Redmak's New Buffalo Chicago,** 2263 North Lincoln (312-787-4522), has burgers and such for lunch, and dinner.

If your kids are basketball fans, they might like dining at **Michael Jordan's Restaurant,** 500 North La Salle (312-644-DUNK). This mid-priced place offers Jordan's pregame meal of steak and potatoes and other Jordan favorites such as pasta, macaroni and cheese, filet of sole, and peach pie.

The renovated **Navy Pier,** in the heart of Chicago, 600 East Grand Avenue (312-595-PIER), features fifty acres of parks, gardens, shops, and eateries.

House of Blues (312-527-1988), a music-themed restaurant and blues club, opened in Marina City last fall.

DAY TRIPS

More amusements are not too far away at **Six Flags Great America,** in Gurnee, Illinois, I-94 at Route 132; (708) 249-1776. This amusement park has rides for kids and adults as well as an IMAX theater.

If shopping for bargains is your forte, don't miss **Gurnee Mills Outlet,** Gurnee, Illinois, I-94 at Route 132; (800) YES-SHOP. Browse the bargains at this mall's more than 200 manufacturers' and retail outlets.

Head to Indiana for the **Indiana Dunes National Lakeshore** (219-926-7561) and **Indiana Dunes State Park** (219-936-1952). Only a ninety-minute drive south of the city lies Mt. Baldy, the park's tallest dune, along with miles of hiking trails and actual sand beaches.

Make a trip south into Illinois to **Starved Rock National Park** for beautiful woods, trails, rivers, waterfalls, and the famed Starved Rock cliff. The **Wisconsin Dells** also attract lots of Chicagoans. (See the chapter on Wisconsin Dells.)

FOR MORE INFORMATION

Contact the **Chicago Office of Tourism,** Chicago Cultural Center, 78 East Washington Street; (312) 744-2400. Also, travel counselors are available at (800) 2-CONNECT or at http://www.ci.chi.il.US/Tourism.

Emergency Numbers
Ambulance, fire, police: 911
Children's Memorial Hospital: Children's Plaza at Fullerton and Lincoln avenues; (312) 880-4000
Poison Control: the Northwestern Memorial Hospital emergency room; (312) 908-2000
Twenty-four-hour pharmacy: Walgreen's, 757 North Michigan Avenue; (312) 664-8686

THE DELLS

Wisconsin Dells, 55 miles northwest of Madison, Wisconsin, is an area of more than 18 square miles with two distinct personalities. If you're looking for natural beauty, the area (which includes the city of Wisconsin Dells and the village of Lake Delton) offers miles of spectacular dells—unusually shaped sandstone formations rising 100 feet above the tree-lined Wisconsin River. If it's fun, games, and a little glitz you want, the area offers a mind-boggling assortment of man-made wonders including a circus, the nation's largest water park, amusements, 360 holes of miniature golf, and more. Obviously, families find it a winning vacation combination: Wisconsin Dells is the Midwest's largest tourist destination, visited by some 3 million people a year.

GETTING THERE

The airport closest to the Dells area is Dane County Airport in Madison (608-246-3380), which is served by a number of major commercial airlines. Car rentals are available at the airport.

Greyhound Bus tickets and schedule information are available at Broadway Mobil Travel Mart, 802 Broadway; (608) 253-2091. Greyhound also stops at Burger King, Highway 13 off I-90/94, exit 87.

Amtrak (800-USA-RAIL) stops at the downtown Wisconsin Dell train station on Eddy Street (608-254-7700), which is open only when a train is due.

Wisconsin Dells, directly off I-90/94, is easily accessible by car.

GETTING AROUND

While there are some shuttles that run between attractions, there is no public transportation, so a car is a must.

WHAT TO SEE AND DO

Museums

Some of the attractions listed here aren't conventional four-walled museums, but come now—would you really expect to find a stuffy museum in Wisconsin Dells? All of the following offer enjoyable learning experiences.

Circus World, 426 Water Street, Baraboo; (608) 356-0800. The Ringling Bros. Circus actually began in 1884 in this town fifteen minutes from the Dells, the original winter headquarters. The exhibit hall is open year-round and contains fascinating memorabilia, including old circus posters and the world's largest collection of colorful vintage circus wagons. The museum has also acquired a collection of vintage circus instruments, including the Ringling Bros. Bell Wagon, which at the time carried nine gigantic church-style bells. But the big attractions during the summer are the live performances under a 2,000-seat big-top tent, including the circus and magic shows.

Mid-Continent Railway Museum, Walnut Street, North Freedom; (608) 522-4261. Located in a tiny town fifteen minutes south of the Dells, the museum provides a nice change of pace from the area's many purely amusement attractions. Steam passenger trains leave a turn-of-the-century depot for fifty-minute rides through the countryside, giving kids a chance to experience the Golden Age of Railways. On exhibit back at the train yard are steam and diesel engines, passenger cars, wooden freight cars, and other vintage railway equipment. It's open daily mid-May through Labor Day; and on weekends until mid-October, when autumn train rides are especially colorful. A winter Snowtrain runs the third weekend in February. You can visit another steam-powered train ride closer to town—a miniature 15-inch-gauge version—at **Riverside and Great Northern Railway,** a mile north on Stand Rock Road; (608) 254-6367.

Museum of Norman Rockwell Art, 227 South Park Street, Highway 23, Reedsburg; (608) 524-2123. Located fifteen minutes south of the Dells, this museum has the world's largest collection of the popular artist's work—some 4,000 examples—including original magazine covers, ads, posters, book, calendars, and Boy Scout; memorabilia. Rockwell's art has universal appeal; even younger children can relate to its warmhearted

Wisconsin Dells at a Glance

- Miles of natural beauty offering fun, games, and a little glitz

- The Dells—nature's dramatic sandstone formations

- Manmade wonders: a circus, water park, miniature golf, and more

- Performances at Stand Rock Indian Ceremonial

- Wisconsin Dells Visitor and Convention Bureau, (608) 254-8088 or (800) 22-DELLS

humor. Combine this stop with a visit to **Pioneer Log Village and Museum,** highways 23 and 33 (608-524-2123), operated by the Reedsburg Historical Society. The eleven-building complex includes a school, church, blacksmith shop, and country store dating from 1850-65.

Tommy Bartlett Robot World & Exploratory, 560 Wisconsin Dells Parkway, Highway 12; (608) 254-2525. This commercial operation is not technically a museum, but the numerous hands-on experiences offered are on par with those you'll find at many children's exhibits at science museums. Children of all ages learn about electric energy, gravity, air currents, robotics, sound, and more by "doing." They can make their hair stand on end, turn upside down in a gyro ride, interact with a robot (who leads a guided tour), and more. Next door, **Tommy Bartlett's Ski, Sky, and Stage Show** (same phone as Robot World) has been packing them in for more than forty years, offering three shows a day, rain or shine, including an evening laser spectacular.

Animal Attractions

International Crane Foundation, E11376 Shady Lane Road, Baraboo; (608) 356-9462. If you're going to Circus World, it is definitely worth a stop at this nearby attraction to see the world's most complete collection of cranes. The foundation works with other nations, including China, India, and Australia, to save seven endangered species of the fifteen in existence. A pair of each of the fifteen are housed in an exhibition pod. Take a self-guided tour to a restored prairie and marsh to get an up-close view of the graceful birds, or take a guided tour to see the cute crane chicks and adult birds.

Wisconsin Deer Park, 583 Highway 12; (608) 253-2041. Nearly 150 deer roam over this twenty-eight-acre facility—step right in and interact. If your kids have never been around animals, they may be intimidated at first, but once they get up the nerve to pet and feed black deer, white tails, and rare white deer, they'll be completely won over. A big hit: the tiny spotted fawns in the baby nursery. Other wildlife to view include elk and buffalo.

Serpent Safari, 1425 Wisconsin Dells Parkway; (608) 253-3200. This small but interesting museum opened in 1996. Discover exotic reptiles, such as albino snakes, and Baby, a 400-pound snake, the largest in captivity. Besides these slithery creatures, the museum houses and endangered alligator and a snapping turtle. After the self-guided tour, stop in the Safari Store, where educational books and toys are available.

Tours of the Dells

A Winnebago Indian legend attributes the spectacular formations of the dells to the path of a giant serpent; geologists say the dells (from the French word *della,* meaning "slab-like or tile rock") were caused by the erosion of Cambrian sandstone by thousands of years of glacial water. A downtown power dam separates the Upper and Lower Dells; both are worth seeing, although most of the rock formations appear on the lower end. To get the most out of this gift of nature, you really have to take some sort of a tour. A variety of choices exist.

School-age kids, teens, and adults will get the biggest kick out of taking one of the "ducks," World War II amphibious vehicles used in the invasion of Normandy and other famous battles. The vehicles, retired in 1958, now have a new mission: transporting tourists over miles of land and water and back again. They venture through fields of wildflowers, along breathtaking trails such as Black Hawk Gorge with its steep canyon walls, and through pristine water past the sculpted cliffs. As you might expect, the land part of the voyage can be bouncy; if anyone in your group has a delicate constitution, opt for a more traditional boat cruise down the river. One-hour, 8½-mile duck tours are

A ride abord a "duck," one of the amphibious vehicles used during World War II, is an exciting way to tour the Wisconsin Dells.
(Courtesy Wisconsin Dells Visitor and Convention Bureau)

available from Original Wisconsin Ducks, 1 mile south of Wisconsin Dells on Highway 12 (608-254-8751); and from Dells Duck Tours, the Main Duck Dock on Highway 12 (608-254-6080). The latter also runs boat tours. A one-hour Lower Dells cruise features colorful local stories of the logging era, plus Indian history and legends; a 2½-hour Upper Dells tour stops at Witches Gulch and Stand Rock, where you can walk along nature trails and hidden canyons.

Other options: a 1-mile canyon tour via horse-drawn carriage with Lost Canyon Tours, 720 Canyon Road; (608) 253-2781. Badger Helicopter Rides, located at 633 Wisconsin Dells Parkway behind Olde Kilbourn Amusements, has three different rides over the Dells in three different price ranges, mid-May through Mid-October. At Holiday Shores Boat Rentals along the east bank of the Upper Dells (608-254-2878), the choice includes pontoons, canoes, paddleboats, and wave runners. Lake Delton Water Sports, Highway 12, Lake Delton (608-254-8702), offers the same selection of boats and also runs Lower Dells Raft Trips. Ride tall in the saddle over one hundred acres of trail on a horse from the OK Corral, a mile south on Highway 16; (608) 243-2811. Kids ride free with parents, and there's a free petting zoo and pony rides for the younger set back at the corral.

Parks

When you need a break from the nonstop amusements, head to **Mirror Lake State Park,** 8 miles west of Baraboo on Highway 12; (608) 254-2333. The park, partially surrounded by sandstone bluffs, is a haven for fishing, camping, swimming at a sandy beach, and canoeing. It's open year-round and in the winter has cross-country skiing, including candlelight evenings in January and February when they provide lit cooking grills and a warming fire.

There's also a small public beach on the south shores of **Lake Delton,** off Hiawatha Drive.

Other Attractions

Water park fans (aren't all kids?) will love the three massive water parks in Wisconsin Dells. **Noah's Ark,** U.S. 12 and SR 23 (608-254-6351), the country's largest; **Family Land,** a mile south on U.S. 12 (608-254-7766), boasting mid-America's largest wave pool; and **Riverview Park,** ¼ mile south on U.S. 12; (608) 254-2608. Those with young kids might opt for Family Land, with Tiny Tots' Water Slides and a complete kiddie playground; or Riverview Park, with four children's activity pools and kiddie go-carts. Each park has wave pools (Family Land boasts the largest), picnic areas, food, shopping, midway rides, bumper boats, and much more.

Big Chief Kart and Coaster World has two parks near each other (one on Highway 12, the other on County Highway A) that comprise the nation's largest complex. There's a track to suit all ages and levels, including Little Chief tracks for young drivers. The complex has expanded to include two wooden roller coasters, the Pegasus and the Cyclops Coaster. The Pegasus, built to accommodate smaller children, is slower and goes up to heights of 45 feet. Tickets are good at either location; call (608) 254-2490 for information.

Storybook Gardens, 1500 Wisconsin Dells Parkway, is a low-key attraction for the very young. There is a petting zoo and miniature train ride tours of the gardens, plus life-size storybook characters; (608) 253-2391.

Crazy King Ludwig's Adventure Park resembles a Dark Ages castle, but the activities it offers never get old. There are five go-cart tracks, bumper boats, batting cages, a bungee jump, and arcade games.

Anyone for fishing? There's no license required at the following attractions. Try **B & H Tour Fishing,** 7 miles north on Highway 13 (608-254-7280), where there's no limit to the number of rainbow trout you can catch. They furnish poles and bait, clean the fish, and freeze and store them until you go home; so does **Beaver Springs Fishing Park,** 600 Trout Road (608-254-2735/800-236-7288). Seven spring-fed ponds on thirteen acres are stocked with trout, catfish, bass, pike, and more.

SPECIAL EVENTS

All the following annual events have special appeal for families. The Wisconsin Dells Visitor and Convention Bureau (800-22-DELLS, ext. R) can provide exact dates and locations.

January: Flake Out Festival snow-sculpting competition, includes children's events, food, and more.

February: Mid-Continent Railway Museum's Steam Snow Train, third weekend.

May: Automation Fest, which features more than 700 cars including antiques, street machines, and classics.

June: Heritage Day Celebration, Bowman Park, features arts and crafts exhibits, ice-cream social, quilters show, and more. The Great Wisconsin Dells Balloon Rally includes launching and display of more than one hundred hot-air balloons. Kite-flying demonstrations and other entertainment.

July: Ultra Light Fly-In at Yukon Trails Campground is a glider and ultra-light aircraft competition.

September: Polish Fest, Riverview Park and Waterworld, features ethnic food, colorful costumes, dance music, and art exhibit. Wo-Zha-Wa Days Fall Festival, downtown, with arts and crafts, antique flea market, street carnival, and parade finale.

October: Mid-Continent Steam Train Autumn Color Tours, selected weekends; Parson's Fall Friendship Gathering features Native American crafts, artifacts, a Powwow and a wedding ceremony.

Shopping

More than sixty shops of all descriptions are in downtown Wisconsin Dells, just a short walk from most hotels and motels. (If you drive, there's plenty of free parking.) But if you think you'll get away with a few dollars in purchases, guess again. In addition to the shops and some twenty restaurants, you'll find approximately twenty "glitzy" attractions, such as Ripley's Believe It or Not! Bill Nehring's Dungeon of Horrors (with a choice of "subtle and funny" scares for kids), The Skreemer space shuttle simulator ride, Haunted Mansion, Waxy World of the Stars, and Dells Auto Museum, to name but a few. While many of the attractions are fun, this type of razzmatazz is not for everybody, and it can get expensive. Of course, most kids enjoy this, and the attractions can be a welcome refuge on a rainy day. You might want to save a visit here for your last night in town. That way the kids can't beg you to return the next day.

Don't leave the state without Wisconsin cheese! You'll find a good selection at Market Square Cheese and Gifts, 1150 Dells Parkway South, Lake Delton; (608) 254-8388. Genuine Native American handicrafts and art are for sale at Parson's Indian Trading Post and Museum, 2½ miles south on Highway 12; (608) 254-8533. You'll also see artifacts on display.

Performing Arts

As you might imagine, the performing arts in Wisconsin Dells don't consist of symphonies and Shakespeare—just good, old American fun.

At **Wisconsin Opry,** E10964 Moon Road, Highway 12, Baraboo (608-254-7951), everybody will have a knee-slapping, hand-clapping, toe-tapping good time. They're open nightly from mid-May to mid-September and Sunday afternoon. A flea market takes place here on the weekends.

Stand Rock Indian Ceremonial, 4 miles north on Stand Rock Road (608-253-7444), is a fascinating, colorful presentation by Native American musicians and ceremonial dancers (including young children). It's held at Stand Rock, the pillar that has become the symbol of the Dells. You can drive here or take a boat (608-254-8555) that departs from the Upper Dells Landing nightly, mid-June to Labor Day.

WHERE TO STAY

This area offers a huge assortment of accommodations in all price ranges. A complete listing, including a map that pinpoints locations, can be found in the Convention and Visitors Bureau's *Travel and Attractions Guide*. Most Wisconsin Dells' hotels and motels are located along two commercial strips: Highway 13 and Highway 12. These merge into Lake Delton, where you can also find some quieter, lakeside accommodations, including cabins (some with their own sandy beaches). Families with kids are the mainstay of the tourist economy, so most lodgings are extremely family-friendly and are constantly adding amenities for children. Here are a few of the many possibilities.

Wisconsin Dells

Chula Vista Resort, Scenic River Road, has family suites, including new Fantasy Dream Suites. Fantasy settings include a Caribbean Pirate Ship, Space, and the Wild Wild West, where the beds resemble covered wagons. Facilities include indoor/outdoor pools, an athletic club, tennis courts, golf, hiking trails, a kiddie playground, and a full-service restaurant. Kids will love Splash Mountain, part of the resort's indoor water complex. It's a twisting, 40-foot-long water slide that travels through a waterfall. Ask about summer packages. Call (608) 254-8366/(800) 38-VISTA.

Polynesian Suite Resort, Highway 13 north, equips some of its 118 suites with microwaves, refrigerators, and separate living areas. Along with an indoor pool, sauna, whirlpools, and tanning booth are outdoor activity pools, rock waterfalls, a water slide, and a kiddie activity area, featuring geysers, swings, a waterfall, and a toddler water slide. Call (608) 254-2883/(800) 272-5642.

River Inn, 1015 River Road, 2 blocks from downtown, boasts a riverfront location and great views of the Dells from the restaurant and most of the rooms, which include family units and economy rooms. There are indoor and outdoor pools, a playground, and a fitness room. Call (608) 253-1231.

The Copa Cabana Resort Hotel and Suites, 611 Wisconsin Dells Parkway, Wisconsin Dells, WI 53965 (800-364-2672 or 608-253-1511), features its own water park called **Lost Lagoon.** Kids delight in the geysers, shark slide, octopus swing, and children's play area.

Meet Yogi Bear himself and have fun during the special three-day weekend programs offered at **Yogi Bear's Camp–Resort,** located off I-90 at S1915 Ishnala Road, P.O. Box 510, Wisconsin Dells, WI 53965; (800) Go-2-YOGI or (608) 254-2568.

Lake Delton

Sandy Beach Resort, 55 Dam Road, with its own beach directly on the lake, had one- and two-bedroom kitchen cottages and one-room kitchenettes. One week is the minimum stay during the peak summer season. Call (608) 254-8553.

Lighthouse Cove, directly on Lake Delton, offers tastefully furnished one- and two-bedroom shore-side condominiums with fully equipped kitchens. Indoor and outdoor pools, tennis and basketball courts, a beach, and boat docks add to the appeal; (800) 790-2683.

WHERE TO EAT

Name your family's favorite food, and you'll find it in this area. Along with the tried-and-true burger, fried chicken, and pizza places, are these restaurants popular with the locals:

Jimmy's Del-Bar, Highway 12, Lake Delton, designed by Frank Lloyd Wright protégé James Dresser, offers three casual, family-style meals daily, including a summer buffet dinner. A kiddie menu is available. Call (608) 253-1861. **Ishnala Supper Club,** overlooking Mirror Lake, serves steaks, seafood, and more in a lovely natural setting. There are even giant Norway pines growing through the dining area! Call (608) 423-4122. Heaps of hearty ethnic food are served at **American Club & Polish/American Buffet,** 400 County Trunk A and Highway 12; (608) 253-4451.

DAY TRIPS

All ages will be fascinated by **LaReau's World of Miniature Buildings,** south of Pardeeville on Highway 22, under an hour's drive east of the Dells. This is a Lilliputian collection of scale model buildings constructed of wood, styrofoam, metal, and concrete. Re-creations include the White House, Independence Hall, Washington Monument, and the Statue of Liberty. Call (608) 429-2848. Wisconsin Auto Tours (see below) offers an interesting car tour of the area.

FOR MORE INFORMATION

Wisconsin Dells Visitor and Convention Bureau, 701 Superior Street, P.O. Box 390, Wisconsin Dells 53905-0390 (608-254-8088/800-22-DELLS), has a helpful *Travel & Attraction Guide,* plus other useful information. Or, via the Internet, http://www.wisdells.com.

Free Wisconsin travel literature is available from **Wisconsin Tourism Development,** 123 West Washington Avenue, P.O. Box 7606. Call (608) 266-2161 in Wisconsin and neighboring states; (800) 432-TRIP elsewhere). Send for the excellent *Wisconsin Auto Tours,* featuring twenty-three road adventures, including one that details the Wisconsin Dells area. The guide notes which attractions are handicapped-accessible. Or visit Wisconsin on the Internet: http://www.tourism.state.wi.us.

Emergency Numbers

Ambulance, fire, police (Adams, Columbia, and Sauk counties): 911

Poison Control: (608) 253-1171

Two hospitals with twenty-four-hour emergency services are approximately 10 miles from Wisconsin Dells: **St. Clare Hospital,** 707 Fourteenth Street, Baraboo (608-356-5561); **Reedsburg Area Medical Center,** 200 North Dewey, Reedsburg (608-524-6487). The **Dells Clinic,** 1310 Broadway, Wisconsin Dells (608-253-1171), provides general health services from 8:00 A.M. to 6:00 P.M.

There are no twenty-four-hour pharmacies in the area. **Broadway Mobil Pharmacy,** 802 Broadway; (608) 253-2091. For an emergency after hours, call the Wisconsin Dells police, and they will contact a pharmacist.

NORTHWOODS AREA

The vast Northwoods area of Wisconsin offers families an unspoiled, natural setting for a vacation of down-to-earth pleasures. Most northern Wisconsin communities were once lumbering centers, and the lore and legends of those days live on, although the logging industry declined by the early 1900s. Today the Northwoods is a sporting paradise and summer vacation retreat. Families come here for the scenic woodlands and lakes.

While there are no official boundaries for the Northwoods, the region is considered to be the north-central (north of Wausau) and northeastern (north of Green Bay) part of the state. Oneida County, where Minocqua, Woodruff, and Rhinelander are situated, and Vilas County, home to Arbor Vitae and Lac du Flambeau, are its tourist centers. Minocqua, called the "Island City," is one of the area's popular summer resorts, thanks to the lake that surrounds it and its proximity to more than 3,000 lakes and ponds, the largest concentration of freshwater lakes in the world. Pine-scented forests offer hiking and biking trails, and day trips lead to man-made and natural wonders. In winter this area (Minocqua and surrounding towns are referred to as the Lakeland area) is a top snowmobile destination, as well as home to Minocqua Park, an XC-ski facility.

GETTING THERE

The Rhinelander-Oneida County Airport (715-362-3641), 25 miles from Minocqua, is served by major commercial carriers. Taxi service is available at the airport. The Lakeland Airport, 1545 North Farming Road, Woodruff, is available to private planes. Call (715-356-4340). **Greyhound** (715-362-2737) also goes to Rhinelander. There are no nearby Amtrak stations.

GETTING AROUND

Cars, boats, and bikes are the popular transportation modes around these parts. There's no public transportation.

WHAT TO SEE AND DO

Parks

Torpy Park, downtown Minocqua, has a beach with approximately 340 feet of frontage on Lake Minocqua. The beach is safe for kids, as it has roped swimming areas, lifeguards, and a designated boat-landing area. There's a diving area, a kiddie dock, tennis courts, a sand volleyball court, picnic tables, and grills, as well as a band shell for evening activities. In winter dress warmly and come here for ice skating.

Brandy Park, Arbor Vitae, off Highway 51N on Lemona Creek Road, has a beach/swim area with lifeguards, tennis courts, a baseball diamond, rest rooms, and a pavilion with picnic tables and grills.

Bearskin State Park Trail is a wilderness trail that extends for 18.2 miles, from just north of the Lincoln and Oneida County line north to Minocqua. The trail, which you enter from behind the Minocqua Post Office, is a former railroad grade that's been surfaced with crushed red granite for hiking and biking. Deer, raccoon, otter, beaver, and other native wildlife scamper about. You cross the scenic Beaver Creek several times via rustic trestles. In winter snowmobiles are allowed to use the trails, although no other motorized vehicles are permitted. Midpoint on the shore of South Blue Lake, there's a rest area with toilets, picnic tables, grills, and drinking water. Daily admission is nominal, or an annual pass can be purchased at the Minocqua AWV area Chamber of Commerce, as can a guidebook detailing the history and points of interest on the trail.

Minocqua is within striking distance of two forests, both offering wilderness recreational opportunities. **Chequamegon National Forest,** Headquarters, 1170 Fourth Street, Park Falls (715-762-2461), is about 13 miles from downtown Minocqua to the eastern part of this vast for-

Northwoods Area at a Glance

- Unspoiled, natural setting for down-to-earth pleasures

- Hiking, skiing, or snowmobiling in pine-scented forests

- Sheer's Lumberjack Show and the Rhinelander Logging Museum

- Home of the "hodag," a mythical dragon-like creature

- Minocqua AWV area Chamber of Commerce, (800) 44-NORTH; Rhinelander Chamber of Commerce, (800) 236-4FUN

est, which features nearly 850,000 acres of lakes, rivers, streams, northern hardwoods, pines, and meadowlands. There are twenty-four campsites; the **Chippewa Campground** in the Medford District is the only one with warm-water showers and flush toilets. It has a swimming beach and play area. For camping reservations call (800) 283-CAMP. The forest publishes a number of helpful brochures on different aspects of the park, including cross-country ski and hiking trails, scenic overlooks, wetland wildlife viewing areas, historic sites, and fishing and boating areas. Contact the forest headquarters for more information.

Northern Highland–American Legion State Forest, Woodruff, is the other forest, It's about 5 miles north of Minocqua to the southwest fringe of the forest near the Woodruff area headquarters. This forest offers 222,000 acres with 900 lakes, plus woodland, and nature and hiking trails. Families also enjoy picnicking, swimming, and canoeing.

There are nine unsupervised beach and picnic areas throughout the park. The closest to Minocqua is Clear Lake, which also has a rustic campground (no flush toilets or running water) and a swimming area. For more information stop by or contact Woodruff Area Forest Headquarters, 8770 Highway J, Woodruff 54568; (715) 356-5211.

In winter **Minocqua Winter Park,** Squirrel Lake Road off Highway 70 West, offers visitors 75 kilometers of groomed cross-country trails, a certified ski school, a ski shop for retail and rentals, and special trails groomed for small children. The day lodge provides childcare for all ages on Tuesdays, weekends, and holidays, as well as food service. Call (715) 356-3309.

Museums

Dr. Kate Pelham Newcomb Museum, 923 Second Avenue, Woodruff; (715) 356-6896. This museum pays tribute to an extraordinary local woman who reached the sick in a special car outfitted with skis on the front wheels and tractor treads on the rear. To access more remote areas, she used snowshoes. Dr. Newcomb practiced until she died in 1956 at age seventy, and her story, told in this museum, is really an inspiration.

Jim Peck's Wildwood, 2 miles west on Highway 70; (715) 356-5588. This is primarily a petting zoo, where kids feed tame deer, pet a porcupine, and cuddle a llama. There's a bear, too, just to admire. Kids will also like the adventure boat rides and nature walk on this thirty-acre property.

Lac du Flambeau Chippewa Museum & Cultural Center, Peace Pipe Road just south of the Indian Bowl, in Lac du Flambeau; (715) 588-3133. The nearby village of Lac du Flambeau lies in the center of the 144-square-mile Lac du Flambeau Chippewa Indian Reservation. The Museum and Cultural Center, which is open late June through mid-August, appeals to kids. The French name, meaning "Lake of the Flaming Torches," was given by fur traders who saw Chippewas fishing in their canoes by torchlight. Exhibits include an authentic Indian dugout canoe, birchbark canoes, crafts and traditional clothing, ceremonial drums, artifacts, and an exhibit displaying Chippewa activities and clothing. Demonstrations take place regularly.

The **Lac du Flambeau Indian Pow-Wows,** Indian Bowl, take place from late June through mid-August; (715) 588-3346. Kids love the ceremonial dance presented by authentic Chippewa performers. Call for show times and dates.

At the **Lac du Flambeau Fish Hatchery,** on the Chippewa Reservation, Highway 47, there's a fishing pond open from May through August where the entire family can fish without a license and pay only for the trout caught. Call (715) 588-3307.

Sheer's Lumberjack Show, Highway 47, Woodruff. This town, which adjoins Minocqua, used to be a boisterous logging settlement, and this show, offered mid-June through August, brings back some of those colorful days. The kids love the chopping and sawing, canoe jousting, speed climbing, clown acts, and log rolling. It's great fun. Call (715) 356-4050.

Minocqua Museum in downtown Minocqua at 416 Chicago Avenue (715-356-7666), displays the Island City's unique history. Open early June through Labor Day. Call for hours.

Million Dollar Penny, the biggest penny in the world, stands on the Arbor Vitae-Woodruff grounds. It symbolizes 1,700,000 pennies (the net contribution collected during the Million Penny Parade for the building fund of the Lakeland Memorial Hospital).

Attractions

Circle M Corral, 2½ miles west of U.S. 51 on 70 West; (715) 356-4441. This amusement and theme park is guaranteed to keep everyone happy for the greater part of the day. There's a water slide, kids' rides and splash area, bumper boats, go-carts, train and pony rides, miniature golf, horseback riding, batting cages, a shooting gallery, video games, and a food court.

The Min-Aqua Bats, one of the oldest amateur water-ski shows in the United States, presents a show at Minocqua's downtown Aqua Bowl every Wednesday, Friday, and Sunday night from mid-June to mid-August at 7:00 P.M. The show is free, though donations are requested. Call (715) 356-5266.

Rhinelander Logging Museum, Pioneer Park; (715) 369-5004. Rhinelander began as a supply center for the logging camps when logging was in its heyday. Today the museum, open from mid-May through mid-September, boasts a replica of an 1870s lumber camp, complete with bunkhouse, cook shanty, and blacksmith shop constructed of Norway pine logs. Logging artifacts on display include tools and equipment and fascinating photographs. On the grounds are early logging equipment, such as a narrow-gauge locomotive and a rare steam-powered snow snake used to haul sleds of logs over icy highways. There's also a cage containing a black "hodag" (see Shopping for a description of this local mythical creature) and a miniature

Kids love the ceremonial dances presented at the Lac du Flambeau Indian Pow Wow.
(Photo by Chris Driers/courtesy Wisconsin Division of Tourism)

electric sawmill. Stop by the gift shop for a hodag souvenir or other Northwoods item. Most of these items are crafted by senior citizens who work at the museum.

Special Tours

Wilderness Cruises, from mid-May to mid-October, offers narrated tours aboard the *Wilderness Queen.* This boat cruises the unspoiled shoreline of the Willow Flowage, a man-made lake built as a reservoir for regulating the Wisconsin River. The boat has an enclosed, heated lower level and an open upper level. Sights along the way include wildlife (osprey nests, eagles, loons, and sometimes deer), plus islands and coves. Lunch, dinner, and Sunday brunch cruises are available. Wilderness Cruises is in a rural area about 15 miles from Minocqua. Call (715) 453-3310/(800) 472-1516 for directions and reservations.

Old Mountain Llama Treks offers hikes through Northwoods. Call (715) 453-3094.

Performing Arts

Northern Lights Playhouse, 5611 Highway 51, Hazelhurst, 5 miles south of Minocqua, presents different shows weekly, including Broadway smashes, musicals, comedies, and children's shows; (715) 356-7173.

Shopping

There are lots of antique and specialty shops throughout the area. Don't miss the famous Wisconsin fudge at **Dan's Minocqua Fudge Shop,** 521 Oneida Street, downtown; (715) 356-2662. Loons—the symbol of the Northwoods—are the theme of the **Loon Land Trading Co. Twisted Root Emporium,** 207 Front Street, downtown; (715) 356-5179. Buy a loon souvenir; then take a look at the solid wood accessories and log furniture.

If you're in Rhinelander, stop by any gift shop for a souvenir "hodag," a dragon-like creature with white claws and white horns along its back. This mythical creature was "photographed" in 1896 by a local lumberman who claimed to have led a party of loggers to capture the monster in a cave. Later, of course, it was revealed as a harmless hoax—done "to get people talking." Today, the hodag is the name of every athletic team at the local high school, as well as the name of a park, a weekly shopping guide, and numerous area events. (See Special Events for one example!)

SPECIAL EVENTS

Check with the Minocqua AWV area Chamber of commerce for special doings in the area. The Lakeland *Times,* published twice weekly, also includes local events. Some highlights:

February: Snowfest Hot Air Balloon Rally features ice sculpting, sled-dog pulls, ice bowling, XC-ski demos, snowman building, and a hot air balloon race.

March: Howard Young Cup in Minocqua Winter Park. It is the biggest XC-ski race in Wisconsin after the Berkebiner. Call (715) 356-3309.

July: The Fourth Celebration, featuring giant parade, special water-ski show and fireworks, downtown Minocqua. Hodag Country Festival, Rhinelander; this three-day celebration—the largest in the

Northwoods—features an outdoor amphitheater with top country-music entertainment, camping on grounds, food, souvenirs (hodags, anyone?), and family fun.

WHERE TO STAY

There are a variety of accommodations in the area, ranging from motel rooms to housekeeping cottages to luxury suites. The Minocqua AWV area Chamber of Commerce has a visitors guide that lists all types of lodging. Here are a few selections for families.

The Beacons of Minocqua, 8250 Northern Road, is on Lake Minocqua. There are sixty units ranging from one to three bedrooms. Kid comforts include pontoon boats, game rooms, summer activities, and a beach. Call (800) 236–3225.

The Point Resort Hotel, Highway 51S, offers sixty-nine studios and suites on Lake Minocqua. Its features include an indoor pool, a playground, terraces with gas grills, and docking facilities. Only a short walk to family attractions, dining, and shopping. Call (715) 356–4431.

Minocqua Shores, Island City Point. One mile from town, this resort offers three- and four-bedroom lakeside condos with dishwashers and microwaves, one- to three-bedroom cottages. There's a beach area, pontoon, and paddleboat rentals; (715) 356–5101.

New Concord Inn, Highway 51 in downtown Minocqua, has fifty-four rooms, an indoor pool, and a game room. It's across the street from Torpy Park Beach, 1 block from the Bearskin Trail, and within walking distance of the water-ski show. Call (715) 356–1800.

Pine Hill Resort, 8544 Hower Road, 2 miles west on Highway 70 on Lake Kawaguesaga, one of the Minocqua Chain of Lakes. Plain but comfortable two- and three-bedroom lakefront housekeeping cottages have refrigerators and gas stoves. There's a rec room and a safe sandy beach. Call (715) 356–3418.

WHERE TO EAT

Hearty meals are the norm in the Northwoods. The Minocqua AWV area Chamber of Commerce visitors guide lists a number of area restaurants. Here are several families will like.

Paul Bunyan's Lumberjack Cook Shanty, 8653 Highway 51 North, has an 1890s logging camp feel and specializes in hearty camp breakfasts—lunch and dinner served, too. Stop by for the Friday Fish Blast. (Note: Just about every restaurant in town has fish fries on Friday.) Call (715) 356–6270 for information.

Mama's Supper Club, overlooking Curtis Lake, on Highway 70 West, has kid's menus and serves delicious Sicilian fare, including homemade pizza; (715) 356–5070.

DAY TRIPS

Take an excursion aboard the Laona and Northern Railway's steam train, the *Lumberjack Special.* The train departs from the historic depot in Laona, which is about one and a half hours east of Minocqua. The train goes to the Camp Five Museum Complex. The train operates from mid-June to late August, except Sundays, and leaves at 11:00 A.M., noon, 1:00 P.M., and 2:00 P.M. Check ahead for times, and don't miss the train. Unless you arrive at boarding time, there's not much else to do in this rural area. Return trains leave at 11:20 A.M., 12:20, 1:20, and 4:00 P.M. Buy your tickets at the depot, about ⅓ mile out of Laona toward Rhinelander on Highway 8.

The complex, accessible only by train, is about 2½ miles from the depot. Here you'll find a logging museum with artifacts, active blacksmith and harness shops, a lumber company money collection, a thirty-minute video on how the steam engine gets going in the morning, and much more.

There's also an old-fashioned country store, an animal corral, an ecology walk, and a nature center. A half-hour forest tour by surrey is included in the admission fee, or take a hayrack/pontoon boat ride through a bird refuge and along banks of wild rice for a slight additional charge. Call (715) 674–3414 in summer and (715) 845–5544 in winter.

FOR MORE INFORMATION

Contact **Minocqua AWV area Chamber of Commerce,** P.O. Box 1006, Minocqua 54548, for literature on the area, or call (800) 44-NORTH. For Rhinelander information call the **Rhinelander**

Chamber of Commerce at (800) 236–4FUN. For free Wisconsin travel literature, including the excellent *Wisconsin Auto Tours Guide*, featuring the Northwoods and Minocqua, call (800) 432–TRIP. Or visit Wisconsin on the Internet: http://www.tourism.state.wi.us.

Emergency Numbers

Ambulance, fire, and police: 911

Twenty-four-hour physician-staffed emergency service: Howard Young Medical Center, 240 Maple Street, Woodruff; (715) 356–8000

Poison Control: (608) 262–3702 (Madison)

There's no twenty-four-hour pharmacy; the hospital will dispense an overnight supply of medicine after pharmacy hours. **Joe's Lakeland Pharmacy,** Save-More Plaza, Route 51N, Minocqua (715–356–3303), is open from 9:00 A.M. to 6:00 P.M. weekdays and 9:00 A.M. to 4:00 P.M. Saturday (closed Sunday); **Wal-Mart pharmacy,** Highway 70 West (715–356–1609).

9 😊 Minnesota

MINNEAPOLIS AND ST. PAUL

The license plates—"Land of 10,000 Lakes"—are misleading. The number of lakes is actually closer to 15,000. Throw the Mississippi River into the equation, and you can see how the preponderance of water dominates life in the Twin Cities. With thirty-one large lakes lying within the metropolitan area of Minneapolis and St. Paul, outdoor recreation is an important part of people's daily routines. There is an estimated acre of parkland for every forty-three Twin Citians, ranging from grassy city oases and the famed Minnehaha Falls in south Minneapolis to public parks that contain everything from Indian burial mounds to botanical gardens.

The abundant natural beauty that enthralls both visitors and resident of Minneapolis–St. Paul also tantalized seventeenth-century French explorer Jean Nicolet, who traveled south from Canada along the Northwest Passage seeking a route to China. Instead, Nicolet found Dakota and Ojibwa tribes, eager to exchange fur pelts for blankets, knives, tobacco, and tools. The area became a major trading post and, after being fought over during the French-Indian War, eventually became part of Minnesota.

Minneapolis–St. Paul is truly the Midwest—situated midway between the Atlantic and the Pacific. The two cities are quite different in style and design. St. Paul is the older, more traditional city, its European, East Coast feel accentuated by historic buildings, city parks, and a wide boulevard (called Summit Avenue) stocked with breathtaking mansions. Minneapolis is often called "the first city of the West," an aggressively hip place filled with contemporary architecture, a cutting-edge renovated warehouse district, and an overall atmosphere that is quicker paced and grittier than quiet St. Paul.

The winters are severe, but Minneapolis and St. Paul have Skyway systems—enclosed and climate-controlled walkways two levels above the street that connect people to downtown office buildings, restaurants, and attractions. Snow and ice removal is efficient. Summers can be quite humid, but unpredictable summer storms can also bring cool spells. For spring and fall trips, bring jackets and other warm clothing.

Both cities welcome families, so much so that the area is often cited as one of the top ten places in America to raise children.

GETTING THERE

Minneapolis–St. Paul International Airport, (612) 726-5555, located 10 miles from downtown Minneapolis and 8 miles from St. Paul, serves more than two dozen airlines. Car rental companies include **Budget** (800-527-0770), **Hertz** (800-654-3131), **Avis** (800-331-1212), **Alamo** (800-462-5266), **Dollar** (800-800-4000), and **National** (800-227-7368).

Amtrak passengers pull into the St. Paul/Minneapolis Midway Station, 730 Transfer Road in St. Paul (800-872-7245), which is about a fifteen-minute drive from downtown St. Paul and twenty-four minutes from downtown Minneapolis. The **Greyhound/Trailways** bus terminal in Minneapolis is at 29 North Ninth Street and the St. Paul location is at Ninth and St. Peter.

GETTING AROUND

Unless you plan to spend all your time in one downtown area or at the Mall of America in nearby Bloomington, it's advisable to rent a car. The Twin Cities operate an excellent transit system, notably with express buses running between the Twin Cities and to and from the Mall of America. Call the **Capital City Trolley;** (612-223-5600). Historic, rubber-wheeled trolleys circle downtown, the Cultural District, historic Lowertown, and the riverfront year-round. A half-hour circuit stops at most major attractions and retail areas. Rides are offered for a nominal charge, and are free for children younger than five. On Sundays, kids younger than twelve ride free.

There are cabs in the Twin Cities, but it's not really a taxi kind of place. Expressway I–94 connects the Twin Cities, I–35W leads you to most Minnesota sites, and cultural and historical attractions are clearly marked along the streets and highways. Both places are laid out an easily understood grid with a few idiosyncrasies tossed in to make life interesting.

WHAT TO SEE AND DO

Museums

DO NOT TOUCH SIGNS are nowhere to be found at the **Minnesota Children's Museum,** 10 West Seventh Street, St. Paul; (612-225-6000. Families are encouraged to explore their imaginations and our world through hands-on activities. Four permanent galleries are complemented by several changing exhibits. In WorldWorks, kids use tools to discover, change, and understand the world. Kids learn how to protect the environment in EarthWorld. Intercultural community is the focus of OneWorld. And Habitot lets infants and toddlers play in four Minnesota landscapes; for example, toddlers can climb through animal burrows, explore caves, and experience a forest in winter. Other activities include operating a crane, creating a thunderstorm, and climbing through a giant anthill. This downtown St. Paul museum is a big hit with children six months to twelve years old.

The Minnesota History Center, 345 Kellogg Boulevard, St. Paul; (612) 296–6126. An architectural masterpiece made of Minnesota materials—Rockville granite and Winona limestone—the History Center is both an innovative museum and a state-of-the-art research center. The world's largest collection of materials on the State of Minnesota is housed in the Center, including a circa 1890 fire engine, vintage Betty Crocker radio broadcasts, buffalo horns, and Native American artifacts. The hands-on museum is organized around themes such as family, work, community, and place. The historic interpreters in period clothing bring an immediacy to the past, while special events make history anything but musty and dull. The Research Center features a microfilm room with fort-two self-service microfilm stations and a special collections room for fragile items. This spectacular museum has something for all ages, and the friendly staff is superbly trained to dispense boredom-free informa-

Minneapolis and St. Paul at a Glance

- Minneapolis: quick-paced and hip, with contemporary architecture, theater, and arts

- St. Paul: European in feel, with historic buildings and mansions

- Land of 10,000 lakes

- Public parks with everything from Indian burial grounds to botanical gardens

- Minneapolis Convention and Visitors Association, (800) 445-7412; St. Paul Convention and Visitors Bureau, (800) 627-6101

tion. There's a gift shop that will appeal to families, as well as the cafe Minnesota, a surprisingly good eatery specializing in regional food.

Science Museum of Minnesota, 30 East Tenth Street, St. Paul; (612) 221-9488. Pause before entering the Science Museum to gawk at "Iggy," the 40-foot steel iguana created by a sixteen-year-old St. Paul schoolboy. Then walk immediately to the information desk and purchase tickets for the **Science Museum Omnitheater.** Shows quickly fill up, and you don't want to miss the awesome movies projected upon a titled dome that is 76 feet in diameter. The shows engross all ages, but the film *Search for the Great Sharks* may frighten younger children. Educational entertainment is the motto of this huge, wonderful museum dedicated to hands-on, interactive exhibits dealing with natural history, science, and technology. The museum's 1.5 million natural history and science specimens include dinosaur exhibits, an Egyptian mummy, an authentic all-wood Hmong house, and other exhibits designed for science enthusiasts, from preschool to high-school age.

The expanded Paleontology Hall offers up-close and personal looks at dinosaurs, including the 82-foot-long Diplodocus. At Anthropology Hall, you can learn about the food, shelter, clothing, and rituals of the world's cultures. The Science Museum began construction of a new $90-million facility on the Mississippi River. It is scheduled to open in 1999.

The Minnesota Historical Society maintains a "living history museum" at **Historic Fort Snelling,** Highways 5 and 55; (612–726–9430). This 1827 stone fortress sits atop a hill overlooking the Mississippi River. Costumed guides re-create military drills and ceremonies from the period. The fort is open from May through October.

Minneapolis Institute of Art, 2400 South Third Avenue; (612) 870–3131. Adjacent to the Children's Theater Company, the Minneapolis Institute of Art houses more than 70,000 works spanning 25,000 years of history in a structure combining Classic Revival and contemporary steel-and-brick architecture. The complex, situated in lovely Fair Oaks Park, also contains the Minneapolis College of Art and Design, as well as the Children's Theater Company (see Theater).

The museum's diverse collection includes antiquities from around the world, a lustrous collection of Chinese jade, African masks, Impressionist and Postimpressionist works, photography, and a Rembrandt. Popular period rooms, which display the museum's decorative arts collection, are gaily festooned for the holidays. A major magnet for children is the 2,000-year-old mummy, as well as rooms dedicated to pre-Columbian gold objects crafted by the Incas.

The Walker Art Center, Hennepin Avenue and Vineland Place; (612–375–7600); houses one of the nation's finest permanent collections of modern art, both American and European. There are representative works from many famous twentieth-century artists working in the media of painting, sculpture, photography, mixed media, video, and film. The Walker also boasts an enormous print collection. Children's programs are unusual and fun, with most taking place on the weekends. Past events have involved puppet making with local performance artists and a make-your-own video class.

Other Attractions

Adjoining **Como Lake** are an handful of facilities. Concerts are held regularly throughout the summer at the pavilion; (612–266–6400). **The**

With its 400 stores surrounding an amusement park, the Mall of America offers something for everyone. (Courtesy Minnesota Office of Tourism)

Conservatory, 1325 Aida Place (612-487-8200), complements its regular displays of exotic flora with seasonal flower shows. There is also an eighteen-hole golf course. But most appropriate for families is **Como Zoo,** Midway Parkway and Kaufman Drive; (612) 488-5571. Animal demonstrations and public feedings occur daily. Admission is free. In winter the Parks & Recreation Department opens a skating rink in Como Park, 1339 North Lexington; (612) 488-4927).

Cafesjians Carousel, Town Square Park (612-290-2774), is within walking distance of both the Children's Museum and Science Museum. Sixty-eight wooden horses each have their own character. Admission to this 1914 carousel is $1.00.

Mississippi Mile, Plymouth and Hennepin avenues, Minneapolis; (612) 348-9300. Downtown Minneapolis is bordered by the Mississippi Mile, a riverfront parkway offering walking, jogging, and biking paths and scenic river views. Points of interest include **Nicollet Island,** home to the historic Nicollet Island Inn, the Nicollet Island Pavilion, and many examples of nineteenth-century architecture that look small-town perfect. **Our Lady of Lourdes Church,** the oldest Minneapolis church in continuous use, and **St. Anthony Main and Riverplace** are historic structures that have been converted to a nightclub, shopping, restaurant, and movie complex. Tour the **Ard Godfrey House,** the oldest home in Minneapolis, built in 1849, and visit one of the city's liveliest spots, the **Upper St. Anthony Falls Lock and Dam** (at Portland Avenue and the Mississippi River), the uppermost of a series of twenty-nine locks connecting Minneapolis with the Gulf of Mexico. View barges and other watercraft from the lock's observation deck.

Take the ride of your life on the Wild Thing at **Valleyfair Amusement Park,** One Valleyfair Drive, Shakopee; (800–FUN–RIDE). Towering more than 200 feet in the air, this "hyper coaster" sends the daring up, down, and in loops at 74 mph. If coasters don't thrill you, there are forty rides and a great water park. Valleyfair is located twenty minutes southwest of the Twin Cities on Highway 101 and is open daily May through Labor Day.

The Raptor Center, 1920 Fitch Avenue, St. Paul; (612) 624–4745. Located on the St. Paul campus of the University of Minnesota, the Raptor Center annually receives more than 500 injured birds of prey for treatment. This offbeat, thought-provoking museum starts with an audiovisual presentation introducing the medical and educational focus of the facility, followed by a live bird demonstration of hawks, owls, falcons, and eagles, and a tour.

Minnesota Valley Wildlife Refuge, 3815 East Eightieth Street, Bloomington; (612) 854–5900. Operated by the U.S. Fish and Wildlife Service, this center features many hands-on exhibits and computer games that allow children to explore such jobs as wildlife manager, refuge manager of a deer herd, or fire boss on a prescribed forest burn. A spectacular twelve-projector slide presentation is shown regularly in the center's auditorium, and naturalist-led programs are also available.

Special Tours

Padelford Packet Boat Company, Plymouth Avenue and the Mississippi River at Boom Island Park (in the Mississippi Mile complex); (612) 227–1100. Take a breather from hectic sight-seeing and take a languid trip down the Mississippi aboard one of the old-style riverboats. Excursions, accompanied by a colorful narrative about the area, leave from both downtown St. Paul and downtown Minneapolis daily at noon and 2:00 P.M. Minneapolis riverboats leave from Boom Island and travel through the upper lock for a view of St. Anthony Falls and James J. Hill's Old Stone Arch Bridge. The St. Paul cruise leaves from Harriet Island, a short walk across the river from downtown, and follows the mouth of the Mississippi River to old Fort Snelling. In summer there are baseball cruises, Sunday brunch excursions, and Dixieland dinner cruises.

Artvantage Tours, 7304 Clarendon Drive, Edina 55439; (612) 941-1334. Artvantage Tours help visitors connect with the area's burgeoning artistic community. Trips include excursions to corporate art collections, public art installations, galleries, studios, architectural landmarks, and museums—and all tours are staffed by art specialists.

Landmark Center, 75 West Fifth Street, St. Paul; (612) 296-6126. Tour the restored Old Federal Courts Building and site of the famous gangster trials of the 1930s. The docents re-create mobster history so vividly you will swear you can see the pinstripes. The old courtrooms have been elegantly renovated. A ground floor cafe serves toothsome fare (especially desserts), and an added attraction outside is **Rice Park,** St. Paul's oldest and prettiest city park.

The **Minneapolis RiverCity Trolley** (612-204-0000) runs tours of downtown Minneapolis May through November. Two-hour or all-day passes can be purchased at three starting points: the Minneapolis Convention Center, Walker Art Center, or St. Anthony Main. A historical narrative of this old mining town is told during the sixty-five-minute loop.

Three offbeat tours, run by Down in History, Inc., reveal St. Paul's unsavory past. **Saint Paul Gangster Tours,** 827 Portland Avenue (612-292-1200), explores crime sites, speakeasies, and haunts frequented by notorious hoodlums. Stops include Ma Barker's home, Dillinger's apartment, and locations of robberies and murders. The two-hour **Bootleg and Brewery Tour** shares the history of alcohol in the Twin Cities. Stops include Pig's Eye Parrant's whiskey caves, the Hamm and Schmidt breweries, and the Hollyhocks Club speakeasy. Don't be spooked out by the **Haunt Spots Ghost Tour.** Ghosts and poltergeists may or may not be spotted at Fort Snelling, the haunted City Hall, or the Guthrie Theater.

Theater

More than eighty professional theater companies thrive in the area, not to mention numerous community, experimental, and dinner theater troupes.

One child-oriented choice is **The Children's Theater Company,** 2400 Third Avenue South, Minneapolis; (612) 874-0400. This award-winning theater, located in a mammoth white brick building attached to the Minneapolis Institute of Arts, appeals to both kids and adults.

First and foremost are the children, who are accommodated in the 746-seat auditorium with seats specially raked so that smaller theatergoers can see the stage. There's even a crying room for children to sob freely without hampering the enjoyment of other audience members. Shows are lavish and vividly staged, ranging from children's classics—*The 500 Hats of Bartholomew Cubbins* and *Babar*—to innovative renderings of new works—*Strega Nona Meets Her Match* and *Crow and Weasel.*

The Guthrie Theater, 725 Vineland Place, Minneapolis (612-377-2224), was founded in 1963 by the legendary Sir Tyrone Guthrie to prove that classical repertory could exist, and indeed flourish, outside of New York and Chicago. Shakespeare, Chekhov, Ibsen, Molière, Miller, and Euripides are well represented here, and in case you fear your children are not ready for the classics, there are pretheater symposiums before selected performances. Children's guides are available at the box office. Get to the Guthrie early for a pretheater stroll through the **Walker Art Center's sculpture garden,** one of the largest public sculpture gardens in the world. It features works by Claus Oldenberg, Frank Gehry, Henry Moore, and George Segal.

Touring companies of Broadway shows land at one of three locations: **The Ordway,** 345 Washington Street, St. Paul (612-224-7661); **The State,** 805 Hennepin Avenue, Minneapolis (612-339-7007); or **The Orpheum,** 910 Hennepin Avenue, Minneapolis (612-339-7007). The Ordway is a beautiful new theater with impeccable acoustics, while the State and the Orpheum are historic playhouses renovated right down to the gilt trim and painted bucolic murals. Many Broadway productions have passed through the Twin Cities here.

Visitors to the Science Museum in St. Paul may want to drop into the **Great American History Theatre, Crawford Livingston The-**

atre, **Science Museum,** 30 East Tenth Street, St. Paul; (612) 292–4320. Past productions at this cozy, child-friendly theater include dramatizations of F. Scott Fitzgerald's *The Great Gatsby* and a countrified version of *A Christmas Carol.*

Purchase tickets for theater events at individual box offices, or call TicketMaster at (612) 989–5151.

Sporting Events

The Twin Cities offers a variety of sports events. **The Minnesota Vikings** professional football team plays through December at the climate-controlled H.H.H. Metrodome, 501 Chicago Avenue, Minneapolis; (612) 989–5151. Also at the Metrodome, **The Minnesota Twins** run the bases April through October; (612) 375–1116. Over at the Target Center, 600 First Avenue, Minneapolis, (612) 673–1600, catch the court action of the **Minnesota Timberwolves,** the state's exciting NBA team.

The Northern League **Saint Paul Saints** plays baseball to capacity crowds at the Midway Stadium in St. Paul, 117 Energy Park Drive, St. Paul; (612) 644–6659. A Saints game means affordable fun—tickets are reasonably priced. In addition to watching the game, patrons can get a haircut, receive a low-cost massage from a group of massage-therapist nuns, or watch the antics of the team mascot, a pig in a baseball cap.

Shopping

Mall of America, Interstate 494 and Highway 77, Bloomington, Minnesota; (612) 883–8800. Think of your local mall multiplied by six, and you have the overwhelming Mall of America. Many tourists come from all over the world and never leave the mall to explore the Twin Cities. More than 40 million visitors have traipsed through the enormous complex that features 400 specialty shops, eight nightclubs (including Planet Hollywood), 12,750 parking stalls, fourteen movie theaters, a miniature golf course, and anchor stores Nordstrom, Bloomingdale's, Macy's, and Sears.

Children and adults alike will be flabbergasted by the Lego Imagination Center, which features larger-than-life displays of dinosaurs, a fully-operational circus, firehouse, birthday party, and spinning globe and spacecraft—all made out of Legos.

Under Water World (888–DIVE TIME), a 1.2-million-gallon aquarium, was recently added to the lower level of the mall. The 300-foot-long acrylic tunnel was designed to simulate a deep-sea dive. Visitors feel "submerged" as they walk within inches of the 15,000 fish, which include sharks, stingrays, and other exotic creatures. The tanks are filled with fish and features to resemble the Mississippi River, a Minnesota lake, the Gulf of Mexico, and a Caribbean barrier reef. A thirty-five-minute taped narrative is available to complement the walk.

Plopped down in the middle of the mall is **Knott's Camp Snoopy,** a seven-acre indoor amusement park complete with a roller coaster and twenty-two other rides, seven shops, three entertainment theaters, and fourteen eateries. Admission is free, and the park operates on a point pass system whereby you purchase paper tickets at booths or at automated ticket machines placed throughout the park. Be sure to set a spending limit. Parents on a budget should limit their children's rides. Camp Snoopy contains attractions for all ages.

Avoid the games of skill and other carnival attractions and the pricey Ford Playhouse dinner theater. Worthy attractions at Camp Snoopy include Pearson's Wilderness Theater, featuring live animals, and the Northwood Stage, which hosts live musical performances throughout the day.

Exercise caution about excessive spending at the mall, too. Sensory overload—all the bright lights, welcoming sights, and sounds and noises—wear you down after awhile, and you might be tempted to run up your credit card. Take frequent breaks for drinks or snacks at the mall's restaurants, rather than the two chaotic food courts. Taking time out for a movie or to explore the quieter (during the day) fourth level is also an option. Don't try to take in the entire structure in one day.

The crowds can also be daunting, and it's advisable to visit the mall in either early morning or late afternoon. The crowds are smaller during the week than on the often bedlamlike weekends.

If you want to shop but don't like the throngs of people at Mall of America, head to St. Paul's **World Trade Center,** Seventh and Wabasha (612–291–1715), or **Town Square,** 445 Minnesota Street (612–298–0900). These linked shopping complexes run four city blocks and include more than seventy shops and restaurants. While the World Trade Center is a mall that surrounds a three-level atrium,

Town Square is tucked above the world's largest enclosed city park. Dancing waterfalls, an amphitheater, and life-size chessboards offer shoppers a respite.

Bandana Square, 1021 East Bandana Boulevard (612-642-1509), is like most historic districts in cities around the country. Specialty shops and restaurants are housed in buildings listed on the National Register of Historic Places. These 1880s buildings were formerly known as the Como Shops, where Burlington Northern coaches and locomotives were painted and repaired. The Twin City Model Railroad Club is located on the square's second level. Visitors are welcome to watch the club's fantastic model railroad in operation.

SPECIAL EVENTS

January-February: The festival season kicks off in winter's deep freeze with the St. Paul Winter Carnival; (612) 297-6953. It runs for twelve days during the end of January through early February.

More than one hundred events make up the festival, including parades, fireworks, skating, ice-carving contest, an indoor carnival complete with rides and games of chance, treasure hunts, hockey tournaments, fancy dress balls, and the crowning of the Carnival's King Boreas and his Queen of the Snow.

July: In mid-July it's Minneapolis's turn to get silly, with the Minneapolis Aquatennial (612-377-4621), an annual summer salute to water, fun, and families. The ten-day festival draws more than a million spectators and participants with seventy-five events taking place downtown and around the lakes. Festivities include a sand castle/sand sculpture competition; a sailing regatta; bass fishing, skateboard, and volleyball tournaments; as well as arts and crafts, music, pontoon boat rides, special foot races, and other events.

On Independence Day weekend, St. Paul hosts Taste of Minnesota (612-228-0018), on the grounds of the State Capitol. Aurora and Constitution avenues in St. Paul. Tour the Capitol, which contains the largest unsupported marble dome in the world. Eat your way through the Taste of Minnesota with vittles from dozens of Twin Cities restaurants.

August–September: The end of August through Labor Day is the Minnesota State Fair (612-642-2200), more than one hundred years old and the largest twelve-day state fair in the country. Held at the meticulously maintained and landscaped State Fairgrounds at Snelling and Larpenteur in St. Paul, the State Fair is a two-week extravaganza of livestock and crops judging, a midway, a juried art show, crafts, food, parades, and well-known musical entertainers.

City children who think that food comes from supermarkets will be wowed by the fair demonstrations, the agricultural exhibits, and the barns filled with cows, pigs, poultry, rabbits, and horses. If your family has never been to a big midwestern state fair, this is the one to try.

November–December: Holidazzle Parades.

WHERE TO STAY

The Twin Cities have myriad places to rest your travel-wearied head, from big-name chain hotels to all-suite complexes and more modest accommodations. On the high-end, there's the **St. Paul Hotel,** 350 Market Street, St. Paul; (612) 292-9292. This expertly renovated hotel offers superb accommodations, one of the best restaurants in the Twin Cities—**the St. Paul Grill**—and a lovely view of Rice Park, the Ordway Music Theatre, and the Landmark Center.

In Minneapolis, indulge yourself at the subdued opulence of the **Marquette Hotel,** IDS Center, Seventh and Nicollet; (612) 332-2351. You can eat at the hotel restaurant, the same one where Mary Tyler Moore used to dine on her TV show. Two more pricey hotels, but worth it, are **The Whitney,** 150 Portland Avenue (612-339-9300), and **The Hotel Luxeford,** 1101 Lasalle (612-332-6800), luxurious suite hotels. Minneapolis also has a **Hyatt Regency Hotel,** South Thirteenth Street at Nicollet; (612) 370-1234 or (800) 223-1234.

Moderate prices and good value can be found at the **Radisson Hotel St. Paul,** 11 East Kellogg Boulevard; (612) 292-1900. The hotel boasts an indoor pool with a panoramic view of the St. Paul skyline; it is connected to the Skyway system and is within walking distance of the city's most popular attractions. Its counterpart in Minneapolis is the **Radisson Hotel Metrodome,** 615 Washington Avenue East; (612) 379-8888. **Best Inn—State Capitol,** 161 St. Anthony, St. Paul (612-227-8711), and in Minneapolis, the **Best Western Regency Plaza,** 41 North Tenth Street, Minneapolis (612-339-9311).

Suite hotels are sanity savers for families, and a terrific complex is the **Embassy Suites,** 175 East Tenth Street, St. Paul; (612) 224-5400. Here you will find tastefully appointed rooms with balconies offering great views of the city, complimentary breakfast and beverages, and satellite television. There are also some quite attractive weekend package deals.

If you really want to have an unusual hotel experience, check into the **Burnsville Fantasuite Hotel,** 250 North River Ridge Circle, Burnsville (612-890-9550), where you can pick out special suites decorated in futuristic, tropical, prehistoric, and other fantasy motifs.

WHERE TO EAT

People take their chow seriously in Minnesota, with an emphasis on rib-sticking fare such as steaks, wild-rice soup, humongous sticky buns, and walleye pike. Vegetarians and connoisseurs of lighter fare will like **Cafe Brenda,** 300 North First Avenue, Minneapolis; (612) 342-9230. The cafe features luscious and low-fat seafood dishes, pasta, and desserts flavored with honey or maple syrup.

Hearty German cuisine can be found at **Gastof zur Gemutlichkeit,** 2300 Northeast University Avenue, Minneapolis; (612) 781-3860. Specialties include wienerschnitzel, sauerbraten, spaetzle, glorious apple strudels, and black forest torte. Young people love hanging out at the unspeakably hip **Loring Cafe,** 1624 Harmon Place, Minneapolis (612-332-1617), where the elite meet to drink espressos and recite poetry. Parents and children admire the Loring's funky decor and great food, including artichoke dip, designer pizzas, and filling pasta dishes; and it's so noisy in there, unruly children are just part of the scene.

A casual place in Minneapolis where you can kick back and dine is **Market Bar-B-Que,** 1414 Nicollet Avenue, Minneapolis; (612) 872-1111. It's home of some of the most righteous barbecued ribs in the country.

In St. Paul, families love the Old World specialties at **Cossetta's,** 211 West Seventh Street; (612) 222-3476. They are known for cheesy pizza, imported meats and cheeses, and monstrous calzones. The **Heartthrob Cafe,** Seventh and Wabasha (612-224-2783), is a zany place where kids are encouraged to be rambunctious. This fifties- and sixties-inspired diner sports gregarious waitpersons on rollerskates who urge you to try the quesadillas, guacamole-topped hamburgers, and many-flavored malts and milkshakes.

Cafe Latte, 850 Grand Avenue, St. Paul (612–224–5687), features innovative and delicious salads, homemade soups and breads, coffee drinks, and an irresistible spread of pastries and cakes. For steaks you can't beat the **Cherokee Sirloin Room,** 886 South Smith Avenue, St. Paul; (612) 457–2729. The steaks are the size of Buicks, and the baked potatoes are big, too.

DAY TRIPS

Grand Casino Hinckley, Interstate 35 at the Hinckley exit; (612) 449–0057. Gambling is legal in Minnesota and abundant, so if you want to see the state's casinos—which are less glitzy than those in Vegas or Atlantic City—this is probably the best one suited for families. A beautiful hour-and-a-half ride from the Twin Cities, this 90,000-square-foot casino features more than 1,500 loose video slots with individual progressive payouts frequently in excess of $50,000. Also featured for the avaricious types are keno, poker, and blackjack machines, fifty-two blackjack tables, bingo, and the Royal Ascot video derby, a horse-racing game. What separates this casino from others is the **Kids Quest Activity Center,** a 7,800-square-foot professionally supervised children's activity center. The casino also hosts **Powwows** and other **Native American events** on weekends. There's also a video arcade for teens and two restaurants, a 360-seat Grand Casino buffet and the Grand Grill American, both featuring tasty regional fare and live nightly entertainment.

FOR MORE INFORMATION

Visitor Information Centers
City of St. Paul Citizen Service Office: (612) 266–8989
St. Paul Convention and Visitors Bureau (612) 297–6985;
    (800) 627–6101; Internet: http://www.stpaul.gov
Minneapolis Convention and Visitors Association: (800) 445–
    7412; Internet: http://www.minneapolis.org
Minnesota Office of Tourism: (612) 296–5029/(800) 657–3700

Hennepin County Parks and Recreation: (612) 559–9000
Parks and recreation information: (612) 348–2141 in Minneapolis;
(612) 266–6400 in St. Paul.
Other Useful Information and Numbers
Road condition information: (612) 296–3076
Traveler's Aid: (612) 726–5500
Metropolitan Transit Commission: (612) 827–7733
St. Paul area Chamber of Commerce: (612) 223–5000
Greater Minneapolis Chamber of Commerce: (612) 370–9132
The *Twin Cities Reader* and the *City Pages* feature comprehensive
guides to what's happening.

Emergency Numbers

Ambulance, fire, police: 911
Poison Center: (612) 347–3141
Children's Hospital of St. Paul Children's On-Call Line:
(612) 220–6868
Abbott Northwestern Hospital of Minneapolis Emergency
Room: (612) 863–4233
Twenty-four-hour pharmacy: Walgreen Drug Stores,
1550 University Avenue, St. Paul; (612) 646–6165

THE GUNFLINT TRAIL

The Gunflint Trail is a 64-mile paved road in northern Minnesota near the Canadian border, which provides access to the Boundary Waters Canoe Area Wilderness (BWCAW), one of the largest wilderness areas in the United States. Starting in Grand Marais, Minnesota, on the north shore of Lake Superior, the world's largest freshwater lake, the Gunflint Trail winds its way through the Sawtooth Mountain Range and the BWCAW near Ely, Minnesota. Major lakes along the Gunflint Trail include Gunflint (on the Canadian border), Poplar, Saganaga, and Sea Gull, each with links or potages into more remote Boundary Waters areas. Hungry Jack, Clearwater, Flour Lake, East Bearskin, Trout, and Loon Lake are also on Gunflint Trail.

Centuries ago Native Americans fished and hunted northern Minnesota's network of lakes and streams. French-Canadian fur traders followed, plying these routes in the eighteenth and nineteenth centuries. Called *voyageurs,* these traders paddled goods, soldiers, and explorers through these scenic waters. Because the BWCAW, composed of 500 lakes interconnected by small streams and channels, is a U.S. Forest Service wilderness area, use is restricted. Canoes provide the primary means of transportation (no motorized boats are allowed), and camping is restricted to designated areas. One mile away use is less restricted in Voyageurs National Park. Motorboats not only are allowed, but they are the most popular means of enjoying this park.

In summer in the BWCAW and in Voyageurs National Park, families find watery adventures and classic north-country scenery. This is a back-to-basics adventure of lazy days spent paddling along chains of lakes, past islands dotted with pine trees and rimmed with pebbly shores, and of simple nights camping or staying at shoreside lodges.

In winter the area is transformed into a cross-country ski mecca. The Gunflint Trail Association maintains 175 kilometers of groomed, cross-country trails through these pristine woods. The region's lodges offer additional winter fun such as dogsled trips, sleigh rides, and snowshoe tours.

GETTING THERE

As the region is remote, most visitors drive here, some with campers in tow. Gunflint is 43 miles from Grand Marais, Minnesota, and six hours north of Minneapolis/St. Paul, which is served by the Minneapolis/St. Paul International Airport; (612) 726-5848. Many major car rental companies are represented here. International Falls also has the International Falls International Airport. By car Voyageurs National Park is also three hours from Duluth and four hours from Winnipeg, Manitoba.

Four communities located along U.S. Highway 53 between Duluth and International Falls serve as gateways to Voyageurs National Park, providing lodging and dining options. **Crane Lake** and **Orr** provide access for persons arriving from the south. Crane Lake, the southeastern most gateway, is a good place to rent houseboats and is also a supply area for persons heading to the nearby Boundary Waters Canoe Area Wilderness. Another gateway to Voyageurs National Park is **Ash River,** 25 miles north of Orr, County Road 129 and U.S. 53. On the south shore of Lake Kabetogama, Ash River also has houseboat rental companies. **Lake Kabetogama,** about 28 miles north of Orr on County Road 122, along with a park visitor center, features about two dozen cabin and resort properties along the lake. **Island View,** about 12 miles east of International Falls on state Highway 11, is the northwesternmost gateway to Voyageurs National Park. Island view has a park visitor center, a few houseboat rental companies, and several resorts located on Rainy Lake. (See Where to Stay.)

GETTING AROUND

As there is no public transportation in the region, a car is necessary to reach the region's gateway communities. Dozens of outfitters guide visitors through the area by canoe, snowmobile, and dogsled and also on cross-country ski tours. Other outfitters offer advice and rent gear and equipment. Some canoe and ski outfitters provide transportation to their base lodges and outfitting centers for an additional fee. Outfitters include **Whispering Pines Wilderness Adventures** (800-510-2947), which offers canoeing, hiking, snowshoeing, skiing, and dogsledding excursions guided by naturalists. **M+M Border Country Adventures** (218-365-6080) offers two- to ten-day guided dogsledding, fishing, and skiing trips. **Gunflint Lodge & Outfitters,** 143 South Gunflint Lake, Grand Marais, MN 55604-3009, is the Gunflint Lodge's canoe outfitting division; (800) 362-5251.

WHAT TO SEE AND DO

Voyageurs National Park, 3131 Highway 53, International Falls, MN 56649-8904; (218) 283-9821. There is no entrance fee. Voyageurs National Park, 15 miles east of International Falls (an entry point to Canada), provides a good starting point for your Minnesota lakes vacation. One of the premier water-based parks in the United States, with 39 percent of the park covered by water, Voyageurs National Park draws lots of motorboating families. Quiet isn't exactly the norm in the popular motorboating spots, but the woodland and lake views are soothing. Motorboats provide the easiest way to travel between campsites and to explore the main areas of the park. But there's more. With paddling energy and portaging stamina, you can canoe and kayak to the park's interior, marshy, and quieter regions, a trip best for families with older children.

Voyageurs is one of the best mainland parks for spotting bald eagles and active wolf packs. Along the water and land-based trails, keep an eye out for beavers, otters, moose, and bears, too. In May through July, rangers offer a tour boat trip to view nesting gulls and cormorants. Fishing is another popular pastime. The park is known as a prime fishing spot for walleye, northern pike, and smallmouth bass as well as muskie, perch, sauger, lake trout, and crappie. To fish you must obtain a Minnesota fishing license.

One of the more popular boat tours is the North Canoe Voyage, where visitors paddle along in a 26-foot replica of a North Canoe with a costumed ranger aboard. It's best to reserve ahead for these trips along

The Gunflint Trail at a Glance

- In summer, water adventures, wilderness, and north-country wildlife

- In winter, cross-country skiing, dogsled trips, sleigh rides, snowshoe tours

- Family-friendly lodging in campgrounds, cabins, lodges, and resorts

- Soudan Underground Mine

- International Falls Chamber of Commerce, (800) 325–5766; Ely Area Information Center, (800) 777–7281

Kabetogama Lake (218–875–2111) and Rainy Lake (218–286–5740). Also popular are the learn-to-paddle introductory family-oriented canoe trips and the evening two-hour star-watch cruise. Older kids may like the six-hour, round-trip cruise to historic Kettle Falls Hotel, one of the few places you can look south from the United States into Canada. Call ahead to reserve meals and at least one month ahead to reserve lodging; (800) 322–0886.

Voyageurs has hiking trails for all ages and skill levels. Landlubbers with little kids should try the 1-mile (each way), spruce-lined Oberholtzer Trail, the only trail accessible by car from the Rainy Lake visitor center. The 2-mile (each way) Blind Ash Bay Trail, which affords scenic vistas of Kabetomaga Lake, is accessible from the Ash River Visitor Center. The heartier can tackle the 4-mile Locator Chain of Lakes Trail, reached by a 6-mile boat trip. You can also hike into several lakes where the National Park Service keeps canoes and boats that are free to the public. Reserve these at a park visitor center and hike in with appropriate life jackets. The park also features special Kids Explore Voyageurs hikes for ages seven to twelve, as well as summertime evening campfire programs on cultural and natural history.

Mid-July through August the more than 900 islands in Voyageurs bloom with a special treat—blueberries ripe for the picking. A summer caution: Combat summer's black flies and mosquitoes by wearing light-colored, long-sleeved shirts and pants. In winter from late December to late March, when there is sufficient snow (and there almost always is), you can cross-country ski, snowshoe, and snowmobile in the park. Ten miles of groomed cross-country ski trails are available near the Rainy Lake Visitor Center. Twice each winter rangers lead a guided, candle-ski tour along this trail. Obtain maps and information at the visitor centers.

At each of the park's entrances from its four gateway communities, you'll find visitor information. The **Crane Lake Information Station** (218-993-2481) is open daily from 10:00 A.M. to 4:00 P.M. late May to Labor Day. The **Kabetogama Lake Visitor Center** (218-875-2111) is open daily from 9:00 A.M. to 5:00 P.M. early May through September. The **Ash River Visitor Center** (218-374-3221) is open daily 9:00 A.M. to 5:00 P.M. late May through Labor Day, and the **Rainy Lake Visitor Center** (218-283-9821) is open daily from 9:00 A.M. to 5:00 P.M. early May through September and at selected times in winter.

Boundary Waters Canoe Area Wilderness (BWCAW) lies just east of Voyageurs National Park. For information and permits write to the Forest Supervisor, Superior National Forest, P.O. Box 338, Duluth, MN 55801, or visit the Permit Station, located east of Ely on Highway 169, from 6:00 A.M. to 5:00 P.M. daily in summer; (218) 365-7681, (218) 365-7600, or (800) 745-3399. Permits are required for camping between May 1 and September 30. It's a good idea to reserve summer permits as far ahead as possible, even as early as February 1.

With its more than 1,500 miles of water trails, the BWCAW affords prime waters for canoeing and fishing. Less noisy, less crowded, and accessible only to those who want to paddle a canoe or kayak and hike the islands, the BWCAW offers a more peaceful getaway than the main areas of Voyageurs National Park. Families with older children accustomed to pack-in/pack-out wilderness camping and long-distance canoeing should find this experience a get-away-from-it-all foray.

Outfitters, a few of whom offer guided summer trips, take much of the work and worry out of a wilderness camping experience.

The entire family will enjoy a walk in the woods of Northern Minnesota.
(Courtesy Minnesota Office of Tourism)

Other outfitters provide rental canoes and equipment, advice, food supplies, and specially designed lightweight equipment. Many of the canoe rental companies are in **Ely.** For information on outfitters contact the Forest Supervisor and call Ely's Vacation Hotline (800-777-7281).

In winter the BWCAW is a popular cross-country ski area, especially those areas located along the Gunflint Trail. Families with older children and teens who are expert cross-country skiers can ski yurt to yurt along the BWCAW's longest tracked trail, the Banadad. While you ski, outfitters bring your gear and food to the yurts and your car to the trail's end. Several lodges along the Gunflint Trail offer cross-country skiing. Contact **Boundary Country Trekking** (218-388-4487 or 800-322-8327) or visit their web site at http://www.boreal.org/adventures/. For information on skiing in and near BWCAW, contact the Gunflint Trail Association, Grand Marais, MN 55604 (218-338-4487 or 800-322-8327) and see Where to Stay.

Ely

Ely is known for its association with the wilderness and with wolves. A jumping-off point for the BWCAW, Ely, located within the Superior National Forest, is known as the "Canoe Capital of the World." Many visitors come here to rent canoes and equipment for the BWCAW experience and trips along the region's other lakes. This small town has twenty-two canoe outfitters. It is within driving distance of 2,021 lakes more than ten aces in size and 1,975 miles of streams. Ely is situated at the end of the Taconite Trail, one of the most recognized trails in the state and one that meanders through three state forests, one national forest, and numerous historical landmarks. A sweet summer treat along the Taconite Trail and paths in the BWCAW are the berries, ripe for the picking from late June through the raspberry harvest in August.

Like the Gunflint region, the area surrounding Ely also offers winter activities such as cross-country skiing, ice fishing, snowmobiling, and snowshoeing. In winter the Taconite Trail becomes a major snowmobiling path. Located within Ely's city limits, the four-mile Trezona Trail circles Miner's Lake. In summer it's used by hikers and bikers and in winter by cross-country skiers.

The Trezona Trail connects to the must-see **International Wolf Center,** 1396 Highway 169; (218) 365–4695 or (800) ELY–WOLF; http://www.wolf.org. This center educates visitors about one of the world's most misunderstood creatures—wolves. Visitors learn about the natural history of wolves by observing the resident pack and touring the Wolves and Humans exhibit. Kids love observing the resident pack, learning how to track wolves, and going on an evening howling outing where they get to shout back to the distant pack. Participants in the center's programs can track wolves by plane or, in winter, tie on showshoes or go dog sledding to follow the animals along trails.

In summer and in winter the International Wolf Center offers special family programs that include meals and lodging at a nearby resort. At the Pack as Family, a summer favorite, spend a weekend learning how the wolf family is similar to the structure of your own family. The night howling expedition is a highlight. A winter favorite is Winter Adventure in Wolf Country, which includes lectures, dogsled adventures, and other outdoor fun.

Another area kid-pleaser is the **Soudan Underground Mine State Park,** Highway 169 (218-753-2245), Minnesota's oldest, deepest, and richest iron-ore mine. On the one-and-a-half-hour tour, you descend ½ mile underground into the mine, which was in use from 1884 to 1963, and take a short spin on a mining car. Dorothy Molter, a.k.a. the "Root Beer Lady," was a fixture of the BWCAW and known for her legendary hospitality and homemade root beer. **The Dorothy Molter Museum** (218-365-4451) comprises two log cabins that were transported out of the BWCAW to Ely. The Winter Cabin was Molter's home and is furnished just as she left it before passing away in 1986. The Point Cabin houses an interpretive center that documents Molter's and the region's history.

SPECIAL EVENTS

January/February: Ely Voyager Winter Festival: Snow sculptures provide the backdrop for snow-related activities and game tastings.

July: Voyageur Days is held around Crane Lake. Activities include fish fry, craft booth, canoe races, and powwow.

December: Snow City Festival & Parade: a welcome to winter with caroling, winter-themed floats, and candlelight walk.

WHERE TO STAY

Voyageurs National Park, 3131 Highway 53, International Falls, Minnesota 56649-8904; (218) 283-9821. The park offers 130 boat-in campsites on a first-come basis. You can rent a boat from one of the nearby resorts. **Woodenfrog State Forest Campground** (218-875-2602) offers sixty campsites on a first-come basis, and lodging is available in the four communities on the park's outskirts. For something different rent a houseboat. Among rental companies: Rainy Lake Houseboats (218-286-5291) and Voyaguaire Houseboats (800-882-6287).

The four gateway communities to Voyageurs National Park offer lodgings, mostly housekeeping cabins and motels. Some are open year-round but most are available just May through October. For accommodations in the **Kabetogama Lake** area, contact the Kabetogama Lake Association, Box 80, Ray, MN 56669; (218) 875-2621 or (800)

524-9085. For accommodations in the **Crane Lake** area, contact the Crane Lake Visitor and Convention Bureau, P.O. Box 15 VTB, Crane Lake, MN 55725; (800) 362-7405. For accommodations in the **Ash River** area, contact the Ash River Commercial Club, Orr, MN 55771; (800) 950-2061. For accommodations in the **Rainy Lake** and **International Falls** areas, contact the International Falls Area Visitor & Convention Bureau, 301 Second Avenue, International Falls, MN 56649; (218) 283-9400 or (800) 325-5766.

Several lodges and housekeeping cabins offer shelter along the trail. Most offer weekend or week-long packages. Popular family-friendly ones include **Gunflint Lodge,** 750 Gunflint Trail; (218) 388-2294 or (800) 328-3325. The lodge can also be booked through American Wilderness Experience; (800) 444-0099. Set on the shores of Gunflint Lake, Gunflint Lodge offers a string of twenty-three one- to four-bedroom housekeeping cabins available with or without meals. While all have a fireplace in the living room, some also feature saunas, CD players, and VCRs. The resort doesn't receive TV reception, so it offers a free supply of movies. The chef is well known for his tasty cooking, a nice surprise for such a remote lodge. Children under four stay free.

In summer the Gunflint Lodge has an outfitting service for self-guided canoe trips. In winter packages include combinations of cross-country skiing, dogsledding, and snowshoeing. My family liked the dogsledding best, but our next favorite activity was snowshoeing, especially past stands of birch to Bridal Falls, a frozen waterfall swirling down a swath of granite. Along the trickling creek we searched for pine-marten tracks in the snow. Winter Women's Week for women only (take your mom and your teenage daughter) includes four nights' lodging, guided ski excursions, snowshoe trips, a dogsled ride, moonlight skiing, snowshoeing, hot tubs, a sauna, a half-hour massage, a cabin with a fireplace, and all meals, including wine with dinner.

Trout Lake Resort, 230 Gunflint Trail (218-387-1330 or 800-258-7688), is located 12 miles up and 4 miles east of the Gunflint Trail. This lakeside, family-run resort offers seven furnished units that can accommodate between two and ten guests. Appropriate to its name, the lake is known for its trout fishing. At **Bearskin Lodge & Cross Country Ski Resort,** 275 Gunflint Trail (218-388-2292 or 800-338-4170), guests dine family style, accompanied by recorded classical music. All of the resort's fifteen units feature fireplaces, and four also come with private decks. In summer the resort offers hiking trails and boats.

Northwoods hospitality is the norm at the **Golden Eagle Lodge Resort & Nordic Ski Center,** 35 Gunflint Trail; (218) 388-2203 or (800) 346-2203. The only resort on Flour Lake, Golden Eagle has eleven cabins with private docks. All include a fireplace wood stove, and two are handicapped accessible. Five lakes are nearby for canoeing, and Flour Lake is known for its bass, walleye, and pike fishing. In summer there are intermittent nature-oriented activities for children.

On the eastern edge of Voyageurs National Park is the **Kettle Falls Hotel,** 10502 Gamma Road, Ray, MN 56669; (218) 374-4404, (218) 875-2070, or (888) KF-HOTEL. A popular place for families on the Minnesota-Canadian border, this property offers housekeeping lodges with kitchenettes as well as twelve rooms (sharing three baths) in the main lodge.

Ely has a variety of accommodation. **Silver Rapids Lodge,** HC1, Box 2992, Ely, 55731 (800-950-9425), offers lakeside motel suites and cabins with kitchenettes. **Deer Ridge,** P.O. Box 238, Ely (218-365-4075), has ten housekeeping cabins on Garden Lake. Situated on thirty-five acres, Deer Ridge has access to BWCAW and provides canoe outfitting trips. **River Point Resort,** in Ely where the Kawishiwi River joins Birch Lake (800-456-5580; http://www.greatresorts.com/rpr.html), is situated on a peninsula with 2,500 feet of shoreline. The resort features a small beach, a playground, access to the BWCAW, and an assortment of vacation homes for rent. For a traditional, family-friendly hotel, try the **Holiday Inn SunSpree Resort,** 400 North Pioneer Road, Ely, 55731; (218) 365-6565 or (800) 365-5070. This property features an indoor swimming pool, boat rentals, and a summer children's activity program.

A list of lodgings is available from the Ely Vacation Hotline: (800) 777-7281.

WHERE TO EAT

Along the Gunflint Trail, the **Gunflint Lodge** (often described as having the best food between Minneapolis and the Canadian border,

218-388-2294 or 800-328-3325), the **Trout Lake Resort** (218-387-1330 or 800-258-7688), the **Bearskin Lodge & Cross Country Ski Resort,** (218-388-2292 or 800-338-4170, and the **Golden Eagle Lodge Resort & Nordic Ski Center** (218-388-2203 or 800-346-2203) provide family-style cooked meals daily. (See also Where to Stay.)

With a dozen or so restaurants, the Ely area is hardly a culinary mecca, but it is the place to go for the most choice in one convenient area. **Sir G's,** 520 East Sheridan Street (218-365-3688), serves homemade sauces over fresh pasta and pizza. **Vertins' Cafe,** 145 East Sheridan Street (218-365-4041), serves steak, seafood, soup, and sandwiches on its menu; a children's menu is also available. **Cranberry's Saloon and Restaurant** (218-365-4301) specializes in American and Mexican dishes such as steaks and burgers, tacos, and a salad bar. The **Evergreen Restaurant** at Holiday Inn SunSpree Resort, 400 North Pioneer Road (218-365-6565), has lakeside dining and features regional and Continental cuisine as well as a children's menu.

DAY TRIPS

In **International Falls** families can visit the Ground Mound Historic Center, 6749 Highway 11, International Falls; (218) 285-3332. This state historic site is the largest American Indian burial mound in Minnesota. American Indian history and heritage can be learned at the Bronco Nagurski Museum, 214 Sixth Avenue, International Falls; (218) 283-4316. This museum houses American Indian artifacts and exhibits about gold mining and early settlers.

FOR MORE INFORMATION

For state tourism information contact the **Minnesota Office of Tourism,** 100 Metro Square, St. Paul; (612) 296-5029 or (800) 657-3700. Their Internet address is http://tccn.com/mn.tourisnVnmhome.html. The **Gunflint Trail Association** Maintains 132 miles of groomed trails. For maps or lodging information, call (800) 338-6932 or http://www.gunflint-trail.com. **International Falls Chamber of Commerce,** P.O. Box 169 International Falls, MN 56649;

(218) 283-9400 or (800) 325-5766. **Ely Area Information Center,** 1600 East Sheridan Street; (218) 365-6123 or (800) 777-7281; http://www.ely.org.

The non-profit **Lake States Interpretive Association,** 3131 Highway 53, International Falls, MN 56649 (218-283-2103) offers brochures, maps, and books about Voyageurs National Park and Chippewa, Superior, and Nicolet National Forests.

Emergency Numbers

In the Ely area:

Ambulance, fire, and police; 911

Ely Police Department, 209 East Sheridan Street; (218) 365-3222

St. Louis/Lake County Sheriff: (218) 365-3222

Hospital: Ely-Bloomenson Community Hospital & Ely Area Ambulance Service, 328 West Conan Street; (218) 365-3271

Pharmacies: James Drug (open daily), 101 East Chapman Street, Ely (218-365-3130); **Martinetto Drug,** 40 North Second Avenue, East, Ely (218-365-6412)

ST. LOUIS

Among cities, St. Louis is a rare breed. Characterized by the 630-foot-high Gateway Arch, St. Louis is one of a handful of cities with a great urban park. Forest Park, site of the 1904 World's Fair, is a sweet expanse of greenery, just fifteen minutes from the Gateway Arch. Forest Park's 1,300 acres offer families a New Age mix of nature and nurture—art, history, theater, science magic for kids, a well-landscaped zoo, and plenty of sports: tennis, biking and hiking trials, and nine- and eighteen-hole golf courses.

GETTING THERE

The **Lambert-St. Louis International Airport**, 10701 Lambert International Boulevard, is 13 miles northwest on I-70; (314) 426-8000. Most major airlines serve the airport, including **American** (800-433-7300 or 314-231-9505), **Northwest** (800-225-2525), **United** (800-241-6522 or 314-454-0088), and **TWA** (800-221-2000). Taxis and rental cars are available. Rental car companies include **National** (800-227-7360 or 314-426-6272), **Hertz** (800-654-3131 or 314-426-7555), and **Avis** (800-331-1212 or 314-426-7766).

Greyhound/Trailways, 1450 North Thirteenth Street (800-231-2222), and the **Amtrak Station,** 550 South Sixteenth Street (314-331-3300), also offer convenient transportation to St. Louis. For train ticket reservations and information, call (800) USA-RAIL.

GETTING AROUND

Taxis include **Yellow** (314-361-2345), **County** (314-991-5300), and **Allen** (314-241-7722). **Bi-State Transit,** 707 North First Street (314-231-2345), offers inexpensive bus transportation. St. Louis's **Metro Link** (314-231-2345), a light-rail mass transportation system, connects most major attractions within the city, including the airport, Union Station, Busch Stadium, the America's Center, and even the north St. Louis suburbs. Metro Link conveniently offers free transportation in the downtown area weekdays from 10:00 A.M. until 2:00 P.M. Rental cars, however, are still a good option for getting around.

WHAT TO SEE AND DO

Museums

Take your children to the **St. Louis Science Center,** 5050 Oakland Avenue (314-289-4444). Let your kids loose for some hands-on science fun at the Science Center's two connected buildings. Kids' eyes grow wide at the sight of the life-size Tyrannosaurus Rex who moves and roars menacingly in the atrium. Wind your way through his world and the changing habitats to see what the land looked like when these giants roamed it and when dragonflies swooped down on the St. Louis area. At the Human Adventure gallery, explore perception and senses by creating patterns in a kaleidoscope, find out why "pretzels" in your ears help hearing, and how your hands can conduct an electric concert. The Discovery Room is a hands-on place to finger such objects of interest as skeletons, sandboxes, tepees, wheelchairs, and stethoscopes.

The tunnel between the two buildings leads you into an underground domain of pipes and mines. Walk through a coal mine, complete with shoveling noises and canary songs, and simulated sewer where water pipes emit swishing noises. Exhibits in the MedTech and DNA Zone galleries look at medical equipment and advances and pose ethical questions about medical research and behavior. When you get hungry, eat at Einstein's Café, where the snacks are relatively good.

Star-studded skies come alive at the **McDonnell Planetarium** (try to purchase tickets in advance, if possible). Browse the exhibits around the theater, which include an authentic Gemini space capsule, replicated space vehicles, properties of gravity, and the brilliance and power of the sun.

Outside is **Monsanto Science Park,** a hands-on educational play park. Here children image themselves in a human kaleidoscope and a giant prism, crawl through thermal tubes, switch giant gears, toss echoes down a 100-foot chamber, and roll balls across a looping track. The **Exploradome** is an inflated exhibition gallery.

A time line of automobile history is exhibited at the **St. Louis Car Museum,** 1575 Woodson Road; (314) 993–1330. The museum displays 150 cars, including model As, pedal cars from 1920, and everything since then. Kids really like the Lamborghini Countach; "It's a real mean, exotic car," one staff member told us. The museum is currently painting a mural telling the history of Route 66.

The **St. Louis Art Museum,** 1 Fine Arts Drive, Forest Park; (314) 721–0072. Originally the Palace of Fine Arts, the museum is the sole remaining building from the Louisiana Purchase Centennial Exhibition of 1904. Greek columned, eagle crowned, and sited by a reflecting pool, the palace once mirrored East Coast standards of sophistication.

With 1990s renovation adding 30,000 additional feet of gallery space, more of the museum's permanent collection came out of the closet, including ancient Egyptian statues of gods and goddesses, mummies, and gold jewelry dating from 600 B.C. Other interesting features of the museum's permanent collection include dazzling works by Claude Monet and Edgar Degas. There is an exhibit on decorative arts, furniture, and household items as they evolved through history. On occasional Sunday afternoons, the museum holds special festival days for children and families. Call ahead to check.

For aviation history, and a sample of life in the American West, visit the **Missouri History Museum,** in the Jefferson Memorial Building in Forest Park, Lindell and Debalinere; (314) 746–4599. The legendary exhibit of Charles Lindbergh's Spirit of St. Louis memorabilia is of popular interest. Backed by nine St. Louis businessmen, Charles Lindbergh bet his stamina against the tediousness of a 33½ hour trans-Atlantic crossing. The museum's one-room gallery evokes Lindbergh's May 20 and 21, 1927, record-breaking flight. There's an eight-minute film and a collection of memorabilia, including flight suit, arm cup for water, hip chronometer, and diary. Logged at eighteen hours: "I've lost command of my eyelids. . . I've got to find some way to keep awake. There's no alternative but death or failure." For musical firsts, peruse Ragtime to Rock N' Roll, a small exhibition of sheet music, photographs, and memorabilia of St. Louis ragtime, blues, gospel. and jazz musicians including Chuck Berry, Miles Davis, and Ike Turner.

St. Louis at a Glance

- City vitality balanced by alluring green space and parks

- Nature, museums, and sports in Forest Park, site of the 1904 World's Fair

- Stunning views from atop the Gateway Arch

- Dixieland jazz and ragtime bands

- St. Louis Convention and Visitors Bureau, (314) 421–1023 or (800) 916–0040

Also in Forest Park is the **Zoological Park** (314–781–0900), a well-kept eighty-three-acre landscaped treat. Board the miniature train pulled by a small-gauge engine. Your children will love the ride under a waterfall and through a tunnel (warn the little ones of several minutes of darkness). The four strategically placed stops allow you to see most everything and still not have to carry a walk-weary child.

Be sure to allow at least an hour for the zoo's **The Living World,** two halls whose interactive high-tech exhibits, computers, and video screens portray the biological world. In the animal hall, you'll be amazed at the dazzling display of four viewing levels—tanks of coral, screens that flash images of spawning salmon, a look at the live quail hatching, and a computer that defines such terms as "anthropod." In the Ecology Hall, follow your fancy as computers inform you about such natural subjects as bird feeding habits or extinct animals.

If you have limited time, pay a short but rewarding visit to the birds. They swoop and chatter in a free-flight cage, built in 1904 and claimed to be the world's largest. There are also six aviaries, which house a bald eagle, red-billed toucans, and the endangered white neck cranes. The wire that encloses the aviary is designed to fade out of view, so you get the feeling you're really walking in their natural habitat.

Stop by at the Jungle of the Apes and see Fred, a 330-pound silver-back lowland gorilla, the zoo's primate pride. The habitat of the Jungle of the Apes was developed to study great ape behavior; it offers banyan trees, black-haired chimps sunning on rocks like satisfied Buddhas. wizened-faced orangutans, and shy gorillas striking poses behind gray-limbed ersatz trees. Raja, a baby elephant born in 1992, is also quite a crowd-gatherer. Younger children will also enjoy the Children's Zoo, which will reopen in 1997 with more interactive activities. The zoo is adding koala and otter exhibits. The play area will include more displays that combine children and animal activities, such as a giant spider web that kids can climb into.

Then end your day with a stunning sunset stroll along **Forest Park**'s windy lanes and expansive lawns. This special green space educates with museums and learning centers, entertains with eighty-three acres of zoo critters, and, like all great city parks, Forest Park allures and pampers us with space and grace. Forest Park also offers lots of recreational activities including seasonal golf, tennis, and ice skating. Call (314) 535-0100.

St. Louis is rich in black history. Not only did the Dred Scott controversy take place here, but legendary ragtime musician Scott Joplin lived and composed in this city. To celebrate such contributions to American culture, the **Museum of Black Inventors,** 9 South Newstead Street (314-741-5901), was founded in 1993. Visitors can learn through artifacts, photographs, and documents about the contributions of African Americans in medicine, agriculture, and daily life. Tools such as the fire extinguisher, lawn mower, and traffic lights were developed by black inventors.

The Holocaust Museum and Learning Center, 12 Milestone Campus Drive (314-432-0020), opened in May 1995. Using text, videos, and artifacts, such as letters telling Jews in Germany that they could not vote and displays of currency that could only be used in the ghettos, the museum tells the history of the Holocaust. The museum has a special emphasis here on the Jews who immigrated to St. Louis from Europe after World War II.

Six Flags over Mid-America, off I-44 (314-938-4800 or 314-938-5300), celebrates its twenty-fifth year with the opening of **Warner Bros. Backlot,** where guests witness the magic of movie making. Live drama, action-packed sequences, and musicals leap off the stage of five

The busy St. Louis riverfront is a popular family attraction. (Courtesy St. Louis Convention and Visitors Commission)

"movie sets." Guests participate in some re-creations. A company store sells just about everything emblazoned with its trademarked characters.

More Attractions

What's a city without a symbol? St. Louis is synonymous with **the Gateway Arch,** at Market Street on the riverfront; (314) 425 4465. This 630-foot-high stainless-steel curve glinting along the riverfront marks the city's gateway position for the pioneers heading west to possibility. For a bird's–eye view, ride the tram to the Arch's top, but only if you can tolerate tight places. Make reservations when you arrive at the Arch, and be prepared for a two-to-three-hour wait.

There is plenty to do while you wait. You may watch *Monument to the Dream,* a twenty-eight-minute film detailing the Arch's building trials. Or, meander through the nearby **Museum of Westward Expansion,** beneath the Gateway Arch (314–425–4465), and admire such pioneer artifacts as the Native American peace medals, wooden stagecoaches, and recipes for buffalo stew.

One of St. Louis's newer attractions is the **Arch Odyssey Theater,** underground at Gateway Arch; (314) 425–4465. This high-tech theater, with a four-story-high screen, surrounds you with sight and sound.

Just north of the Arch, **Laclede's Landing,** between Eads and King bridges on the Riverfront (314–241–5875), is named for Pierre Laclede, who came ashore here in 1763 to establish a fur trading post. Now, these cobbled walkways and reclaimed warehouses sport shops, bars, and restaurants.

Just downriver, and across from the Arch, commercialism floats a more tacky existence. Here paddleboats are turned into moored casinos (which don't welcome those under twenty-one). You may want to climb aboard the *Tom Sawyer,* or the *Becky Thatcher* and enjoy dinner on the Mississippi. You can enjoy a one-hour harbor cruise aboard a paddle wheeler, or two-and-a-half-hour dinner/dance cruises with **Gateway Riverboat Cruises,** 500 North Leonor K. Sullivan Boulevard; (314) 621–4040.

Green Spaces

At the **Missouri Botanical Garden,** 4344 Shaw Boulevard (314–577–5100), find a still point and a vista from the meditation huts and tranquil stone paths in the Japanese Garden. With fourteen acres, this is the largest formal Japanese garden in the United States. Then, tour the Climatron, the first geodesic-dome greenhouse, and the blooming rose gardens, lily ponds, and flower-bedecked paths. Dozens of individual gardens delight the senses, particularly the Scented Garden. It features flowers noteworthy for their fragrance and texture, sculptures and fountains that fill the garden with the sounds of water and chimes, and braille markers that make this garden especially appreciated by blind visitors. End your visit with a tour of the Chinese Garden and take in the scents of lotus, gardenias, and camellias. The pavilion and the carved marble bridge, which spans the central pool and a narrow stream, are gifts from Nanjing, St. Louis's sister city.

At the **Laumeier Sculpture Park,** 12580 Rott Road (314–821–1209), a 125-acre outdoor park, the landscape blooms with modern sculpture, some of huge proportions such as the red 100-foot-long Alexander Lieberman statue *The Way.* On these rolling hills among the pines and oaks, the angles, lines, and massive size of these innovative modern sculptures delight your eye.

Other Attractions

Just a few minutes from Laumeier is **The Magic House,** 516 South Kirkwood Road (Lindbergh Boulevard); (314) 822-8900. This is a fun house of interactive exhibits. Here kids (and adults) explore sensory and scientific awareness by dancing with their shadows, tapping morse code, trying computers, and crawling through tunnel mazes, Tots one to seven especially enjoy A Little Bit of Magic, their own place for sliding, climbing, jumping, turning steering wheels, and sand painting with colored lights.

Tour the **Anheuser-Busch Brewery,** I-55 and Arsenal Street (314-577-2626), the largest brewer in the world. Visitors can watch how beer is brewed in the expanded Brew House. From three stories high, check out the functioning brewery equipment. There are also some antique pieces in the Brew House, including a copper kettle and a huge hop-vine chandelier that, according to legend, belonged to the Belgian exhibit at the 1904 World's Fair. See everything from the packaging plant to the lager cellar to the Budweiser Clydesdale stables. Parents can enjoy free samples of Anheuser Busch beers. The gift shop caters to the whole family, with items ranging from beer mugs to Budweiser T-shirts.

St. Louis has another claim to fame: offbeat museums. The **Bowling Hall of Fame and Museum,** 111 Stadium Plaza (301-231-6340), has actual bowling alleys you can use; compare old-time alleys to modern-day lanes.

If you've ever collected toy trains, and wished for miles of track, visit the fifty-acre **Museum of Transport,** 3015 Barrett Station Road; (314) 965-7998. Here you'll be dwarfed by the yardful of big engines like the Union-Pacific steam locomotives, the 1890s Black Diamond, and Big Boy, a 600-ton steam locomotive from the forties.

Do you have a canine among your best friends? If so, you won't want to miss a visit to **The Dog Museum,** Queeny Park, 1721 South Mason Road; (314) 821-DOGS. Paintings, figurines, a dog-specific video theater, and a gift shop are all on the grounds of the Jarville House, a Greek Revival mansion. Bring home a souvenir for your fuzzy pal.

Sports

Brings the kids to a **Cardinals** baseball game, Busch Stadium; (314) 421-3060. They can sit, if seats are available, in the special Kids Corner with the team mascot, Fredbird. Kids can test their sports skills in the Busch Stadium Family Pavilion, which has batting cages and pitching mounds along with displays of old uniforms. Periodically, there are chances to meet current and former players. Also check for hockey games and times for the sports arena. Come early to **Busch Stadium,** 250 Stadium Plaza (314–421–3060), and tour the **St. Louis Cardinal Hall of Fame,** 100 Stadium Plaza (314–421–FAME), which features films and sports memorabilia. **Blues Hockey** is played at Kiel Center, 1401 Clark Avenue; (314) 622–5400.

More Recreational Spaces

Creve Couer Park, Dorsett Road (314–889–2863), has facilities for sailing, canoeing, camping, hiking, and picnicking. Winter brings ice skating and sledding; and in the spring, call about fishing and boating in the park. For more outdoor activity, **Queeny County Park,** 550 Weidman Road (314–391–0900), features the Greensfelder Recreational Complex with skating rinks, outdoor pool, and tennis courts. The park also hosts the St. Louis Symphony Pops in the summer.

Shopping

The shopping in St. Louis is as much an attraction as an activity. **Plaza Frontenac,** 97 Plaza Frontenac, Clayton and Lindbergh (314–432–5800), features ritzy apparel at Saks, Gucci, Montaldo's, and Rodier. The **St. Louis Union Station,** Market Street, between Eighteenth and Twentieth streets (314–421–6655), offers scores of shops in a century-old renovated train station. The **St. Louis Centre,** 515 North Sixth Street (314–231–5522), is a large, enclosed shopping center with four floors. Shops of interest in the **Saint Louis Galleria,** I-170 and Highway 40 (314–863–6633), include FAO Schwarz, Godiva, Crayola Kids, and Ann Taylor.

Nightlife and Performing Arts

Take a walk along Laclede's Landing to find some lively nighttime entertainment in St. Louis. It won't be long before you begin to hear the swinging brass of the dixieland jazz and ragtime bands playing in bars and restaurants. *The Riverfront Times,* distributed at no charge in restaurants and offices throughout the city, and the *St. Louis Magazine,*

612 North Second Street (314-231-7200), list calendars of events and nightly entertainment.

St. Louis also has a thriving performing arts scene. At **Powell Symphony Hall,** 718 North Grand (314-533-2500), listen to the **St. Louis Symphony Orchestra,** one of the oldest symphony orchestras in the country, led by Maestro Hans Vonk. **Dance St. Louis** is located at 634 North Grand (314-534-5000); **The Muny on Forest Park** is at the **Riverport Performing Arts Center,** 14141 Riverport Drive, Maryland Heights, (314-298-9944); and the **West Port Playhouse** is at 600 West Port Plaza (314-576-7100).

The **Fox Theater,** 527 North Grand Boulevard (314-534-1678), an ornate Siamese-and-Byzantine-style theater, opened in 1929 and was restored in 1981. Today it features Broadway productions such as *Phantom of the Opera,* comedians such as Seinfeld, as well as concerts and dance.

Entertain the entire family with **Bob Kramer's Marionettes,** 4143 Laclede Avenue; (314) 531-3313. These puppet shows delight the child in everyone. See demonstrations of puppet making Monday through Saturday at 10:00 A.M. and 1:00 P.M. and the show Puppet Follies happens every Saturday at 11:15 A.M. and 2:15 P.M. The store sells great puppets. There is an admission fee, and call in advance for specific shows.

Gambling: Not for Kids

The **Casino Queen,** 200 Front Street (800-777-0777), offers gambling excursions on the Illinois side of the river six times daily. Breakfast, lunch, and dinner cruises are available, but plan your child care in advance with a hotel or service because guests must be twenty-one years or older to board.

The **President Casino on The Admiral,** 802 North First Street (800-878-7411), is a large dockside casino, with slots, blackjack and craps tables, and a restaurant and delicatessen.

SPECIAL EVENTS

January: The Missouri Botanical Garden features the Annual Orchid Display.

February: Historic Soulard hosts a Mardi Gras Celebration, with a charity ball, Creole cook-off, jazz music, and parade.

March: Downtown turns green for a day, and copes alive with the luck and spirit of the Irish, during the St. Patrick's Day Parade. Near the end of the month, jazz talent from across the land unites in St. Louis for the Mid-America Jazz Festival.

April: Six Flags Over Mid-America reopens, and the St. Louis Cardinals kick off their new season. The Storytelling Festival offers professional tales from early May.

May: Riverboat races between modern day Becky Thatcher and Tom Sawyer commemorate National Tourism Week. See the clowns, acrobats, and zany circus antics reminiscent of the travelers of the 1800s, at Circus Flora. Jefferson Barracks Park hosts American Indian Days, featuring food, dancing, and celebration at an intertribal pow-wow. The Children's Zoo opens its outdoor area to visitors.

June: Zoo and Aquarium Conservation Day, at the zoo. Get a Taste of West Ports you sample foods from more than fifteen different restaurants. At the month's end. the Sand Castle Festival, Laumeier Sculpture Park, features huge sand castles.

July: Fair St. Louis is said to be one of the largest Independence Day celebrations in the United States, each year attracting millions to the Gateway Arch and to the St. Louis waterfront. From July 3 to July 5, festivities include hot air balloons, sky diving, jet fighters, and fireworks, plus more than 150 international craft and food vendors.

August: Artisans and craftspeople strut their stuff at the Festival of the Little Hills.

September: Early fall brings the Annual Bevo Day. A parade, plenty of food, rides, markets, and arts-and-craft shows take this festival into the night. Downtown hops during the St. Louis Blues Heritage Festival, featuring live rhythm-and-blues, jazz, rock-and-roll, and gospel music. Also, the St. Louis County Fair and Air Show feature exhibits, demonstrations, and other attractions.

October: Faust Park hosts the Faust Folk Festival, with nineteenth-century-style performing arts and a crafts sale. Missouri Chili Cook-Off and the Applebutter Festival, in Historic Kimmswick (twenty-minute drive from downtown St. Louis), invite with homemade apple butter, carriage rides, and entertainment.

December: During the holidays, St. Louis jumps into the season with the Light Up Ceremony, the Christmas Parade (314-851-1441), and the Annual Way of Lights (314-397-6700). Keeping with tradition, the *Nutcracker* plays at Fox Theatre.

WHERE TO STAY

For a luxury hotel stay, look into the **Hyatt Regency St. Louis Union Station,** One St. Louis Union Station; (314) 231-1234. Other hotels include **Courtyard by Marriott,** 2340 Market Street (314-241-9111), **Hampton Inn Union Station,** 2211 Market Street (314-241-3200), **Holiday Inn Downtown Convention Center**, Ninth Street at Convention Plaza (314-621-8200), **Regal Riverfront Hotel,** 200 South Fourth Street (314-241-9500), and **Days Inn at the Arch,** 333 Washington Avenue (314-621-7900), **Mayfair Suites,** 806 St. Charles Street (314-421-2500), features a bar and grill, a wide variety of rooms, and easy access to all the attractions of St. Louis, making this a popular lodging choice. Families take priority at the **Summerfield Suites Hotel,** 1855 Craigshire Road; (314) 878-1555 or (800) 833-4353. A spacious living area complete with television and VCR joins two separate bedrooms with their private baths. Fully equipped kitchens make feeding little ones easier and cheaper.

Resort

To combine a St. Louis visit with a resort stay, try the **Tan-Tar-A Resort and Golf Club,** Osage Beach, (800) 826-8272, about three hours from St. Louis. The resort features championship golf courses, five pools, tennis, racquetball, and dozens of other activities plus the Lake of the Ozarks. Children's programs offered in season.

WHERE TO EAT

Tony's, 410 Market Street (314-231-7007), is one of only a few Mobil four-star rated restaurants in the United States. Come early—by 6:00 P.M. if you can. No reservations are taken. Dinners come with three bread courses, attentive service, and scrumptious food. Among the specialties: veal, rigatoni, quail.

For the best burgers in St. Louis, munch at **O'Connel's Pub,** 4652 Shaw Street; (314) 773-6600. For dinner with a view and nightly entertainment, make reservations at **Top of the Riverfront Restaurant,** 200 South Fourth Street; (314) 241-3191.

For relaxed dinners, try the **Old Spaghetti Factory,** 727 North First Street (314-621-0276), where pasta and special sauces dominate the menu. **Ozzie's Restaurant and Sports Bar,** 645 West Port Plaza (314-434-1000), provides comfortable atmosphere, wood furnishings, twenty-two televisions, and many hockey, baseball and other jerseys adorning the walls.

Fitz's Bottling Company, 6605 Delmar (314-726-9555), is a root beer microbrewery where customers can see the root beer being brewed and watch the old bottling line. Daily specials often feature barbecue and burgers. For Italian cuisine, try **Zia's** 5256 Wilson Avenue (314-776-0020), and taste the St. Louis specialty of toasted raviolis. For Nouvelle American cuisine, make reservations for **Faust's** in the Adam's Mark-St. Louis, Fourth and Chestnut streets; (314) 342-4690. For the best bakery in town, try **Amighetti's Bakery and Cafe,** 3151 Wilson; (314) 776-2855. Voted one of the best in St. Louis, the breads, pizza, and ice cream are treats.

DAY TRIPS

Plan a day to visit **Six Flags Over Mid-America,** P.O. Box 60 Eureka, Missouri; (314) 938-5300. Secure your stomach for the mindblowing Ninja—the black belt of roller coasters—and cool off from the summer heat on the Log Flume or the rapids of Thunder River. Looney Tunes Town give the kids a chance to meet Bugs and other characters, and at the end of the day, you enjoy Batman Nights with lasers and fireworks. Take I-44 to exit 261, about 30 miles from St. Louis.

Among the 5,000 caves that gave Missouri the nickname the "Cave State," the **Meramec Caverns,** one hour west of St. Louis by way of I-44, in Stanton, are the most well-known. Discovered more than 200 years ago, the Caverns feature rock formations that are more than 70 million years old. You'll be amazed at the colors, the formations, the "onyx mountain," the natural pools of water, and the enormous size of the Cavern. Kids marvel at the Jungle Room, named for its resemblance to a swampy jungle full of rocky "vegetation." Outside, restaurants and gift shops await.

Instead of grabbing a bite at a crowded concession, pack a picnic for **La Jolla Natural Park,** adjacent to the Caverns, along the banks of the Meramec River and enjoy a picnic or barbecue.

FOR MORE INFORMATION

The St. Louis Convention and Visitors Bureau: (314) 421-1023 or (800) 916-0040, for free information about lodging, restaurants, and important numbers; Internet: http://www.st-louis.mo.us.

Fun Phone: (314) 421-2100, for information about special events

Missouri Information Center: Interstate 270 in North St. Louis, Riverview exit; (314) 869-7100

St. Louis County Department of Parks and Recreation: 41 South Central Avenue, 63105; (314) 889-2863

St. Louis Visitors Center: Seventh Street and Washington Avenue

Emergency Numbers

Ambulance, fire, police: 911

For Highway Patrol: (314) 434-3344

Children's Hospital: The Cardinal Glennon Children's Hospital, 1465 South Grand Street; (314) 577-5600

Twenty-four-hour pharmacy: Walgreens, 4 Hampton Village Plaza Shopping Center; (314) 351-2100

Poison Control: The Cardinal Glennon Children's Hospital features a poison control center. Call the hotline: (314) 772-5200.

THE BLACK HILLS, THE BADLANDS, AND MT. RUSHMORE

South Dakota' natural beauty and unusual geological features, plus its Wild West history and Native American presence, combine to offer families, especially city dwellers, an interesting landscape for a family vacation.

The Sioux Nation, despite being driven from the Black Hills after the discovery of gold in the area in 1874, still maintains a sizable presence in South Dakota. More than 50,500 Native Americans, most of the Lakota, Dakota, and Nakota tribes of the Sioux Nation, live within the state's boundaries, both on and off reservations.

GETTING THERE

South Dakota has two major airports; the one in **Rapid City** provides better access to the Black Hills and Badlands areas. The **Rapid City Regional Airport** (650–394–4195), 9 miles southeast of town, is served by several carriers, including **Northwest** (800–225–2525), **Skywest** (800–221–1212), and **United Express** (800–241–6522).

Among Rapid City's car rental companies are **Avis** (800–331–1212), **Hertz** (800–654–3131), **Budget** (800) 676–0488), **National** (800–227–7368), and **Thrifty** (800–367–2277).

Jack Rabbit Lines runs routes between Rapid City and Sioux Falls; (605) 336–0855. **Amtrak** does not provide any service to South Dakota. **I-90** and **I-29** are two of the major highways leading to Rapid City.

GETTING AROUND

With a lot of wide open spaces, South Dakota is best seen by car. For those who prefer not to drive, **Gray Line** of Rapid City (605–342–4461) offers tours of the Black Hills and the Badlands.

WHAT TO SEE AND DO

The Black Hills, approximately 70 miles wide and 110 miles long, have much to offer families, including four national park areas: Mount Rushmore National Memorial, Wind Cave National Park, Jewel Cave National Monument, and Devils Tower National Monument, which lies just west of South Dakota in Wyoming. East of the Black Hills lies another not-to-be-missed site, the Badlands National Park.

The Black Hills

The **Black Hills National Forest,** 10 miles west of Rapid City on U.S. 16, covers 1.2 million acres. In 1874 when General George Custer led a military expedition through the Black Hills, the region was sacred Sioux land. The Lakota Sioux named the region *Paha Sapa,* or "Black Hills," a place to communicate with *Wakan Tanka,* the "Great Spirit." Despite this, much of the land was taken from the Sioux after gold was discovered here in 1874. Among the Black Hills highlights are the following.

The **Mount Rushmore National Monument,** P.O. Box 268, Keystone, South Dakota 57751 (605–574–2523), is about 23 miles southwest of Rapid City off U.S. 16A, and 2 miles southwest of Keystone. It's what first comes to mind when people think of South Dakota. The chiseled faces of George Washington, Thomas Jefferson, Abraham Lincoln, and Theodore Roosevelt, carved by Gutzon Borglum in monumental scale, gaze out at the land. Each head is about 60 feet long, twice the size of the Sphinx in Egypt. Borglum began sculpting this massive project in 1927 at age sixty, and he died in 1941 before completing the carvings, which were to feature also the shoulders, chest, and waist of each president. For the most spectacular light, arrive at dawn. Visitors can now get a closer look at the memorial if they go on the Presidential Trail, which opened in 1995. This nature trail, at the base of the monument, allows visitors to realize the enormity and complexity of the structure.

The Black Hills and the Badlands at a Glance

- Dramatic landscapes plus Wild West history and Native American presence

- 20,000 artifacts in the Indian Museum of North America

- Mount Rushmore National Monument

- Gold rush ambiance and activities

- Black Hills, Badlands, and Lakes Association, (605) 341-1462

The thirteen-minute film at the visitors center details the crafting of the monument, as do the photographs and tools on display.

In May 1998, an interpretive center telling the history of Mount Rushmore is scheduled to open. Visitors will be able to see the flag used in the unveiling of the sculpture and the tools used in the carving of the four presidents. At the new amphitheater, there are nightly ceremonies and special park presentations.

Seventeen miles southwest of Mt. Rushmore, a fifth face takes shape in stone. Still being built is the **Crazy Horse Memorial** on U.S. 16-385; (605) 673–4681. When completed, this tribute to the Lakota Sioux leader will be the largest mountain carving in the world at 563 feet high and 641 feet long. Lakota Chief Henry Standing Bear invited sculptor Korczak Ziolkowski to carve this monument because, wrote Standing Bear, "My fellow chiefs and I would like the white man to know the red man has great heroes, too." Ziolkowski began the project in 1947, and although he died in 1982, his family continues this monumental carving.

Ziolkowski, desiring not to depict a realistic image of this Sioux leader, but rather a rendering of the Sioux spirit, portrayed Crazy Horse astride a steed, his arm extended, responding to the goading question "Where are your lands now?" asked by a white man after the Battle of Little Big Horn when many Sioux were pushed into reservations. The dramatic and dignified warrior points, answering "My lands are where my dead lie buried."

Once a year, during the first weekend in June, visitors can actually hike the mountain where Crazy Horse is being carved. At other times, visitors can view the memorial in progress from an observation deck, which offers and interesting look at the rare art of mountain carving. Admission is charged.

A huge visitor center houses the **Indian Museum of North America,** featuring more than 20,000 artifacts of North American tribes. A special wing is devoted to the Lakota, a majority of whom live in the Dakotas.

A high-tech tour of the Black Hills history, The Journey, is new. Conveniently located near Mount Rushmore at 625 Ninth Street (605–394–6923), this $12.5-million structure explores 2.5 billion years of the area's history. Collections from the Sioux Indian Museum, the Minnilusa Pioneer Museum, the Museum of Geology at South Dakota School of Mines and Technology, the Duhamel Plains Indian Artifact Collection, and the State Archeological Research Center tells the history and heritage of several tribes. While you watch the twelve-minute orientation film, fog seeps from the walls, creating a mystical atmosphere. Be sure to visit the outdoor geological field camp; watch the video wall puzzle that, when solved, depicts a prehistoric woman; and tour the three tepees that allow visitors to touch items such as buffalo hide and listen to a hologramlike image of a woman telling stories.

The **Jewel Cave National Monument** (605–673–2288) is 59 miles southwest of Rapid City and 13 miles west of Custer on Highway 16. It features more than 100 miles of accessible passageways, making it the fourth longest cave in the world. Unusual calcite formations hang from the ceiling. Three tours, each covering about ½ mile, offer different views of the cave. While the Scenic Tour follows a paved lighted path, the Historic Tour, conducted by candlelight, traces the route of the earliest cave explorers, and the Spelunking Tour, more rigorous for ages sixteen and older, winds through undeveloped passages and caverns. Hiking boots are required. Whatever tour you choose, be sure to wear layers of warm clothing as the average cave temperature hovers at a chilly 47 degrees Fahrenheit.

Every member of the family will be awed by the epic faces of Mt. Rushmore.
(Courtesy South Dakota Tourism)

Forty-two miles north of Rapid City is **Deadwood,** an 1876 gold rush boom town in the northern section of the national forest, off I-90 on U.S. 85 and U.S. Alt. 14; (605) 578–1102. Although the city is a designated National Historical Landmark with the facades of many buildings along Main Street sparkling with a turn-of-the-century flair, the town is not exactly as it was in the gold rush days. Now more than eighty gambling establishments lure tourists. While these might contribute to the Wild West spirit of this frontier village where Wild Bill Hickok was murdered, the gaming also lends a somewhat tawdry air, which detracts from the family allure. Deadwood, however, has recently begun catering to families. Attractions include an amusement park, Sherman Street Trolley Station, and the Adams Museum.

One mile from the town the **Mount Moriah Cemetery,** known also as "Boot Hill," features the graves of such western legends as "Wild Bill" Hickok and Calamity Jane. If your kids crave wax museums,

Deadwood's **Ghosts of Deadwood Gulch,** Old Towne Hall, Lee Street (605-578-3583), features eighteen scenes of pioneer days.

For some more gold rush days ambiance, take an underground tour of the once prosperous **Broken Boot Gold Mine,** on U.S. Alt. 14; (605) 578-2250. It brought up gold from 1878 until 1904. Or, explore the surface workings of one of the oldest and largest gold mines in the western hemisphere, the still-operating **Homestake Gold Mine,** in **Lead,** 3 miles from Deadwood, Main and Mill streets; (605) 584-3110. Children under four are not permitted.

Nearby, **Terry Peak** and **Deer Mountain** offer downhill and cross-country skiing.

Custer State Park

Adjacent to the Black Hills National Forest is **Custer State Park,** 42 miles southwest of Rapid City on Highway 16A, HC 83 Box 70E, Custer 57730; (605) 255-4515. Featuring 73,000 acres of rolling grasslands and pine forests, the park is home to about 1,400 head of buffalo, one of the nation's largest herds. Besides eyeing these formidable beasts, symbols of the West, you're likely to see deer, elk, pronghorn antelope, and bighorn sheep.

Among the park's highlights are three scenic drives. Along the 14-mile **Needles Highway Scenic Drive,** on Highway 87 from Legion Lake to the base of Harney Peak, the highest mountain in the Black Hills, you thread through the towering granite pinnacles, popular with rock climbers. On the **Iron Mountain Road,** which spans alternate 16, for 17 miles from Custer State Park to Mount Rushmore, you drive through granite tunnels, past Black Hills overlooks, and through stands of spruce and pine. You're likely to see buffalo, coyotes, prairie dogs, wild burros (the only wildlife in the park that it's okay to feed), and elk, especially in the early morning or at dusk along the **Wildlife Loop Road,** which forms an 18-mile loop passing the Wildlife Station and three of the park's resorts (see Where to Stay).

Pick up park information at the **Peter Norbeck Visitor Center,** 15 miles east of Custer on Highway 16A; (605) 255-4464. **Sylvan Lake,** 7 miles north of Custer on Route 87 and 89, is known for its setting amid massive rock formations, and for its fishing, and **Legion Lake** has good fishing, swimming, and family-oriented budget cabins.

Wind Cave National Park

Wind Cave is the highlight of the 18,000 acres of grasslands of the **Wind Cave National Park,** 53 miles south of Rapid City, near Hot Springs and south of Custer State Park; (605–745–4600). It's a sure winner for kids fascinated by underground wonders. Said to be the world's sixth longest cave, this attraction offers more than 78 miles of mapped passages, with lots of boxwork ceiling formations. Remember warm clothing and good walking shoes. Above ground keep an eye out for the frequent buffalo, elk, pronghorn, and deer herds.

The Badlands National Park

The Badlands, 83 miles east of Rapid City (605–433–5361), exits 110 and 131 off I-90, will intrigue your family. Designated by Congress as a National Monument in 1939, and upgraded to a National Park in 1978, the Badlands has dense deposits of fossils from the Oligocene Epoch, the Golden Age of Mammals, including giant turtles, three-toed horses, and saber-toothed tigers. Once a saltwater sea, later a marsh, the area is now a remnant of one of the world's great grasslands, with jutting peaks, twisting canyons, and vast prairies. The formations reveal amazing colors as erosion has exposed the formations' layers of purple, yellow, tan, gray, red, and orange. Some of the best colors can be seen at sunup and sundown.

Wind and water created the wild assortment of pinnacles, cones, gorges, and other geologic oddities that caused the Lakota Sioux to label the region *Mako Sica,* or "Land Bad." French trappers and traders referred to the area as *Mauvaises Terres à Traverser*—"Badlands to Travel Across." Soon after these trappers came soldiers, miners, cattlemen, and homesteaders who struggled with each other and the Sioux for the land. After the Wounded Knee Massacre, the Lakota were confined to reservations.

The park offers a variety of programs, including a Junior Ranger Program during the summer for ages five to twelve, which reward kids with a badge (parents pay a nominal fee) after they answer questions about the park and about ranger-led programs they attended.

Look for deer, buffalo, and pronghorn antelope, but don't settle for just driving through the Badlands. Spend some time on foot. Obtain information about the hiking trails from the **White River Visitor Center,** open Memorial Day through mid-September, Highway 27 in the Stronghold Unit, 20 miles south of the town of Scenic. Hiking information is also available year-round from the **Ben Reifel Visitor Center at Cedar Pass,** off Highway 240, on the park's eastern side. Kids like the Touch Room with its fossils, rocks, and plants.

It's a completely different experience to walk among the unusual knobs, pyramids, and points. Six developed trails cut through the Badlands. **The Fossil Exhibit Trail,** west of the visitor center on S.D. 240, south of Wall, is great for kids. This ¼-mile loop, which is wheelchair and stroller accessible, features replicas of area fossils. **The Cliff Shelf Nature Trail,** another ¼-mile loop just east of the visitor center on 240, passes through a juniper grove and a cattail marsh that attracts Badlands wildlife. While easy, a few steps make this not wheelchair accessible.

For teens **the Castle Trail,** northeast of the visitor center on 240, above the Cliff Shelf Trail, offers a 5¼-mile one-way stretch through rolling grasslands and Badlands formations, or a 6-mile loop when combined with the **Medicine Root Trail.** As weather changes can be sudden in the Badlands, be sure to take proper clothing and provisions, including adequate food and water, when hiking any distance. Check out the National Park Service Internet site, http://www.nps.gov.

Special Tours

For western adventure while in Custer, sign on with **Dakota Badland Outfitters,** P.O. Box 85, Custer, (605) 673-5363. Born-and-raised Dakota cowboys guide you through the Black Hills wilderness and the Badlands on day or overnight trips. Ride horseback or, more suitable with young ones, sit in a mule-drawn ranch wagon as guides relate local history and legend, and provide picnic lunches. For more adventure, book an overnight pack trip into the Badlands backcountry.

Black Hills Balloons, P.O. Box 210, Custer 57730 (605-673-2520), floats you over such scenic spots as Mount Rushmore, Crazy Horse Memorial, and herds of grazing buffalo. Check on minimum age and height requirements for children.

MORE ATTRACTIONS

In Rapid City the free **Story Book Island,** 1301 Sheridan Lake Road (605-342-6357), is a good place to let little ones romp on replicas of popular storybook characters. A moat leads to a "fairy-tale castle."

At **Bear Country U.S.A.,** off U.S. 16, 8 miles south of Rapid City (605-343-2290), roll up your windows and surround yourself with grizzly bear, timber wolves, mountain lion, buffalo, moose, bighorn sheep, and black bear as you drive through this 220-acre natural Black Hills habitat. After the drive, take the kids to see the young animals in the Welcome Center or go for pony rides.

In season two ski areas not far from Deadwood offer downhill fun. **Terry Peak Ski Area,** P.O. Box 774, Lead 57754, 3 miles west of Lead, is open generally Thanksgiving through Easter. Call (605) 584-2165 or (605) 342-7609; twenty-four-hour ski conditions, (800) 456-0524. The 20 miles of trails make this facility relatively easy to manage. There's also **Deer Mountain,** southwest of Lead on Highway 85, P.O. Box 622, Deadwood 57732; (605) 584-3230 or (605) 578-2141. It features 25 downhill trails, plus groomed cross-country trails and a ski school.

Shopping

In Rapid City, **Rushmore Mall** offers department stores and traditional mall shops. Stroll down **Main Street** and **St. Joseph's Street** for the specialty shops, including the Prairie Edge Galleries, Sixth and Main, for authentic Plains Indian arts and crafts.

Theater

Call the **Rushmore Plaza Civic Center,** 444 Mt. Rushmore Road (800)-247-1095), to find out about upcoming performances and events.

Sports

The **Rushmore Plaza Civic Center,** 444 Mt. Rushmore Road (800-247-1095), has times and schedules for the **Rapid City Posse** basketball team.

SPECIAL EVENTS

January: Black Hills Stock Show and Rodeo, Rapid City.

June: Crazy Horse Memorial Volksmarch held the first weekend of June. The only time of year when the public can climb Crazy Horse Memorial. Fort Sisseton Historical Festival, Fort Sisseton.

July: Black Hills Heritage Festival, Rapid City, featuring arts, crafts, music, entertainment, and ethnic foods.

At the Black Hills Powwow and Arts Expo, Rapid City, celebrate Native American dancing and art.

The Black Hills Roundup, Belle Fourche, a top three-day rodeo.

Gold Discovery Days, Custer, features a pageant, a parade, and a park festival.

Mammoth Days, Hot Springs, brings out Fred Flintstone-type characters for the prehistoric theme event. Eat a mammoth burger and enjoy the mammoth games.

Days of '76, Deadwood, features reenactments of the gold rush, plus a rodeo.

August: Sturgie Rally and Races, a world-renowned motorcycle extravaganza.

September: Crazy Horse Open House and Night Blast, Crazy Horse Memorial, lights up the night with a actual dynamite blast of the monument.

At the Deadwood Jam, Deadwood, bands play all day on Main Street.

October: At the Buffalo Round-up, Custer State Park, see a buffalo herd corralled by rangers and wranglers.

WHERE TO STAY

A good base in Rapid City, which has lots of lodging choices. The **Radisson Inn,** 445 Mt. Rushmore (at Main Street), Rapid City (605–348-8300 or 800-446-3750), has moderately priced rooms, plus a pool.

The **Holiday Inn-Rushmore Plaza,** 505 North Fifth Street, is another moderately priced lodging with a pool; (605) 348-4000 or (800) 465-4329. At the **Best Western Town and Country,** 2505 Mt. Rushmore Road, Rapid City (605-343-5383 or 800-528-1234), there are both indoor and outdoor pools. **The Quality Inn,** 2208 Mt. Rushmore Road, has two outdoor pools and some suites with Jacuzzis; (605) 342-3322 or (800) 221-2222. The **Alex Johnson Hotel,** 523 Sixth Street, has a downtown location, a Native American and western decor, and often special family rates; (605) 342-1210 or (800) 888-2539.

Keystone and **Hill City** are close to Mt. Rushmore. In Keystone the **Powder House Lodge,** U.S 16, Keystone (605–666–4646), offers cabins and motel rooms. In Hill City, the **High Country Ranch Bed and Breakfast,** 12172 Deerfield Road (605–574–9003), provides some western flare with free half-hour horseback rides; family rates.

Custer State Park offers four lodges as well as campgrounds. **Blue Bell Lodge and Resort,** Highway 87S, has rustic cabins with modern amenities, plus horseback rides and chuck-wagon cookouts; (605) 255–4531 or (800) 658–3530. The **State Game Lodge Resort** (605–255–4541 or 800–658–3530), where President Calvin Coolidge summered in 1927, offers lodge rooms, motel units, and cabins, as well as a restaurant and grocery store. Nearby Grace Coolidge Creek is noted for its trout. The **Sylvan Lake Resort** (605–574–2561 or 800–658–3530) overlooks—what else—Sylvan Lake. It's in the shadow of Harney Peak, the highest peak east of the Rockies. The resort has guest rooms, cabins, and a restaurant. **Legion Lake Resort,** Legion Lake (605–255–4521 or 800–658–3530) offers twenty-five rustic cottages; it's a good spot for swimming, fishing, and paddle-boating.

You can also camp at one of the seven campgrounds. Some sites are on a first-come basis, whereas others may be reserved by calling (800) 710–2267.

The **American Presidents Resort** is on Highway 16A, 1 mile east of Custer, P.O. Box 446, Custer 57730; (605) 673–3373. It has cabins, many but not all of which feature kitchens. The grounds have RV hookups and tent sites. Kids like the pool and the free miniature golf.

The Deadwood/Lead area offers several motels and hotels, including the **Best Western Golden Hills Resort,** 900 Miners Avenue, Lead 57754 (605–584–1800 or 800–528–1234); and the **Best Western Hickock House,** 137 Charles, Deadwood 57732 (605)–578–1611 or 800–837–8174).

Shearer's Western Dakota Ranch Vacations, HCR1, Box 9, Wall (605–279–2198), 9 miles from Wall, features horseback and wagon rides, chuck-wagon suppers, and all the chores you want. Stay in the ranch home, log cabins, tents, or tepees.

WHERE TO EAT

Try the **Flying T Chuckwagon Suppers,** on U.S. 16, 6 miles south of Rapid City; (605) 342–1905. Sample a cowboy chuck-wagon meal of barbecued beef, beans, baked potatoes, and biscuits served up in tin plates and cups. Live country and western music along with western decorations add to the atmosphere. Meals are moderately priced, and reservations are recommended.

Just a few miles outside of Rapid City, check out the **Chute Rooster,** U.S. 385 in Hill City; (605) 574–2122. Traditional western meals are served in the barn-turned-restaurant. In summer kick up your heels and join in the square dancing.

While visiting Mt. Rushmore, a convenient place for lunch is the **Buffalo Room** (605-574-2515), an inexpensive cafeteria overlooking the memorial.

When you visit **Wall Drug Store,** 510 Main Street, Wall (605-279-2175), sample the cafeteria. Although the food is plain, the atmosphere and collection of western art are not. While you peruse the murals and memorabilia, munch on a buffalo burger, and linger over homemade pie. A cup of coffee is still only 5 cents.

In Custer State Park, check out the **Pheasant Dining Room,** U.S. 16A, Custer; (605) 255–4541. This **State Game Lodge** restaurant serves hearty fare and good homemade desserts at moderate prices.

More than sixty restaurants serve first-class meals at bargain prices as a loss-leader to the gambling houses. **BJ's Grinder King,** 902 Main Street, Rapid City (605-348-3166), serves the best pizza in town.

DAY TRIPS

A stop at **Wall Drug,** 510 Main Street (605-279-2175), north of the Badlands on I-90, is a must. This small 1930s family drugstore got its boost by offering free ice water to hot and weary drives during the Great Depression. Today Wall Drug often serves 20,000 visitors each day. If you're wondering how a store in a town of 800 attracts so many visitors, you've never driven the highways of South Dakota where signs relentlessly beckon you to come on by. This is the place for kids to stretch their legs, climb on the outdoor covered wagon, and get a photo with a 6-foot-tall rabbit. Inside they can search for souvenirs and admire the funky western decor. Internet: http://www.state.sd.us/state/executive/tourism/20reasons/wall.htm

Evans Plunge, in **Hot Springs,** just 9 miles south of Wind Cave, is a naturally heated, 87-degree mineral-water spring. This indoor-outdoor swimming complex features three water slides and a spa. Also in Hot Springs, visit the **Mammoth Site,** on Highway 18; (605) 745–6017 or (800) 325–6991. It boasts the world's largest concentration of Columbian and woolly mammoth bones discovered in their primary context.

For trout fishing go to **Spearfish,** 45 miles northwest of Rapid City on I-90; (605) 642–2626 or (800) 626–8013. Spearfish Creek and the area's lakes offer peaceful blue-ribbon trout fishing. A walk through the nearby canyon reveals waterfalls. The **Black Hills Passion Play** is another Spearfish event. Set on a stage 2 blocks long and peopled with 200 actors, this play recounts the last seven days of Christ's life.

FOR MORE INFORMATION

South Dakota Department of Tourism, 711 East Wells Avenue, Pierre, South Dakota 57501-3369; (605) 773–3301 or (800) 732–5682; http://www.state.sd.us.

Black Hills, Badlands and Lakes Association, 900 Jackson Boulevard, Rapid City, South Dakota 57702; (605) 341–1462

Deadwood Visitors Bureau, 3 Siever Street, Deadwood, 57732; (605) 578–1102

Wall Chamber of Commerce, Box 527, Wall 57790; (605) 279–2665

Rapid City Convention and Visitors Bureau, 444 Mt. Rushmore Road N., Rapid City 57709; (605) 279–2665

Emergency Numbers

Ambulance, fire police: 911

Hospital: Rapid City Regional Hospital, 353 Fairmont Boulevard: (605) 341-1000 (emergency: 605-341-8222)

Pharmacy: Although there are no twenty-four-hour pharmacies in Rapid City, **Albertsons,** 855 Omaha Street, is open weekdays 9:00 A.M. to 9:00 P.M., and Saturday 9:00 A.M. to 6:00 P.M.; (605) 343-8542.

POISON CENTER: (800) 952-0123

WICHITA

Wichita, the largest city in Kansas and a major aviation and agriculture center, is cosmopolitan without being too slick; residents sport a friendly, open manner and are happy to help tourists. There are plenty of attractions in town, and Wichita also makes an excellent base from which to explore such exciting sites as a Cosmosphere and Space Center just a day trip away.

GETTING THERE

Mid-Continent Airport (316-946-4700), 5 miles west of downtown on Highway 54, is served by a number of major airlines. Car rentals, taxis, and shuttles (many hotels run their own) are available at the airport.

Amtrak (800-USA-RAIL) doesn't stop in Wichita (the closest stop is in Newton, 30 miles north).

Greyhound/Trailways provides transportation nationally from the depot at 312 South Broadway; (316) 265-7711 or (800) 231-2222.

GETTING AROUND

Metropolitan Transit Authority buses (316-265-7221) run regular daytime routes in Wichita, except for Sunday. Three nineteenth-century-style trolleylike buses serve downtown and major tourist destinations.

WHAT TO SEE AND DO

Museums and Historical Attractions

Children's Museum of Wichita, 435 South Water: (316) 267-2281. This museum truly has something for all ages. The Tot Tug for toddlers comes complete with preschool toys and a model train. Younger kids love the colorful three-story maze that looks like a small village from the outside; inside are challenging crawling and climbing spaces. Playacting is encouraged: Kids can be judges, doctors, or fire fighters, thanks to true-to-life costumes and props. Kids can time travel in the Prairie House with its miniature furniture, tepee, and chuck wagon. Older kids like the challenging, science-related exhibits, such as the Infinity Chamber, where they see hundreds of their own images. Weekends are lively, with original puppet shows on Saturday and a Sunday Concert Series. Also on Sunday, kids can talk to other youngsters around the world (some in other children's museums) at the Ham Shack, with the help of local licensed amateur radio operator volunteers. Frequent traveling exhibits add spark to this already dynamic facility.

Omnisphere and Science Center, 220 South Main: (316) 264-6178 for current show lists or 264-3174 for information. There is a nominal admission to this museum of hands-on exhibits that teach kids the basics of physics, chemistry, and astronomy. There's an extra fee for the changing planetarium shows and live science demonstrations with audience participation. In the summer, the museum's magician and illusionist performs, and other kids' programs are offered.

Sedgwick County Historical Museum, 204 South Main; (316) 265-9314. Inside this imposing 1892 City Hall building (a National Historic Site) are some delightful exhibits that kids enjoy, including the Child's World area with doll and toy collections, a 1910 drugstore, a Victorian home, and a Wichita-built Jones Six automobile.

Five minutes west of downtown are three riverside museums that, along with the botanical gardens listed below, comprise the **Museums on the River:**

The Indian Center Museum, 650 North Seneca; (316) 262-5221. The museum is inside the arrow-shaped Mid-American All Indian Center, a Bicentennial gift to all Native Americans from the people of Wichita. The location: at the confluence of the Big and Little Arkansas (pronounced "arKANSAS" in these parts) rivers where the Wichita tribe camped more that one hundred years ago. At this meeting point stands a striking, 44-foot-tall sculpture, *The Keeper of the Plains,* that kids find quite impressive. The center displays changing exhibits of

---

Wichita at a Glance

- Friendliness, fun cultural attractions for the family

- An inside view of aviation at the Cosmosphere and Space Center

- Bison and antelope roaming the prairie at the Sedgwick County Zoo

- Covered wagon trips with campfires, hearty pioneer meals, and tall tales

- Wichita Convention and Visitors Bureau, (315) 265-2800 or (800) 288-WICHITA

---

traditional and contemporary Native American works. Try to come on Tuesday when volunteers prepare American Indian cuisine, including Indian tacos, meatpies, and fry bread. An annual powwow (see Special Events) is held here, with some events usually held at the town park.

Lake Afton Public Observatory, 247th Street West and Thirty-ninth Street South; (316) 794-8995. Located 15 miles southwest of Wichita, this place is a lovely spot to spend an evening (open Friday and Saturday after sunset and Sunday evenings during the summer). See Saturn's rings, the moon, star clusters, and galaxies through the 16-inch telescope. Kids can make their own telescope and play astronomy computer games. The Observatory is across from **Lake Afton Park** (316-794-2774) where there's fishing, boating, and camping.

Continuing with the celestial theme, just outside Wichita is the **Kansas Cosmosphere and Space Center,** Eleventh and Plum, Hutchinson; (316) 662-2305 or (800) 397-0330. The Hall of Space Museum holds the largest collection of space suits, a moon rock, and full-scale replicas of spacecraft and rovers. There is a multimedia planetarium and an Omnimax Theater, which envelops visitors with its dome screen and digital sound.

Old Cowtown Museum, 1871 Sim Park Drive; (316) 264–0671. Relive Wichita's frontier days at this historic village museum, a circa 1865–1880 town with authentically furnished homes and businesses. Located on seventeen acres along the Arkansas River, Old Cowtown includes original buildings, such as the Munger House, built in 1869, the town's first log house/hotel. There's lots for kids to like, including a main street straight out of a Western movie, a fully stocked General Store, the town's first jail, a one-room schoolhouse, a blacksmith at work, and a livestock area with Texas longhorn cattle. Costumed interpreters answer questions, and on selected days in July and August, Girl Scouts in period clothing reenact childhood activities, from attending school to helping with washboard laundry.

Summer weekends bring activities including reenactments, nineteenth-century music, theatrical performances, or cooking demonstrations. The museum, open weekends year-round and daily March through October, also holds several special events (see Special Events).

The Wichita Art Museum, 619 Stackman Drive: (316) 268–4921. This museum is worth a stop if you have time—it's free except during selected traveling shows. The beautiful mother-and-child paintings by Mary Cassatt invariably appeal to youngsters. Other American works by such artists as Charles Russell, Winslow Homer, and Edward Hopper are also on display. A changing interactive gallery of art experiences is intriguing for both kids and adults.

Parks, Gardens, and Zoos

Botanica, 701 Amidon; (316) 264–0448. At this "living museum of plants," your senses will be delighted by nine-and-one-half acres of colorful tulips, irises, daylilies, mums, wildflowers, and other flowers. From spring to fall, more than 300 varieties of roses bloom in the Rose Garden. Reflecting pools, streams, and a pond of goldfish and Japanese Koi add kid appeal to this fragrant facility. The Woodland Walk, a one-quarter-mile wood-chip trail laid out by Boy Scouts, is full of native plants, birds, and small wild animals. A natural area with poisonous plants is a good place to show kids how to identify poison ivy, poison hemlock, and other no-nos. Special events, including festivals, parties, concerts, plus seasonal flower shows, are held throughout the year. Catered lunches are sold on Wednesdays and Fridays, and guided tours are offered April through October; both require reservations.

Sedgwick County Zoo and Botanical Garden, 5555 Zoo Boulevard (northwest edge of town, just off I-235); (316) 942-2212. This fine zoo, open 364 days a year, allows compatible groups of animals to roam within natural barriers in habitats resembling different geographic areas of the world. A recently opened exhibit is the North American Prairie, with a skywalk over a habitat where bison and antelope roam. Elsewhere, birds fly free in a tropical rain forest, reptiles and amphibians slither and crawl through a dark herpetarium, and tigers, rhinos, zebras, elephants, lions, and monkeys roam. Visitors can pet and feed domestic animals in the farm area. Have lunch or a snack at the restaurant on the premises.

Other Attractions

FantaSea Water Park, 3330 North Woodlawn; (316) 682-7031 for taped information, or 682-8656. The only water-oriented theme park in the state, FantaSea runs the gamut from small wading pools with slides for tiny tots to large water slides and a giant wave pool. Grab a bite at the concession stand, or bring your own cooler (no glass or alcohol allowed). The park is open May through Labor Day; call for specific days.

The **Joyland Amusement Park,** 2801 South Hillside; (316) 684-0179. This typical amusement arena has adult and kids' rides, an arcade, picnic grounds, bumper cars, and a miniature train tour. The park is open April through October.

The 21st Century Pyradomes, 3055 North Hillside; (316) 682-3100. Drive by to see the eight distinctive geodesic domes designed by H. Buckminster Fuller and a 60-foot pyramid inspired by (what else?) the pyramids of Egypt. Should you desire, tours are offered on weekday afternoons.

Tree Trunk Art, as it's known, can be found at numerous spots throughout town. Artist Gino Salerno has recycled old tree trunks into delightful pieces of art that kids adore, including Wizard of Oz characters, which can be found at **Watson Park,** 33044 South Old Lawrence Road. For other locations, call the parks department at (316) 268-4361.

Wichita Boat House and **Arkansas River Museum,** 335 West Lewis; (316) 267-9235. Situated on the east bank of the Arkansas

History comes alive at the Old Cowtown Museum. (Courtesy Old Cowtown Museum)

River, the Boat House offers boat rides, rentals, and relaxation on the water. Displays include the *Jayhawk,* one of three racing yachts used by Wichita native Bill Koch to win the America's Cup.

Sportsworld, 1010 North Webb Road (316–682–3700), is the area's largest family sports complex. It features two miniature golf courses, batting cages, go-cart tracks, and a video arcade.

Theater, Music, and the Arts

The Convention Bureau's Fun Fone (316–262–7474) offers daily updates of entertainment and special events. The downtown Century II complex is where most cultural activities take place, including Metropolitan Ballet (316–687–5880), which performs the *Nutcracker* each Christmas season; Music Theatre of Wichita (316–265–3107), staging five different productions each summer; Wichita Symphony Orchestra (316–267–7658), whose performances include Young People's Concerts; and Wurlitzer Pops (316–263–4717), featuring the grand old organ from New York's

Paramount Theater in several concerts throughout the year. **The Wichita Children's Theatre,** 201 Lulu (316-262-2282), performs both here and at their own theater.

Shopping

Dorothy and Toto hailed from Kansas, so it's only natural that Wizard of Oz artifacts are sold at shops throughout the town and state. At **The Best of Kansas** at the Hay Market, 5426 East Central (316-685-0611), you'll find Oz memorabilia as well as native arts, crafts, and food products. Get yourself and your pardners outfitted with boots, jeans, and cowboy hats at **Shepler,** the world's largest western store, 6501 West Kellogg; (316) 946-3600. Wichita is also the home of Coleman products, an extensive line of camping items. The **Coleman Factory Outlet Store and Museum,** 239 North St. Francis (316-264-0836), offers a wide assortment of discounted products as well as a display of vintage Coleman items.

Sports

The **Wichita Wings,** a Major Soccer League team, play at the Kansas Coliseum, I-135 at Eighty-fifth Street North; (316) 262-3545. **Wichita Wranglers,** an AA minor league baseball farm team for the Kansas City Royals, go to bat at Lawrence-Dumont Stadium, 300 South Sycamore; (316) 267-3372. The **Wichita Thunder** hockey team (316-264-GOAL) also plays at the Kansas Coliseum.

SPECIAL EVENTS

Contact the Wichita CVB for details on the following annual events.

April: Renaissance Faire, with arts and crafts, dramatic and musical performances, authentic games and activities.

May: Wichita River Festival, ten days of parades, bike and bathtub races, old-fashioned socials, hot air balloons, and the grand finale—Wichita Symphony's *1812 Overture* (young kids might not like the cannons, but they will like the fireworks that follow); Kansas Polkatennial, with three days of nonstop polka music and dance.

July: Inter-Tribal Mid-America All-Indian Powwow is an opportunity to learn cultural heritage, such as traditional dances.

August: National Baseball Congress, with top-quality nonprofessional teams playing at Lawrence-Dumont Stadium.

September: Wichita Arts Festival, weekend of dance, theater, music, and art; Mexican Independence Day Celebration, with music food, games, and sport tournaments; Kansas State Fair, Hutchinson.

October: Wichita Asian Festival, with traditional costume fashion shows, dances, skits, karate demonstrations, and Asian food; Old Sedgwick County Fair, first weekend, at Old Cowtown Museum, re-creates an 1870s fair with music, craft demonstrations and sales, antique buggies, wagon rides, steam-operated carousel, traditional foods, costumed reenactments, and theatrical performances.

Late November–December: Old-Fashioned Christmas, Cowtown, Monday through Saturday evenings after Thanksgiving, with music, programs, and refreshments.

December: Wichita Winter Fest, a weekend of strolling carolers, roasted chestnuts, cider, activities, and entertainment.

WHERE TO STAY

The Wichita CVB has a Lodging Guide that lists a few bed-and-breakfast inns, though there is no B&B reservation service. A wide assortment of reasonably priced accommodations range from budget motels, including **Super 8 Motel,** 527 South Webb Road (316-686-3888 or 800-848-8000), to full-service hotels. Be sure to ask about weekend packages. Some choices: **Guild Plaza Hotel,** 125 North Market; (316) 263-2101 or (800) 876-0240. This hotel has a cafe, free cribs, an indoor pool, and an airport van. **Wichita Suites,** 5211 East Kellogg (U.S. 54); (316) 685-2233 or (800) 243-5953. Choose from studio or one- and two-bedroom suites, all with refrigerators. There's also a heated pool, exercise equipment, and free cribs (but no rollaways). The **Wichita Marriott,** 9100 Corporate Hills Drive (316-651-0333 or 800-228-9290), has good-sized rooms and an indoor and outdoor pool. The **Residence Inn,** 411 South Webb Road; (316) 686-7331 or (800) 331-3131. This all-suite hotel offers lots of space with equipped kitchens and complimentary breakfasts.

WHERE TO EAT

The Wichita CVB has a helpful restaurant listing. An interesting note: Wichita is the birthplace of **Pizza Hut,** and the chain sometimes opens up prototypes in town to test new architecture or new menu items. Check locations with the CVB.

A few family friendly selections: **Spaghetti Warehouse,** 619 East William Street (316-264-7479), serves Italian and American lunch and dinner, with a kid's menu available. Youngsters like the tableside hibachi cooking at **Kobe Steak House of Japan,** 650 North Carriage Parkway (316-686-5915), open for dinner seven days a week and offering a kid's menu. Reservations are suggested.

DAY TRIPS

The Kansas Travel and Tourism Division's *Attractions Guide* has a helpful listing divided by geographical areas and other tourist literature.

For swimming and other water sports, head thirty minutes northeast of town to **El Dorado State Park,** Highway 177 (316-321-7180), which sports the state's largest recreational lake. Enjoy fishing and swimming at two beaches (no lifeguards) as well as a marina (no boat rentals), hiking trails, and picnicking. The town of El Dorado is also the home of the **Flint Hills Overland Wagon Trips,** 120 South Gordy; (316) 321-6300. Trips leave on selected spring, summer, and fall weekends for picturesque overnight rides on horses, covered wagons, and stage coaches. Meals, campfires with singing and tall tales, plus hearty pioneer meals and snacks, are included. All ages are welcome, but we wouldn't advise this with very young or fussy kids who might find the trip bumpy and boring once the novelty wears off.

Hutchinson, 45 miles northwest of Wichita (and the site of the annual State Fair in September) is a must. There's lots to see, but the real star is the **Kansas Cosmosphere and Space Center,** 1100 North Plum; (316) 662-2305 or (800) 397-0330. Tourists frequently are surprised to find such a comprehensive collection of NASA space artifacts housed in the Hall of Science, which features hands-on exhibits and the world's largest public display of space suits. An Omnimax Theatre shows larger-than-life films daily (sometimes too realistic for very young children), and a Planetarium offers sky shows on weekends year-round, summer weekdays, and certain holidays. Your kids may want to return someday for their five-day Future Astronaut Training Program for students entering the seventh, eighth, or ninth grade.

Hutchinson is also home to the **Dillon Nature Center,** 3002 East Thirtieth; (316) 663-7411. This thirty-acre site has woods, prairie, marshes, and ponds that attract hundreds of different wildlife species. Two miles of trails, picnic areas, a fishing pond, and a garden make this a pleasant stop. Admission is free, although there are sometimes fees for special programs. Just west of Hutchinson on Highway 96 is another treat for kids: the **Hedrick Exotic Animal Farm;** (316) 422-3296. Joe and Sondra Hedrick raise and train animals for petting zoos and for camel, ostrich, and pig races throughout the country. The assortment of animals on this working farm also includes zebras, llamas, goats, kangaroos, and exotic birds. Open daily, the farm offers tours for a fee.

There's lots more in the Hutchinson area, including two state parks, a small zoo, and the nearby **Yoder Amish Community,** with shops selling handicrafts, furniture, and baked goods. Contact the Greater Hutchinson Convention/Visitors Bureau for more information; (316) 662-3391 or (800) 658-1777.

Winfield, 60 miles south of Wichita, is the home of **Binney & Smith Crayola Factory,** 2000 Liquitex Lane; (316) 221-4200. Your kids will be fascinated by the plant tour, which shows how crayons are created, from the beginning right to the final packaging. This is an extremely popular tour for kids, and during the school year, groups book as much as a year in advance. Summer visitors will find it easier to get in—but we advise reserving as soon as you know your travel plans.

Another interesting tour for kids: **Country Critters Puppet Factory** in Burlington, 95 miles northeast of Wichita, 217 Neosho; (316) 364-8623. See how the puppets are created, sewn together, decorated, and packaged for shipment. The tours are offered twice daily on weekdays; call first to reserve. And if you're in Burlington on a Saturday night, stop by the **Flint Hills Opry,** 404 Neosho (316–364–5712), for downhome performances by local (and occasionally Nashville) singing talent.

For more information

Wichita Convention and Visitors Bureau: 100 South Main, Suite 100; (315) 265–2800 or (800) 288–WICHITA. Two satellite offices on I–35 are open summers only, both inside Hardee's Restaurants: Towanda Service Area, 20 miles north of town, and Belle Plaine Service Area, 20 miles south of town.

The Kansas Travel and Tourism Division: 700 Southwest Harrison, Suite 1300, Topeka 66603-3712; (800) 2–KANSAS

Emergency Numbers

Ambulance, fire, police: 911
Twenty-four-hour Poison Control Information Center: (316) 688–2277
Hospital: Medical Center, 550 North Hillside: (316) 688–2468
Pharmacy: Cumming's Pharmacy, 501 North Hillside, near Wesley Medical (316–682–4565), is open every day of the year from 8:00 A.M. to midnight.

14   Colorado

DENVER

The Mile High City is a green, tree-lined metropolis that, you may be surprised to know, is not in the mountains—but rather on high, rolling plains (flatter than Manhattan) *near* the mountains. With the edge of the Rocky Mountains just 30 miles west, Denver is a year-round recreational mecca—and with a rich selection of museums, plus the largest performing arts complex outside of New York's Lincoln Center, Denver is a cultural mecca as well. Add to that more than 300 days of bright sunshine a year, a summer that's comfortably dry, a winter where the snow comes and goes (the heavy snows usually fall in the mountains and you can frequently golf in January), and you have the makings for a family vacation paradise.

GETTING THERE

Denver International Airport, the world's largest airport, covering 53 square miles (twice the size of Manhattan Island), is 4 miles from downtown Denver. Public buses (see Getting Around) transport passengers into town, and private shuttle service taxis, and car rentals are available.

Amtrak, Union Station, Seventeenth and Wynkoop (800-USA-RAIL), is a hub on the major east-west routes, with three arrivals and three departures daily. (The basement of the station contains one of the largest model railroads, which can be viewed the last Friday of every month.)

Greyhound (800-231-2222) is at Denver Bus Terminal, Nineteenth and Arapahoe.

Denver is at the crossroads of several major highways: I-70 from the west and east, I-25 from the north and south, and I-76 from the northeast.

GETTING AROUND

Beyond downtown, you will need a car or public transportation.

Regional Transportation District (RTD) (303-299-6700) provides public transit for metropolitan Denver/Boulder. The **RTD Cultural Connection Trolley** (303-299-6000), which operates from Memorial Day to Labor Day, goes to Denver's top cultural attractions (leaving every thirty minutes) for an all-day nominal fare. The shuttle buses on the Sixteenth Street Mall are free and take visitors for 1 mile through the heart of downtown on the pedestrian promenade.

The Ski Train, 555 Seventeenth Street (303-296-1-SKI), makes a two-hour journey through the Rockies, through twenty-six tunnels, stopping at the foot of Winter Park's major lifts. The train operates Saturdays and Sundays throughout the ski season.

WHAT TO SEE AND DO

Museums and Historical Sites

The Children's Museum of Denver, 2121 Children's Museum Drive, I-25 and Twenty-third Avenue; (303) 433-7444. Be prepared to have fun at this top-notch facility. Older kids are invariably drawn to the miniature TV studio, where they read the news or work the camera. The Bank on It area is a superb way for kids to learn that money doesn't grow on trees. At KidSlope, a mountain made out of plastic, kids learn to ski year-round (in fact every fifth grader in Denver must take a ski lesson here). On the first Friday of every month, admission is free during Friday night, 5:30 to 8:00 P.M. Ask about special workshops and programs.

Take the Denver Trolley along the South Platte River from the museum to the **Forney Transportation Museum,** 1416 Platte Street, (303-433-3643), where antique and classic automobiles, plus a steam locomotive, are on display.

The Colorado History Museum, Thirteenth and Broadway (303-866-3682), is a wonderful place to learn about this state's colorful past. Dioramas, photos, artifacts, and exhibits portray the rich western heritage of covered wagons, Indian dances, buffalo hunts, miners, pioneers, fur trappers, and cowboys—stuff that most kids love.

Denver at a Glance

- Green, tree-lined metropolis with 300 days of bright sunshine a year

- Cowboy and mining history at the Black American West Museum

- A feast for sports fans: professional baseball, basketball, and football teams

- Day trips to ski country

- Denver Visitor Information Center, (303) 892-1112

At the **Colorado Railroad Museum,** 17155 West 44th Avenue, Golden (303-279-4591 or 800-365-6263), train lovers enjoy viewing the more than fifty historic locomotives and cars exhibited on eleven acres. Inside are model railroads and other train memorabilia.

Colorado State Capitol, Broadway and Colfax; (303) 866-2604. While younger kids may be bored stiff at the Colorado State Capitol, older kids should appreciate a visit to this building, modeled after the U.S. Capitol in Washington, D.C. Free tours are offered weekdays from 9:00 A.M. to 3:00 P.M. The fifteenth step on the west side is exactly 1 mile high. The dome is covered with 200 ounces of 14K gold, but the building's really valuable material is the rare Colorado rose onyx. The entire world's supply was used as wainscoting in the building. The Rotunda offers a splendid panorama.

The Denver Art Museum, Fourteenth Avenue and Bannock Street; (303) 640-2793. The largest in a fourteen-state radius, this museum is a work of art itself, resembling a medieval fortress, with twenty-eight sides and ten stories covered with more than a million Corning gray glass tiles that each reflect light in different ways. The museum recently incorporated a number of interactive learning tools during the renovation and reinstallation of all its galleries, making the

The whole family will have fun on a horse and carriage ride along Denver's 16th Street Mall, a mile-long pedestrian plaza lined with shops, department stores, and outdoor cafes. (Courtesy Denver Metro Convention and Visitor Bureau)

museum especially appealing to younger visitors. Kids like the Western and American Indian galleries, complete with dugout canoes, totem poles (housed in a two-story atrium), toys and games, and what many consider to be the world's finest examples of Native American art. Try to visit on Saturday, when admission is free. Twice a month, there's a Saturday for Families program.

Many black cowboys helped settle the West as Paul Stewart, founder and curator of the **Black American West Museum, the Dr. Justina Ford House,** 3091 California Street (303-292-2566), discovered. At this museum, which contains one of the best collections of western black memorabilia, listen to the oral histories of wranglers, miners, and entrepreneurs. Learn how rodeo star Bill Pickett came to invent the art of "bulldogging" (steer wrestling). Find out about freed slave Clara Brown, who traveled to California on a wagon train, became a laundress of miners' shirts, and saved and invested wisely to amass a small fortune, which she used to buy freedom for her friends and relatives in Kentucky.

The Denver Museum of Miniatures, Dolls and Toys, 1880 Gaylord Street; (303) 322-3704. There's a delightful assortment of tiny treasures housed in the historic Pearce-McAllister Cottage, an 1899 Colonial Revival house. Although the building itself and the period furnishings may bore kids, the upstairs rooms filled with period toys and dollhouses won't. Pick up a "treasure hunt" sheet so that your kids can answer the questions and receive a small token from the gift shop. Saturday Art Workshops are held on the first Saturday of each month.

The Denver Museum of Natural History, 2001 Colorado Boulevard, City Park, (303) 322-7009. This is the top visitor attraction in town, and this family spot deserves its popularity. The dioramas are especially appealing in the renovated Explore Colorado: From Plains to Peaks Hall, with eleven scenes depicting the state's diverse plants and wildlife. Kids light up discovery boxes in front of each scene to reveal such things as a quail nest with eggs—plus information on how many eggs are laid each year and how many chicks are hatched. Interactive videos explore subjects such as animal families and Colorado weather patterns. The Hall of Life is another winner: Visitors use a magnetic "life card" to activate exhibits and store information on height, weight, blood pressure, and pulse rate. Seventeen of the thirty-eight exhibits (which range from nutrition and fitness to substance abuse) are programmed to encode information on the card. At the end of the tour, visitors receive a printout of their basic health information, fascinating info for kids. At the Navaho Hall there's an authentic hogan (a Navaho dwelling) that shows how Native Americans live.

Prehistoric Journey: The History of Life on Earth, a $7.7-million permanent exhibit, which opened in October 1995, starts swimmingly. At the time-travel theater, you get an underwater view of ancient seas where the first life forms appeared. Then a land trail leads you through Beartooth Butte, Wyoming, dateline 395 million years ago. Meander into Cretaceous Creekbed, a Nebraska Woodland, and along the Kansas Coast (yes—Kansas was shorefront property 295 million years ago, when much of America lay underneath a great inland sea). Kids like peering at the scientists at work, reconstructing fossils in the fossil laboratory. The museum's famed dinosaurs (twelve skeletons, including the 80-foot-long *Diplodocus)* feel at home in this setting. Arrive early to get a timed ticket to this exhibit.

Don't leave without visiting the Schlessman Family Earth Sciences Laboratory, where scientists prepare and study fossil specimens, magnified to one hundred times their size so that visitors can view them via a live color-television monitor. There's also an open storage area where the museum's collection of fossils can be viewed.

The T restaurant facility's restaurant offers snacks and is a good place to take a break before visiting the IMAX Theater or Gates Planetarium (separate admission for each).

United States Mint, West Colfax at Cherokee Street; (303) 844-3582. Don't miss a chance to show your kids how coins are made: More than five billion coins are produced here each year, and 40 million coins are stamped each day. This is the second largest storehouse of gold bullion in the nation, after Fort Knox. The free tours, weekdays from 8:00 A.M. to 2:45 P.M., reveal the fascinating process, from stamping to counting and bagging. Your chances of gaining admission are better if you line up in the morning; if possible, try to be in line before 1:30 P.M. Chances are you won't leave without buying a unique coin souvenir (not sold elsewhere) from the gift shop.

Amusement Centers and Parks

Elitch Gardens, I-25 and Speer Boulevard, across the river from Mile High Stadium and not far from Coors Field; (303) 455-4771 or (800) 354-8247. This fifty-eight-acre amusement park, with a 105-year-old history, received a new face-lift and a new location in May 1995, when the park relocated into downtown Denver from the city's northwest. Of the twenty-one thrill rides, twelve reopened bigger and better. Coaster enthusiasts scream happily on Twister II, the longer and taller version of the famed wooden coaster. Other park picks are Disaster Canyon, a simulated white-water raft ride and the scenic Rocky Mountain views from Total Tower, and the sweeping downtown vista from atop the Ferris wheel. Kiddieland features ten tot-pleasing rides, not the least of which is the handcrafted carousel. Formal flower gardens, waterfalls, and evening concerts, musical revues, and circus acts add to the festive atmosphere.

Lakeside Amusement Park, I-70 and Sheridan Boulevard; (303) 477-1621. Lakeside has fifteen kiddie rides, Cyclone Roller Coaster, plus forty other rides and a scenic miniature train.

Tiny Town, 6249 South Turkey Creek Road; (303) 790-9393. This teeny, tiny town will tickle tykes, with a steam train ride around one hundred handcrafted miniature structures, including newly added Old West buildings. It's open May through October and decorated with Christmas lights during the holiday season.

Water World, Eighty-eighth Avenue at Pecos Street; (303) 427-SURE. Water World has everything from twisting water slides and oceanlike wave pools for the older crew to Wally World for younger folks. It's open Memorial Day through Labor Day.

Parks and Zoos

Denver has the largest city park system in the nation, with 205 parks in the city and 20,000 acres of mountain parks. The most prominent is City Park, Seventeenth Avenue and Colorado Boulevard. Here you'll find the Museum of Natural History as well as two lakes, picnic sites, play grounds, playing fields, tennis courts—and the beautifully landscaped Denver Zoo, East Twenty-third and Steel Street; (303) 331-4100. The zoo's seventy-three acres house more then 1,300 exotic animals in barless enclosures (imagine staring a Bengal tiger in the eye).

A major zoo attraction is Primate Panorama. Walk through an African village of bamboo, thatched-roof houses and a bazaar to a setting of waterfalls and thick vegetation. Here you encounter a Sumatran orangutan, a Celebes black ape, or one of the twenty-seven other primates. The design enables you to stand as close as 15 feet from a gorilla and observe tree-dwelling monkeys swing and scamper in a four-story-high enclosure. Primate Panorama already has its celebrities: Kondu, a 550-pound silverback, and Jo-Ray-Kay, who became proud parents of Cenzoo, a baby male gorilla, in February 1996. The Northern Shores exhibit, where polar bears and sea lions can be viewed from glass-walled underwater areas, is another not-to-miss exhibit. Tropical Discovery features exotic venomous snakes, alligators, crocodiles, piranhas, leopards, and anacondas.

The zoo, consistently rated as one of the country's top ten, is open every day of the year.

More than 1,200 vibrantly colored butterflies surround visitors at the **Butterfly Pavilion and Insect Center,** 6252 West 104th Avenue (off U.S. Highway 36), Westminster; (303) 469-5441. Flitting from leaves to flowers, the butterflies sometimes alight on the shoulders or heads of surprised children and adults. This simulated tropical forest is humid (take your coats off before you enter) with 80-degree temperatures and 70-percent humidity—a great place to warm up in winter. Besides ducking the winged beauties, children like learning about these real "morphing" heroes of the rain forests and observing their dry, leaflike chrysalis, the cocoon from which the butterflies emerge. More things that fly, creep, and crawl on display include Madagascar hissing cockroaches, a hive of bees, and a rose-colored tarantula.

Another Denver park: **Buffalo Bill's Memorial Museum and Grave,** Top of Lookout Mountain, I-70 exit 256; (303) 526-0747. This famous frontier scout and showman wanted to be buried in Wyoming, but because he died in Denver, he is buried on this site, some twenty minutes west of town. Along with the gravesite are guns, outfits, and posters from his Wild West Show and exhibits on the Pony Express and frontier life. If everyone has taken his or her Dramamine, hold on as you leave the museum for a drive on the curving Lariat Loop Trail to Golden.

Stop and smell the roses at **Denver Botanic Gardens,** 1005 York Street; (303) 331-4000 or 4010 (recorded information). There are also Japanese and Rock Alpine plant gardens and a tropical rain forest along with other exotic species, located both indoors and outdoors on twenty-one lovely acres. Seasonal flower shows are held at this year-round facility. The garden is undergoing a twenty-year, $40-million redevelopment and will soon start construction on a Children's Exploration Garden with mazes, a tree house, and interpretive gardens.

Shopping

Downtown at the **Sixteenth Street Mall,** with its pedestrian promenade, you find dozens of shops, outdoor cafes, and plenty of restaurants. The mall gets even merrier with the addition of the **Denver Entertainment and Fashion Pavilion,** adjacent to the Adam's Mark Hotel. Scheduled to open in fall 1997, this complex is anchored by Niketown, a mega-store complete with its own basketball court. Other stores will include Virgin Records and a Hard Rock Cafe.

Lower downtown (also called LoDo) is the old section where Victorian warehouses have been converted into art galleries, discos, pubs, restaurants, and condo lofts.

The 140 upscale stores of **Cherry Creek Mall,** 1000 East First Avenue (303-388-3900 or 800-424-6360), include Saks, Neiman Marcus, and—hold on to your wallets—F.A.O. Schwarz. A number of shops around town sell Native American and southwestern art, jewelry, and furnishings. By fall 1997 in LoDo, **Stadium Walk,** a square-block complex of shops and restaurants to include a Planet Hollywood, should be completed.

Built to be suggestive of a Rocky Mountain Ski Lodge, the **Park Meadows Shopping Center,** junction of C-470 and I-25, about 12 miles south of Denver in Douglas County, houses Colorado's first Nordstrom department store. The ski ambiance comes from the wood-beam ceiling (the largest in Colorado), two massive stone fireplaces, and a red rock "mountain" with trees, waterfalls, and wildflowers. If you like to hunt for bargains, head to the outdoor **Mile High Flea Market** (303-289-4656), held weekends and Wednesdays on eighty paved acres at I-76 and Eighty-eighth Avenue. Along with the hundreds of vendors, there are food stalls and amusement and pony rides for the kids.

Theater, Music, and the Arts

There's always something entertaining going on in Denver—from evening concerts at the Botanic Gardens and the Zoo to big-name tours at the city's two large amphitheaters (Red Rocks and Fiddlers Green). Tickets for many events can be purchased at the Ticket Bus on the Sixteenth Street Mall at Curtis Street.

Cultural events abound at the **Denver Performing Arts Complex** (The PLEX), Fourteenth and Champa Street. Call (303) 893-4100 or (800) 641-1222 for tickets and show schedules. Second only to New York's Lincoln Center in capacity, this complex, with 9,000 seats in ten theaters, offers symphony, opera, theater, and dance performances year-round. Event listings can be found on the Internet at www.denver.org.

Sports

Denver's National League baseball team, the **Colorado Rockies** plays in Coors Field. Purchase tickets by calling (303) ROCKIES (762-5437).

The **NBA Denver Nuggets** play from November to April at the McNichol Sports Arena; call (303) 893-6700. The American Professional Soccer League Team, the Colorado Foxes, plays at Englewood

High School Stadium, 3800 South Logan, from May to August. Call (303) 840–1111 for information. The **NFL Broncos** play at Mile High Stadium, 1700 Federal Boulevard: (303) 433–7466. Hockey fans can watch the Colorado Avalanchers play and soccer fans enjoy the Colorado Rapids.

SPECIAL EVENTS

Check with the Convention and Visitors Bureau for details on these events:

January: National Western Stock Show and Rodeo includes Children's Ranchland, junior show and sale, buffalo, goats, and lots more.

March: Powwow brings Native American tribes to the Denver Coliseum.

June: Cherry Blossom Festival, Sakura Square; Juneteeth, celebration commemorating the end of slavery with food and events, parade, open stage, Gospel Extravaganza.

July: Buffalo Bill Days, Golden, with parade, crafts fair, and Wild West Show; Denver Black Arts Festival features African American artists and entertainers in City Park.

Late August–Early September: Colorado State Fair, the state's largest single event.

September: Octoberfest, Larimer Square.

WHERE TO STAY

A listing of accommodations, ranging from bed-and-breakfast inns to all-suite hotels, can be found in the *Official Visitor's Guide*. For accommodations refer to Vacation Planning Guide. Three packages designed by the Convention Bureau feature discounted hotel rooms, tickets, and car rentals; call (800) 489–4888. **Bed and Breakfast— Rocky Mountain,** 639 Grant Street, 80203 (303–860–8415), is a free reservation service for inns and home stays throughout the state.

Downtown hotels include a number of well-known chains. The all-suite **Residence Inn by Marriott,** 2777 Zuni (303–458–5318), offers free breakfast daily and free light dinner and cocktails on weekdays. **Embassy Suites Hotel and Athletic Club** at Denver Place, 1881 Curtis

(303-297-8888 or 800-733-3366), also offers complimentary breakfast and cocktails. **The Hyatt Regency Denver,** 1750 Welton Street (303-295-1234 or 800-233-1234), has an outdoor pool, a jogging track, and tennis courts. **The Westin Hotel,** 1692 Lawrence Street (303-572-9100 or 800-228-3000), offers large rooms and heated indoor and outdoor pools. A bargain downtown, **Comfort Inn-Downtown,** Seventeenth Street and Tremont (303-296-0400 or 800-4-CHOICE), was once part of **Brown Palace,** the city's Victorian landmark, and shares the hotel's distinctive atrium lobby. Complimentary breakfast is included. The **Westin's Tabor Center,** 1672 Lawrence Street, Denver, Colorado 80202 (303-572-9100 or 800-228-3000), offers the new Westin Kids Club amenities. These include child-friendly rooms, children's sports bottle or tippy cup upon check-in, as well as a safety kit with a nightlight, Band-Aids, and emergency phone numbers. Rooms feature bath toys and bath products for kids, and parents can request—at no charge—jogging strollers, potty seats, bicycle seats, and step stools. Restaurants and room service also feature children's menus.

WHERE TO EAT

Denver's *Official Visitor's Guide* offers a descriptive listing of restaurants. Don't be surprised if you find buffalo steaks on the menu: The city, considered the buffalo capital of the U.S., serves more of the meat (said to be lower in fat, calories, and cholesterol than beef) than any other city. A restaurant, **Denver Buffalo Company,** 1109 Lincoln Street (three blocks from the State Capitol), (303) 832-0880, serves their own ranch-raised buffalo along with seafood, poultry, pasta, and other dishes. the complex also has a trading post and art gallery.

For something completely different, take the kids to **Casa Bonita,** 6715 West Colfax (at Pierce); (303) 232-5115. This huge facility seats 1,200 and serves Mexican and American food in a Mexican village setting, complete with strolling mariachis, high divers, gunfights—and a volcano.

DAY TRIPS

Colorado is ski country, and Denver is a fairly short drive from a variety of top notch areas. Winter Park, about 70 miles northwest of

Denver, is a popular ski destination. (The Ski Train, detailed in Getting Around, delivers skiers right to the base of the mountain.) Winter Park (303-726-5514 or 800-453-2525) features more than 130 trails of diverse terrain.

For parents who want to catch up with their kids' ski skills, and for kids who want to learn, Winter Park offers an excellent kids' ski school and special workshops. Discovery Park, with 20 acres of trails, terrain gardens, gentle slopes, and three chairlifts, gives even the most skittish beginner enough space to learn. In addition, Winter Park has a nursery for infants two months and up and a nonski program for ages through five. Most kids ages three and four enjoy the ski-and-play programs on their own little "mountain." Older kids and teens perfect skills in day-long kids' classes.

In Summit County, ninety minutes west of downtown Denver, there are several ski areas, all with good kids ski programs: Keystone Resort/Arapahoe Basin (303-468-2316 or 800-222-0188), Copper Mountain (303-968-2882 or 800-458-8386), and Breckenridge (303-453-5000 or 800-800-BREC). (For summer vacationers, gold, tennis, horseback riding, mountain biking, and sailing, on nearby Lake Dillon, are the main attractions.)

Vail/Beaver Creek (303-949-5750 or 800-622-3131) is 100 miles west of town. For details on area ski resorts, contact Colorado Ski Country at its airport booth or in town at 1560 Broadway, Suite 1440, Denver 80202; (303) 837-0793.

Denver Convention Bureau's Ski Lift Line, (800) 489-4888, can arrange transportation from your hotel to the lifts, lift tickets at ten area resorts and ski equipment rental (including clothes, if you need them).

FOR MORE INFORMATION

The Denver Visitor Information Center, (303) 892-1112, 225 West Colfax (across the street from the U.S. Mint), offers more than 500 free brochures and maps. **Wheelchair Getaways of Colorado,** (303) 674-1498 or (800) 238-6920, rents accessible full-size luxury vans by the day, week, or month.

Emergency Numbers
Ambulance, fire, police: 911
Poison Control: (800) 882-2073
Pharmacy: Clay Drug, 9297 Federal Boulevard, (303) 426-8901,
    is open until midnight.
Hospital: Saint Joseph Hospital, 1835 Franklin Street;
    (303) 837-7240

GRAND TETON NATIONAL PARK AND JACKSON

Jagged, snow-capped, and glistening in the sun, Grand Teton's mountain peaks, rising as high as 13,770 feet, fulfill the vision of the American West as both rugged and beautiful. The Gros Ventre and Shoshoni tribes called the 40-mile range *Teewinot,* a word meaning "many pinnacles." The mountains ascend sharply on the park's western side, above mirror-like glacial lakes and a deeply forested valley. Grand Teton National Park, stretching for 310,521 acres across fields, mountains, and lakes and cut through by a river, is often bypassed on the way to the more famous, and more crowded, Yellowstone National Park to the north.

But don't pass this beauty by. While sharing much of Yellowstone's larger-than-life scenery, Grand Teton is less crowded and less well-known. As a result, on a visit here, families leave the throngs behind. You can hike on quiet trails, float down the Snake River, canoe on pristine lakes, and enjoy the frequent sightings of moose, deer, and elk.

GETTING THERE

The **Jackson Hole Airport,** 1250 East Airport Road (307–733–7682), hosts about fifteen daily flights from connecting Salt Lake City and Denver. The **Grand Teton Lodge Company,** Box 240, Moran 83013 (307–733–2811), offers a shuttle from the airport to Jackson Lake Lodge. Among the taxicab/shuttle services are **All Star Taxi** (307–

733-2888), **Alltrans Taxi/Charter** (308-733-1799), **Buckboard Cab** (307-733-1112), **Gray Line of Jackson Hole** (307-733-4325), and **Jackson Hole Transportation. Jackson Hole Express** (SLC to JAC) can be reached at (307) 733-1719.

A car is important in order to get easily around the park at your own pace. Among the airport rental car companies: **Avis** (307-733-3422 or 800-331-1212), **Budget** (307-733-2206 or 800-533-6100), and **Hertz** (307-733-2272 or 800-654-3131). Note: Reserve a rental car well in advance. In tourist season cars become scarce, and you don't want to be stranded without one. Note that Yellowstone is closed to car traffic during winter.

When driving to the Grand Teton National Park from the south, pass through Jackson and continue north on U.S. 26/89/191, a highway that is open year-round, covers the length of the park, and continues to Yellowstone. From the east enter the park at Moran Junction, on U.S. 26/287.

Public transportation is minimal. **Greyhound** services Rock Springs, Wyoming (nearly 200 miles away); (307) 362-2931. They also go to Idaho Falls in neighboring Idaho, about 100 miles from Grand Teton; (208) 522-0912. The nearest **Amtrak** station is in Pocatello, Idaho, about 150 miles away from the park.

GETTING AROUND

A car is a must. If you want to tour the park by mountain bike or canoe, rent these in Moose, just outside the southern park entrance.

WHAT TO SEE AND DO

Getting Oriented

Your first venture should be to the **Moose Visitor Center,** Drawer 170, Moose, Wyoming 83012; (307) 739-3300. It's about 12 miles north of Jackson near the park's southern border. Talk to the rangers about trails, sites, and activities that appeal to your family. Pick up a free map, songbird guide, and the *Teewinot,* the park newsletter. The newsletter lists hikes, lodgings, and naturalist programs (including summer campfire programs and full-moon walks), ranger-led hikes, and children's programs. Be sure to obtain a copy of the *Young Naturalist*, a brochure that sparks kids' interest with park information, nature questions, and a list of activities necessary to earn a Young Naturalist souvenir badge. (While kids must earn this, parents must pay a nominal fee for this award.)

Browse the Visitor's Center bookstore. *Short Hikes and Easy Walks in Grand Teton National Park*, available for a small fee, is a great resource as it offers suggestions to families, especially those with small children, and those who want to experience the wilderness without the hard work. The parks department also has handouts with hiking information. *Day Hikes*, a free publication, contains a map of the trailheads and lists mileage and elevation. The publication lists less strenuous and time-consuming walks of thirty minutes to the more involved, and often more strenuous, treks that could keep you on the move for fourteen hours. *Teton Trails*, available for a moderate fee, includes detailed descriptions of hiking trails and details what you might encounter in the way of flora and fauna of the Teton Range.

Grand Teton's many wonderful recreational pleasures—from easy scenic drives to simple hikes, boat rides, and peaceful canoe trips to difficult backpacking treks—suit families with diverse outdoor temperaments.

Scenic Drives

If pressed for time on this family push, you could just drive through the park by entering at Moose and continuing north along **Teton Park Road.** This windy stretch continues for about 50 miles, becoming U.S. 287/191/89 near the park's northern border as the road heads into Yellowstone. Some scenic places to stretch your legs: about 8 miles north at **Cottonwood Creek** and **Lupine Meadows.** If your visit can only be brief but does allow for time out of the car—a necessity—continue north to pristine **Jenny Lake,** where a brief boat ride and a short walk lead to a picnic spot by a waterfall. Be aware of the schedule for the return boat rides; after the last trip you must either spend the night or take a long hike back, about two and one-half hours (see hiking section later in this chapter).

Back on Teton Park Road, the trip north leads you by the 7,593-foot **Signal Mountain** and **Jackson Lake,** an impressive stretch of clear waters with wooded shores. At **Colter Bay Visitor Center,** take

Grand Teton National Park and Jackson at a Glance

- Snow-capped mountains meet glacial lakes and forested valleys

- Breathtaking scenic drives, hikes on quiet trails, rafting down gentle rivers

- Ski trails for kids of all ages and abilities

- Jackson Hole Summer Rodeo

- Jackson Chamber of Commerce, (307) 733–3316

time to check out the educational programs and to browse in the **Indian Arts Museum,** where Native American artists demonstrate their crafts daily from June through early September.

Hiking and Canoeing: the Southern Park

One of the most popular hikes is the 1½-mile trek to **Hidden Falls,** a cascade of water on the south shore of Jenny Lake. But an easier way to reach these falls—especially if you have young children—is to board the ten-minute shuttle boat ride across Jenny Lake. From the dock follow the sound of rushing water ¼ mile to **Inspiration Point,** 400 feet above Jenny Lake, for a scenic view. Continue along the trail for .2 mile to the falls. This spot may be crowded, but for solitude continue to hike 3½ miles along level ground to the glacier-carved boulders of **Cascade Canyon,** habitat of the yellow-bellied marmot and golden-mantled ground squirrel. You're sure to see some of these scurrying around as you admire the wildflowers that bloom throughout the summer.

Just north of Jenny Lake lie two nearly connected bodies of water: **String Lake** and **Leigh Lake** both offer easy hikes, easy canoeing, and scenic views. The **String Lake Trail** circles this body of water for a flat 3½ miles (allow about three hours), and the **Leigh Lake Trail** (park at the String Lake parking lot) leads 2 miles (about one hour) to the lake's south shore. For some extra fun combine a canoe and hiking trip. Put in your canoe at String Lake and paddle to the northern edge; then portage about 100 yards to Leigh Lake. Paddle along this pristine lake, pausing to hike along the shores. You can picnic at almost any spot along this trail and be sitting pretty with a scenic view of 12,605-foot **Mount Moran,** a peak partially covered by Skillet Glacier. Let your kids dangle their toes in the lake and look for deer in the woods.

Note: You can rent canoes from **Dornans' Moose Enterprises,** 10 Moose Street (307-733-2522), as well as from several park concessions. Dornans' also sells groceries and sandwiches.

Hiking and Canoeing: the Northern Park

Jackson Lake, nearly 20 miles long and fed by the Snake River, dominates the northern section of the park. This lake, more heavily forested and generally quieter than the lakes in the southern section, affords easy access to canoe rentals at **Signal Mountain Marina** on Jackson Lake; (307) 543-2831.

The rangers at the nearby **Colter Bay Visitor Center** offer helpful information and nature programs, including slide shows on such local denizens as coyote and bald eagles. To see live animals head out along the nearby **Hermitage Point Trail,** which begins at the visitor center and loops for 3 miles around **Swan Lake** and **Heron Pond** through pine forests, meadows, wetlands, and lakes. Because this path is less traveled, you are likely to catch sight of beaver, otter, elk, and moose. Listen for the hornlike sounds of the hard-to-find trumpeter swans that can sometimes be spotted here. Be careful of the turnoffs. A round-trip hike of the entire 8.8-mile Hermitage Point trail takes about four hours.

For very young children and bird lovers, the **Lunchtree Hill Trail,** a half-mile hike beginning at Jackson Lake Lodge, winds through marshy meadows that are home to songbirds and hummingbirds.

For a moderate hike that rewards you with a climb through woods to a summit with a panoramic view, opt for the **Grand View Point Trail,** a 2.2-mile, two-hour round-trip trek that pleases older children (and parents too).

Swimming

Swimming is allowed in **Jenny, Leigh,** and **String** lakes, but with

Autumn is a magical time among the majestic Grand Tetons.
(Courtesy Wyoming Travel Commission)

these glacier-fed lakes' waters hovering at about 54 degrees Fahrenheit, only those impervious to cold go for the plunge. Most people settle for toe dangling. For the intrepid, String Lake offers the shallowest water, and Leigh Lake invites with quartz sand and a beautiful view. While fishing is allowed on **Bradley** and **Taggert** lakes, as well as on the **Snake River,** swimming is not.

River Float Trips and Fishing Trips

A float trip down the Snake River gently weaves you through the spectacular landscape, providing ample opportunity for wildlife viewing. Especially nice are the dinner trips with **Barker-Ewing Float Trips;** (800) 365–1800. These leave the Moose Visitor Center at 6:00 p.m. for a 10-mile drive upstream. Your float downstream on a twelve-person raft takes about three hours (dress warmly). While no wildlife sightings are guaranteed, you're more likely to see animals at dusk than during the day. Often great blue herons dance above the water, and eagles nest in the tall pines. Look sharply and you might even see a moose. After 5 miles the guides pull into an encampment where you dine and watch the sun set over the Teton peaks. Other companies offering float trips include **Grand Teton Lodge Co. Float Trips** (307-543-2811) and **Triangle X Float Trips** (307-733-5500), which offers trips with overnight accommodations in a tepee.

If you're angling to do some fishing, twenty-six Jackson Hole businesses offer guided trips. Call Westbank Anglers (800-922-3474). For a listing of other outfitters and the best fishing sites, contact **Wyoming Game and Fish;** (800) 423-4113.

Mountain Biking

The hearty can take to their fat wheels for a scenic foray through the park. Rent some two-wheelers from **Adventure Sports,** P.O. Box 39, Moose 83012; (307) 733-3307. But be careful; don't pedal along the often crowded park roads. Instead, be safe and bike along a designated mountain trail.

Horseback Riding

For horseback riding, the area east of Jackson Lake is a good place. At the **Jackson Lake Lodge Corral,** Jackson Lake (307-543-2811), saddle up for a guided breakfast or evening excursion. The **Grand Teton Lodge Company** (307-543-2811) operates one- and two-hour treks for riders ages eight and up.

Hot-Air Ballooning

Less demanding, but equally pretty, is an aerial journey with **Wyoming Balloon Co.,** (307-739-0900), which has you floating over the Snake River and Jackson Valley.

Other ways to take in the spectacular views of the Jackson Hole valley are by airplanes, helicopters, and paragliding. Call **JH Aviation** (307-733-4767), **JH Paragliding** (307-739-8620), **Mountain Rotors** (307-733-1633), and **Satellite Aero, Inc.** (307-739-1999).

Jackson Attractions

On this vacation allow some time to explore the town of Jackson (Jackson Hole is the valley), a cowboy town 12 miles south of Grand Teton National Park's Moose headquarters. Jackson's small-town, Old

West flair and friendliness intrigue kids. With little kids, hop aboard the **stagecoach,** at the corner of the town square next to the ticket booth, for a short spin through town.

You'll notice right away that the town square differs from most local parks as it's adorned at all four corners with arches made of real elk antlers collected by the local Boy Scouts who gather these after the local herd sheds them. Be around this square in the summer on a Monday through Saturday night at 6:30 P.M. when the town's good guys shoot it out with the bad guys, a special treat for elementary school kids. (Warn little ones of the guns' noise, and assure everyone that it's safe. No real bullets are fired.)

There's more rough riding at the **Jackson Hole Summer Rodeo,** Rodeo Grounds, Snow King Avenue (307-733-2805), every Wednesday and Saturday evening through Labor Day. Kids love the steer roping, barrel racing, and quick horsemanship.

The **National Museum of Wildlife Art,** 2820 Rungius Road (307-733-5771), features 250 works by well-known painters and sculptors, plus a private collection of big game wildlife art. The **Jackson Hole Museum,** 105 North Glenwood Street (307-733-2414), focuses on Jackson's history with archaeological artifacts, fur-trade exhibits, as well as mounted game heads (which often scare little kids and annoy environmentally concerned adults).

Golf. Jackson Hole sports two championship golf courses, both with scenic views: The **Jackson Hole Golf and Tennis Club,** P.O. Box 250, Moran 83013 (307-543-2811—winter and 307-733-3111—summer); and the **Teton Pines Golf Club** (307-733-1733). Apparently the high altitude (6,209 feet above sea level) carries golf balls 10 percent farther than at sea level. For younger kids **Alpine Golf,** Snow King Resort (307-733-7680), offers eighteen holes of miniature golf.

Scenic Mountain Views. Get a bird's-eye view of the summer and fall scenery, even if you don't ski, by riding the **Snow King Scenic Chairlift,** Snow King Resort; (307) 733-5200 (see Skiing). If you hike up, the ride down is free. For a nominal fee **Teton Village's Aerial Tram,** Teton Village (307-733-2292), offers splendid views as well.

Winter Fun
Alpine (Downhill) Skiing
The Jackson Hole area offers excellent skiing at three facilities. The

slopes at **Snow King Ski Resort** (307–733–5200), Wyoming's original ski area, nearly swoop down into town. Open to skiers from mid-December to April, with night skiing available Tuesday to Saturday, Snow King has a 1,571-foot vertical drop and lots of beginner and intermediate trails.

Outside of town, skiers have both **Grand Targhee Ski Resort** (800–TARGHEE) and **Jackson Hole Ski Resort,** Box 290, Teton Village; ski area (307) 733–2292. On the sunny west side of the Teton mountains is **The Grand Targhee Ski Resort,** Box Ski, Alta, Wyoming, via Driggs, Idaho 83422; (307) 353–2300 or (800) TARGHEE. The ski area offers 3,000 acres of terrain, about 70 percent of it intermediate.

Grand Targhee has nursery facilities for tots two months and older. Children age three can have private lessons, while ages five to seven take a learn-and-play program. The ski school also has ski programs for ages five through twelve. Children five and under always ski free, and children fourteen and under generally ski free when one adult purchases a three-day or more lodging package. At Grand Targhee it's hard for kids to get lost since all trails funnel down into the same base area.

The **Jackson Hole Ski Resort** (307–733–2292 or 800–443–6931) is the area's most well-known resort. Twelve miles from Jackson, located at Teton Village, P.O. Box 290 83025, this ski area boasts a 4,139-foot vertical rise, among the steepest in the United States. Jackson Hole, while offering some top-notch, difficult terrain, also has more than 22 miles of groomed beginner and intermediate trails. Rendezvous Mountain is a challenge; most families start and even keep to the less demanding trails on Apres Vous.

At the **Jackson Hole Ski School** classes are available for adults, kids ages three to five in their Rough Rider Ski Program, and six to thirteen in the Explorer Ski Program. A nursery is available for ages two months to eighteen months, and child care is provided for ages nineteen months to five years. Children five and under ski free. Call the ski school for new program information at (307) 739–2663.

Nordic (Cross-Country) Skiing

Ski-skating tracks are available at Jackson Hole Nordic Center, Grand Targhee Nordic Center, Spring Creek Nordic Center, and at Teton Pines Nordic Center.

For those who like the easy, gliding pace of cross-country skiing, the

Jackson Hole Ski School Nordic Center, P.O. Box 290, Teton Village 83025, (307) 733-2292, rents cross-country skis and offers several kilometers of groomed trails. A variety of cross-country programs are offered for children and families.

The **Grand Targhee Nordic Center,** Box SKI, Alta (307-353-2300 or 800-TARGHEE), has 15 kilometers of groomed trails. The **Teton Pines Nordic Ski Center,** next to the J.H. Racquet Club (307-733-2992), features between 10 and 13 kilometers of trails plus lessons for children and adults as well as day-care facilities and rentals. The **Spring Creek Nordic Center,** Box 3154, (307) 733-8833, offers 14 kilometers of trails that wind through a nature reserve, making it likely you'll spot some deer, elk, maybe even moose. Rentals and lessons are available.

In **Grand Teton National Park,** check with the rangers for trail conditions, but generally when there's snow, favorite cross-country trails include the beginner's 3-mile **Swan Lake-Heron Pond Loop,** near the Colter Bay Visitor Center, and the longer 9-mile **Jenny Lake Trail.**

Off-the-Slopes Winter Recreation

Nonskiers and those who want a break from the moguls have plenty of choices. At the **National Elk Refuge** east of Jackson, thousands of elk come to feed during the winter. A sleigh ride through the refuge with **National Elk Refuge Horse Drawn Sleigh Ride,** Box C, Jackson 83001 (307-733-9212), is available from mid-December through April. The whole family, even little ones, will like seeing these majestic animals close-up.

For more wildlife head out on a guided safari with naturalists from the **Great Plains Wild Life Institute,** Box 7580, 83001; (307) 733-2623. Use the van's telescopes and binoculars for up-close looks at bighorn sheep, moose, and bald eagles. Wildlife Discovery tours include the extra fun of lunch at a local ranch plus a snowshoe nature walk. A half-day sunrise tour is offered, too. Call ahead to book.

For a special treat you and the kids are not likely to forget, take a **dog sled trek.** This is a cozy and easy way to get into the backcountry. The huskies do the work while you savor the woodland peace and the wildlife. For this tour all you'll hear are the wind in the trees, the swoosh of the sled, and the panting of the dogs. Among the area's companies **Jackson Hole Iditarod Sled Dog Tours,** Box 1940, 83001 (307-733-7388), is led by Frank Teasley, a professional musher and veteran of Alaska's grueling Iditarod. His guided runs take you east to Granite Hot Springs, past wildlife trails and to a 108-degree hot-springs soak (wear a suit). Other routes go through Grand Teton National Park. **Washakie Outfitting** (307-733-3602) is another choice.

Ask about the size of the sled. For most runs two smaller kids or one adult and one small child can usually snuggle in the sled, while another adult, if the guides permit, can stand on the back of the sled. Ask how many sleds will be required for your group.

The south entrance to **Yellowstone National Park** (see chapter Yellowstone National Park) is about two hours away. In winter, most of the roads are closed to public vehicles, but the animals are out. With young children opt for a tour by heated park snowcoach (a bus equipped for the deep snow). Call **Yellowstone Reservations** (307-344-7311).

With teens or preteens try a snowmobile run from Yellowstone's south entrance to Old Faithful. Pass by bison and elk, track coyotes, and watch out for the mule deer as you roar up to this steamy geyser surrounded by snow—quite a sight in winter.

Outfitters include **Rocky Mountain Snowmobile Tours,** (307-733-2237 or 800-647-2561), **Flagg Ranch Village** (307-543-2861 or 800-443-2311), **Heart Six Snowmobile Tours** (307-543-2477 or 800-647-2561), and **Jackson Hole Snowmobile Tours** (307-733-6850 or 800-633-1733).

Theater and the Arts

Yes, Jackson has theater, but the fare tends to be good old western family goings-on. From Memorial Day through Labor Day, check out the musical comedy at the **Jackson Hole Playhouse,** Deloney Street between Millward and Glenwood streets; (307) 733-6994. The **Mainstage Theater,** P.O. Box 20264 (307-733-3670), at times, also sports what they call "elegant and rowdy family fun." The town is big enough for two chuck-wagon shows: **Bar J Chuckwagon,** Teton Village Road (307-733-3370), and **Bar-T-Five,** 790 Cache Creek Road (307-733-5386).

Shopping

Boutiques, western-wear shops, and nearly forty museums and art galleries, specializing in western landscapes and paintings of cowboys and

Native Americans, ring the town square and adorn the side streets. Pop in and out of the galleries until you find one that appeals to you; you won't have a problem. Other good bets: **Trailside Americana,** Town Square and Center Street, Drawer 1149 (307-733-3186), and **Martin-Harris Gallery,** upstairs at King and Broadway streets (307-733-0350). Many stores offer Native American jewelry and crafts. Know what you're buying and comparison shop. The **Valley Bookstore,** 125 North Cache, Town Square (307-733-4533), features a good selection of maps, mountaineering books, field guides, and children's books.

SPECIAL EVENTS

Check with the Visitors Bureau for more specific information about these events in the Grand Teton and Jackson areas.

February: International Rocky Mountain Stage Stop Sled Dog Race; Cowboy Ski Challenge.

April: The Pole-Pedal-Paddle, a ski-cycle-canoe relay race starts at Jackson Hole and finishes at the Snake River.

May: The Elk Antler Auction, Jackson town square; Old West Days with Native American dancing, cowboy poetry, and Mountain Man rendezvous; Teton Village Mountain Man Rendezvous.

June-September: Wednesdays and Saturdays see the Jackson Hole Summer Rodeo near downtown Jackson.

July-August: Nightly concerts at the famed Grand Teton Music Festival, Teton Village.

August: Grand Targhee Bluegrass Festival with musicians from the Rocky Mountain region, children's entertainment, and crafts.

September: Jackson Hole Fall Arts Festival of gallery shows, artist's workshops, and dance.

October: Quilting in the Tetons, exhibits and workshops.

December–April: Ski races for amateurs.

WHERE TO STAY

Lodging is limited within Grand Teton but widely available in nearby Jackson. Within the park, one of the best lodges for families is **Signal Mountain Lodge,** Box 50, Moran; (307) 543-2381. They offer lakefront cabins, apartments, and motel units. **Jackson Lake Lodge,** Box 240, Moran, is also lakefront and a good family choice with motel-style units; (800) 628-9988. **Colter Bay Village,** Box 240, Moran (307-543-2855), rents log cabins.

Grand Teton National Park has five campgrounds. **Jenny Lake,** with only forty-nine sites, is the most popular; this campground tends to fill before 8:00 A.M., so arrive early. Another popular spot is **Lizard Lake** with sixty sites; this tends to fill by 2:00 P.M.

Outside the park grounds there are several facilities. **Snake River KOA,** 12 miles south of Jackson Highway 89-191, Star Route Box 14A (307-733-7078), features showers and also arranges horseback riding and float trips. Trailers and tents are welcome.

For familiar chain lodgings, try **Best Western Lodge at Jackson Hole,** Box 7478 (307-739-9703 or 800-458-3866); or **Best Western Inn at Jackson Hole,** in Teton Village (307-733-2311 or 800-842-7666). **Days Inn,** which offers free continental breakfast, is a mile south of downtown Jackson, 1280 West Broadway; (307) 739-9010, (800) 833-5343, or (800) 325-2525. The Jackson Hole Chamber of Commerce has a complete listing of all area accommodations.

In Jackson Hole the **Wildflower Inn** (307-733-4710), a bed and breakfast 10 miles from the park's south entrance, welcomes families. This hand-hewn log home sports pleasing country decor, a glass-enclosed hot tub, and friendly hosts. Stay here for a real western welcome. For additional bed-and-breakfast options, call the **Bed and Breakfast Association;** (307 734-1999).

Another option is **Teton Village,** Teton Village Property Management, Teton Village; (307-733-4610 or (800) 443-6840, twelve miles northwest of Jackson on Wyoming 390. The company has 125 condominiums spread out at the base of 10,536-foot Rendezvous Peak. Besides condominiums, Teton Village has other lodgings, including the **Inn at Jackson Hole,** P.O. Box 348; (307) 733-2311. Twenty-nine of the eighty-three units have cooking facilities.

Snow King Resort, P.O. Box SKI, Jackson 83001 (307-733-5200 or 800-522-5464), has hotel rooms, suites, and condominiums. For more Jackson Hole accommodations, call **Jackson Hole Central Reservations,** Box 2618, Jackson 83001; (307) 733-4005 or (800) 443-6931.

Another ski resort that makes an ideal summer spot for families, especially those with tots, is **Grand Targhee,** about an hour's drive from Grand Teton National Park, Box Ski, Alta 83422; (307) 353-2300 or (800) TARGHEE. The Kids Club Day Camp has activities for ages four to ten from 9:00 A.M. to 5:00 P.M. Although the weekly **Targhee Institute Science Explorers** program for grades four through seven fills up with locals, check to see if space is available for your visit. Grand Targhee's accommodations include motels and condominiums.

Spring Creek Resort Hotel & Conference Center, Box 3154, Spring Gulch Road (307-733-8833 or 800-443-6139), is situated on a 1,000-acre nature preserve atop a butte. This casually upscale resort is both family friendly and rated four-diamond from AAA. Rooms and condominiums are available. Great views and some of the area's best dining make Spring Creek a treat. Kids especially like looking out the dining room windows to count the wildlife that roams by. The resort also provides transportation to the ski areas and has its own cross-country center. In summer the resort can arrange day forays from white-water rafting to hiking and horseback riding.

Go western with a dude ranch stay. The **Triangle X Ranch,** P.O., Box 120T, Moose 83012 (307-733-2183), is a **dude ranch** complete with nature hikes, scenic float trips, western dancing, and cookouts. Winter activities include cross-country skiing and wildlife viewing. **Lost Creek Ranch,** 25 miles northeast of Jackson, P.O. Box 95, Moose 83012 (307-733-3435), has two-bedroom cabins, an outdoor heated pool, tennis court, and a children's program. Ride the range or head off to a secluded fishing spot. **R. Lazy S Ranch,** a mile north of Teton Village, P.O. Box 308, Teton Village 83025 (307-733-2655), has twelve cabins and separate riding programs for adults and kids over six, as well as pack trips, hikes, and boating.

WHERE TO EAT

Before setting out to explore the park, stock up at **Dornans' Deli,** 10 Moose Street (307-733-2415), with muffins, sandwiches, and drinks, or sit down at an outdoor picnic table and your food as you gaze over the Teton peaks. In the park, take a meal break at the **Jackson Lake Lodge Pioneer Grill,** Jackson Lake Lodge; (307) 543-2811.

Jackson, like any town that swells in season with tourists, serves up a variety of eateries. The tourist map of town lists most of the restaurants, including the familiar fast-food places just like the ones back home.

For some western pizzazz with your plateful of baked beef and chicken, go to the **Bar J. Chuckwagon and Original Western Show,** off Wyoming 390; (307) 733-3370. After your meal, go country with a medley of cowboy singing, poetry, foot stompin' fiddle playing, and dancing. In town, **Bubba's Bar-B-Que,** 515 West Broadway (307-733-2288), dishes up moderately priced ribs, chicken wings, and a salad bar. In winter go to dinner by horse-drawn sleigh with the **Bar--T-Five Outfitters,** P.O. Box 2140, Jackson 83001; (307) 733-5386. Layer-up for this moonlight-and-stars ride to a pioneer cabin for barbecue and chicken followed by medleys performed by the Bar-T-Five Singin' Cowboys.

DAY TRIPS

For more river adventures, contact **Barker-Ewing River Trips,** 45 West Broadway, Box 3032B, Jackson 83001; (307) 733-1000 or (800) 448-4202. They offer a white-water overnight raft trip down the Snake River, on a section that is scenic but not in the Grand Teton National Park. Minimum age is six. This trip is a delight, but remember to dress warmly and bring rain gear and gloves just in case. (You're not in Kansas anymore.)

Even with little tots you can re-create the pioneer days with **wagon train trips** lasting two to six days. Families ride in renovated wagons that have cushions to soften the bounce (an amenity not available to our stalwart pioneers). You can also ride horseback alongside. The trips include campfire cookouts and, with some outfitters, staged "Indian" attacks just to simulate the frontier fears and create some excitement. Among the outfitters: **Wagons West,** Peterson-Madsen-Taylor Outfitters, P.O. Box 1156A, Afton 83110; (307) 886-9693 or (800) 447-4711.

FOR MORE INFORMATION

The **Moose Visitor Center** (307-733-2880), 12 miles north of Jackson Hole, is at the park's southern end. **Colter Bay Visitor Center,** near

Jackson Lake (307-543-2467), is in the north area of the park. **Grand Teton National Park,** Drawer 170, Moose, Wyoming 83012. **Wyoming Division of Tourism,** I-25 at College Drive, Cheyenne, Wyoming 82002; (307)777-7777 or (800) 225-5996. **Wyoming State Museums and Historic Sites,** 2301 Central, Barrett Building, Cheyenne 82002; (307) 777-7014. **Wyoming Recreation Commission,** 122 West Street, Herschler Building, 2 West, Cheyenne 82002; (307) 777-7695.

For a *Jackson Hole Vacation Planner,* call **Jackson Chamber of Commerce;** (307) 733-3316. Weather and road conditions, (307) 733-2220. Via Internet: info@jacksonhole.com.

Before your trip obtain a copy of the sixteen-page *The Kids Guide to Jackson Hole,* available from Nancy Brumsted and Jan Segerstrom, Teton County Schools, P.O. Box 568, Jackson County 83001. The guide, written by local schoolchildren, gives other kids inside tips.

Emergency Numbers

Ambulance, fire, police: 911

Local sheriff: (307) 733-4052

Local police: (307) 733-1430

Local fire department: (307) 733-2331

Hospital: St. John's Hospital, 625 East Broadway in Jackson; (307) 733-3636

Twenty-four-hour pharmacy: Albertson's Grocery Store, 520 West Broadway; (307) 733-9222

Poison Control Hotline: (800) 422-2704

YELLOWSTONE NATIONAL PARK, CODY, AND BIG HORN NATIONAL FOREST

No family member will ever be bored in a national park as spectacular as Yellowstone. This important and impressive geothermal region continues to display some of the powerful forces deep within the earth. Old Faithful erupts spraying steam hundreds of feet into the air. But this well-known geyser, with a habit of spouting on schedule, is just one of many that mark the landscape. Yellowstone offers much more than geysers. Admire the canyon, hike through forests along trails that lead to waterfalls, take scenic boat trips on the lake, fish for trout, ride horseback, and just look out your car window to see bison, moose, and bighorn sheep in their native habitat.

GETTING THERE

The Yellowstone Regional Airport (307–587–5096), Cody, serves the Big Horn Basin and is serviced by **SkyWest/Delta Connection** and **Mesa Airlines/United Express. Jackson Hole Airport** (307–733–7695) is larger and serviced **by Delta, SkyWest, American**

Airlines, **Continental Express,** and **United Express. Hertz, Budget, Rent-A-Wreck,** and **Avis** rental-car companies have airport facilities.

Greyhound (406-587-3110) offers bus service to Bozeman, Livingston, and West Yellowstone, Montana. **Karst Stage** (406-586-8567 or 406-587-9937) offers connecting bus service from Bozeman and Livingston to the park's north entrance. The **Rock Springs Busline** (406-669-3208) serves Jackson, Wyoming; **Powder River Bus Lines** (307-754-3914) serves Cody. From most of these towns you can take bus transportation to Yellowstone National Park. **Powder River Transportation** (307-527-6316 or 307-587-5544) provides bus service from Cody to Yellowstone's east entrance. There is no direct rail service to the park.

To enter Yellowstone National Park by car coming from Montana in the north, take U.S. 89; from the northeast, take U.S. 212; from Cody, which is east of Yellowstone, take U.S. 14/16/20 or the Chief Joseph Scenic Highway to the northeast entrance. If traveling from the south, take U.S. 287/191/89; if arriving from the west, take U.S. 20 to the park's west entrance. The park's entrance fee is good for seven days. If you plan to stay longer, have a disability, or are over sixty-two years of age, look into an annual Yellowstone Passport, Golden Eagle, Golden Access, or Golden Age Passport.

GETTING AROUND

A Grand Loop Road that cuts a figure eight, stretching for 142 miles through the park, takes you by most of the major attractions. Those who prefer that others do the driving should contact **AMFAC,** the park's concessionaire, Yellowstone National Park 82190; (307) 344-7311. They offer bus tours that cover the Grand Loop, or choose either the Lower Loop or the Upper Loop. These drive-by tours, however, don't do much more than literally allow you to "glimpse" Yellowstone.

The best way for families to experience Yellowstone is by spending time here. Let the family vehicle lead you to some of Yellowstone's wonders, and allow yourself to savor these at your own pace. Be sure to get out of the car: Stroll, hike, horseback ride, and walk. Only by getting off the road can you truly gain a sense of Yellowstone's grandeur.

WHAT TO SEE AND DO

Spring, summer, and early fall before the snows arrive are the best times for families to visit Yellowstone. To avoid the busiest times however, schedule your arrival by late spring or early June. Because Yellowstone is most popular for families in warm weather, particularly when school's out, the hiking, driving, and sight-seeing information listed below applies to the warm seasons unless otherwise stated.

If you can get away in late spring or in early autumn, your visit may be more satisfying. Not only do the crowds dissipate at these times, but so does the heat. In spring wildflowers dot the meadows, and in fall the aspens turn the color of spun gold, creating fairy-tale vistas of mountains and ridges.

Winter in Yellowstone brings a special rustic peace. The park's vast fields of snow make Yellowstone a haven for cross-country skiers and snowmobilers. In places icicles arch over the falls while elsewhere a meadow remains perennially green, thanks to the warmth of a nearby hot spring. Eagles float overhead, gliding on an updraft of air warmed by the boiling geysers. Winter does, however, make for some closed roads and deep snow. Snowmobiles are available, and the cross-country skiing on groomed trails or in the backcountry is superb—if you know what you are doing. AMFAC offers a day trip by heated snow coach to accessible park highlights. (See In Winter and Where to Stay.)

Yellowstone can be divided into five different regions: Geyser Country, full of fumaroles, mudpots, hot pools, and home to Old Faithful; Mammoth Country, a thermal area of hot springs; Roosevelt Country, where the park offers stagecoach rides and rugged scenery; Canyon Country, made dramatic by the Grand Canyon of Yellowstone; and Lake Country, where moose, and sometimes bear, roam the shores of Yellowstone Lake, where the native cutthroat trout is plentiful.

Geyser Country

In Geyser Country the star is **Old Faithful,** named for its regular schedule of eruptions; check the chalkboards at the visitors center, the local shops, and ice-cream parlors for the expected time or simply watch the crowd getting thicker. Ask the rangers at the **Old Faithful Visitor Center** (307-545-2750) for tips on trails to take.

Old Faithful won't disappoint. Splashing steamy water 100 to 180 feet into the air, the geyser is a reminder of earth's primal forces. The area around Old Faithful, however, is disappointing, overbuilt, and overcrowded. With all the parking lots, lodging, eateries, and traffic jams, this bit of the park often seems more reminiscent of a mall than a majestic natural wonder.

Don't settle for just a view from the benches surrounding Old Faithful. Obtain a map of the Upper Geyser Basin from the Visitor Center, and select any number of easy boardwalk trails that wind past forty steamy geysers, and hot bubbling pools. Note: Be careful to stay on the boardwalk. Do not walk on the ground, as the crust around these thermal areas can be dangerously thin. Visitors have been burned and some killed by the scalding water. Also tell your kids ahead of time to resist the urge to throw pennies, sticks, or anything else into the boiling springs. This is not good for kids or the thermal attractions. Hold little ones by the hand, or put them in the stroller as the boardwalk makes for a perfect pathway.

Some popular and not-too-long trails include the Geyser Hill Loop, a 3-mile track that takes you over bubbling ground. Look for Beehive Geyser, which can spray more than 180 feet in the air—but alas, not as predictably as Old Faithful—and Doublet pool, which is a beautiful blue color. In recent years, however, eruptions have occurred twice daily.

As you meander along the boardwalk past these geothermal wonders, keep an eye out for bison. Often several will simply sit near the boardwalk. Admire them from afar, and don't attempt to create a catchy photograph of your child next to a big bison—for that could be the last photo. However peaceful these animals may look, they are wild, unpredictable, and potentially dangerous.

Back on the road from Old Faithful toward **Mammoth Hot Springs,** stop at **Midway Geyser Basin** and explore the colorful pools.

Allow at least one-half hour to visit **Fountain Paint Pot,** a colorful area where algae and bacteria surrounding these muddy water holes have turned them to shades of pastel pinks and blues.

Near here, the road north from Geyser Country to Mammoth Country takes you past great sweeps of plains, often with herds of bison grazing, especially near Gibbons Meadows.

Yellowstone at a Glance

- Geysers, hot springs, and pastel-colored water holes

- Stagecoach rides and rugged scenery

- Yellowstone's canyon, 20 miles long and 4,000 feet across

- Wildlife galore: elk, bison, mule deer, and bears

- Buffalo Bill Historical Center in nearby Cody

- Yellowstone Park camping, dining, lodging, and tour information: AMFAC, (307) 344-7311

Mammoth Country

Near the northern border of Yellowstone and just minutes away from Gardiner, Montana, is **Mammoth Hot Springs,** where, even in high season, the crowds thin out a bit. We prefer staying here for its rustic but serviceable lodging and the long scenic stretches of road that lead here.

As the acidic waters of Mammoth Hot Springs pass through the limestone, calcium carbonate remains. Eventually the build-up causes the unusual-shaped terraces you see. The springs, which continue to grow, cover an entire hillside.

Also in Mammoth Country are the park headquarters. At the **Albright Visitor Center** (307-344-2263) look at the films, slides, and photographs of the park.

In the Mammoth area, several day hikes and walking trails are worth the trouble, but these are not for beginning hikers. The **Beaver Ponds Trail,** for example, puts you to the test, gaining 500 feet in elevation.

As this area is less crowded, Mammoth is a good place to go horseback riding. With luck you may come upon a herd of elk. Even a brief foray off the road does much to enliven your sense of Yellowstone's wonders.

Roosevelt Country

Roosevelt Country drew the first tourists here with its lodging facilities. Less dramatic than the geyser or canyon areas, Roosevelt Country has the simple serenity and peaceful good looks of forests, meadows, streams, lakes, and marshes. A rewarding and not too difficult hike, especially with young children, is **Tower Fall Trail.** This waterfall cascades 132 feet and then flows into the Yellowstone River. Admire the setting of white water and mountain peaks from the visitor's platform; then hike the half mile of switchback trails down to the falls. Deer often rest on the rocks at the river bottom, where the tumbling waters create a thunderous display. Rest awhile before you attempt the half-mile hike back uphill. Horseback and stagecoach rides can be arranged at the lodge. (See Special Tours.)

If you continue from the center of Roosevelt Country toward the northeast entrance of the park, you'll see **Lamar Valley** and **Lamar River,** known for its good viewing of bison, elk, and mule deer. Small ponds for fishing are nearby and so is the **Yellowstone Institute,** Box 117, Yellowstone National Park, Wyoming 82190; (307) 344–2294. This nonprofit organization offers a variety of summer classes.

Canyon Country

Don't miss **Canyon Country;** many think of this as Yellowstone's most dramatic feature. The canyon, 20 miles long and 4,000 feet across, captivates with its bands of pink, yellow, and orange. Two waterfalls, the **Lower Falls** and the **Upper Falls,** cascade into the misty canyon. During your exploration, bypass Canyon Village, a touristy spot, but check out maps at the **Canyon Visitor Center** (307–242-2550).

Popular overlooks include **Inspiration Point,** a short, paved walk to a spectacular overlook of the canyon, and **Grandview Point,** another short walk to a canyon view. Along the South Rim stop at **Upper Falls Overlook** (handicapped accessible) and try the **Clear Lake Trail,** a hike through large rolling meadows and forested areas to **Clear Lake.**

Just a few miles south of the canyon lies the **Hayden Valley,** an expanse of wild grass and sage that attracts elk, bison, and bears. Be careful as you are in bear country.

A llama trek is a fun and unique way to experience Big Horn National Forest.
(Courtesy Wyoming Travel Commission)

Lake Country

More than 100 miles of shoreline surrounded by the natural landscape of tree-covered mountains and blue skies make **Yellowstone Lake** not only North America's largest mountain lake but another park highlight. Look for Canada geese and trumpeter swans. Stop at the **Fishing Bridge Visitor Center** (307–242–2450, ext. 6150) to find out about fishing areas. Ask about **Elephant Back Mountain Trail,** which leads you on a 4-mile hike to a panoramic view of the lake and into Pelican Valley.

Lake Yellowstone Hotel, a nearby lodge, surprises with beautiful lake views. From June to September, sign up for a one-hour narrated, scenic cruise. Remember to watch for bear and moose that graze along the shoreline and bald eagles as they swoop down to catch trout.

Head to **Steamboat** and **Lake Butte** for a sunset picnic.

Beyond the five areas described is the backcountry. You need a permit if you plan to trek through this area, and you will have to inform the various ranger stations of your exact plans. The wilderness can be beautiful, but take proper precautions. Ask the rangers for information about campsites, trails, hiking guides, and bears.

Special Tours

In warm weather. AMFAC, Yellowstone National Park, 82190 (303–297–2757), the park's concessionaire, offers a variety of exciting off-the-road trips. Call them well before your visit to book any of these trips.

With little time, go for the one- or two-hour guided horseback rides. While limited to easy "walks," these trail trips take you through the woods and into the hills, where herds of elk or deer may be plentiful. Instead of hearing car engines and the chatter of other tourists, on these rides listen to the cries of female elk, the wind rustling the leaves, and the birds. Roosevelt, Canyon, and Mammoth offer guided trail rides in the summer. Beginning and ending dates vary a bit, so check each location. Minimum age is generally eight; check with the reservationists or stable hands. With kids too young for horses, sample a pioneer journey with a scenic, but short, ride in a replica of a **Concord stagecoach.** These depart from the Roosevelt Lodge corrals early June through August and tour the Roosevelt-Tower region.

Something different for dinner? Climb aboard a horse-drawn wagon for a western-style campfire steak dinner with old **West Dinner Cookouts**, early June through August, Roosevelt.

Other possibilities include cruises on Yellowstone Lake, boat rentals from the marina, and guided fishing trips at Bridge Bay Marina from Yellowstone Lake. To fish, anglers twelve years and older must obtain a fishing permit. These are available throughout the park at Ranger Stations, visitor centers, and the Hamilton general store. For information and reservations, call (307) 242–2650.

In winter. Covered with snow, Yellowstone serves up a special kind of peace. In winter, park roads are restricted to over-the-snow vehicles. The elk, bison, deer, and coyotes still roam the park, but the majority of tourists do not. From the **Mammoth Hot Springs Hotel** (see Where to Stay), you can rent snowmobiles, go ice skating, or rent skis. If cross-country skiing is your prime interest, book a stay at **Old Faithful Snow Lodge,** near the famous geyser. The ski shop rents equipment including snowshoes, and nearby 40 miles of relatively short trails glide through the Old Faithful area, taking you past steaming hot springs, shooting geysers, and some big game—elk and bison. Additional short trails are available in the Blacktail Deer Plateau area and the Lamar Valley. To get to some of the trailheads, hop aboard a snow coach or the van shuttles. Warming huts are spaced throughout the park for snowmobilers, skiers, and snow-coach passengers. But dress appropriately. This is real winter. **The Heart Ski Ranch,** Moran (307-543-2477), offers family friendly snowmobile trips in winter.

WHERE TO STAY

Book your park accommodations as soon as you know the dates of your stay. Especially in season, Yellowstone is busy, and lodgings fill up fast. For reservations, call (303) 297-2757.

The park cabins and lodges offer a range of family-friendly rooms for a variety of budgets. There are ten accommodations in six locations within the park. Most of these are basic, without televisions, radios, and telephones; some are without private baths.

Mammoth Hot Springs Hotel, open December to early March and late May through late September, offers hotel rooms and cottage-style cabins, some with full bath, and some without. This is the only park lodging fully accessible by automobile in winter. From here you can rent snowmobiles.

Roosevelt Lodge and Cabins, open June through the end of August, has rustic charm and simplicity. Limited number of family cabins.

Canyon Lodge and Cabins, open June through the end of August, is half a mile from Yellowstone's canyons, and cabins are simple but have private baths.

Fishing Bridge R.V. Park, open at the end of May until September, allows RVs up to 40 feet in length, hard-sided only—no pop-ups or tents. Electric, water, and sewer hookups and laundry and shower facilities are available.

Lake Yellowstone Hotel & Cabins, open mid-May until the end of September, was renovated in 1991 and is among the park's best. New suites are available, but rooms in their annex building are less expensive.

Lake Lodge Cabins, open beginning of June until September, offers cabins. The property has laundry facilities and a restaurant.

Grant Village, open June 1 through September, is situated on the shore of Yellowstone Lake and provides the southernmost overnight accommodations in the park. Rooms have private baths and there are laundry facilities and a steak house on the property.

Old Faithful Inn, open early May through early October, is a National Historic Landmark standing near Old Faithful. This stately log hotel has a dining room, lounge, and gift shop.

Old Faithful Lodge Cabins, open late May through mid-September, also has a view of Old Faithful and accommodates visitors with simple cabins with or without private baths.

Old Faithful Snow Lodge, open mid-May through mid-October, and again in winter, is popular with skiers. While the rooms do not have baths, the cabins do. In winter this lodging is accessible only by over-the-snow vehicles. AMFAC's snow coaches arrive here daily for excursions.

All reservations can be made through the **Reservations Department,** AMFAC, Yellowstone National Park, Wyoming; (307) 344-7311. Rooms at Yellowstone book quickly, so it's best to make reservations at least four months in advance. About twelve campgrounds are also available, most on a first-come basis.

Outside the park near the eastern entrance is Buffalo Bill's original lodge (with a few modern changes). **The Pahaska Tepee,** 183 Yellowstone Highway, Cody 82414; (307-527-7701), has cabins, and offers fishing, overnight pack trips, and trail rides.

WHERE TO EAT

Yellowstone offers a variety of dining choices. Dress is always casual, and cafeterias and fast food are easy enough to find. The restaurants at **Mammoth Hot Springs, Lake Yellowstone Hotel, Old Faithful Inn, Grant Village,** and **Canyon Lodge** offer a variety of choices on their menus, including children's meals. Breakfast and lunch are served, and reservations are required for dinner; call (307) 344-7901. Family-style restaurants are located at **Roosevelt Lodge** and **Old Faithful Snow Lodge.** Roosevelt Lodge offers an Old West Barbecue. **Lake Lodge,**

Old Faithful Lodge, and **Canyon Lodge** all offer cafeterias with choices of salads, sandwiches, pasta, chicken, and more. If your stay is short and every minute counts, fast food is available at **Mammoth Hot Springs, Old Faithful,** and **Canyon Lodge.** As a convenience for hikers and fishers, box lunches can be ordered from any dining room or cafeteria and can be picked up the next morning.

Day Trips: Cody and the Big Horn National Forest

Situated conveniently between Big Horn and Yellowstone on Route 14/16/20, is the town of Colonel William "Buffalo Bill" F. Cody founded in 1896. A day trip, or better yet an overnight, in Cody, 52 miles from Yellowstone National Park's east entrance, is a must. First of all, the drive, which parallels the river, leads through the scenic Shoshone National Forest and the Wapiti Valley, an area President Teddy Roosevelt once dubbed "the most scenic 52 miles in the U.S." Not much has changed along this route since Roosevelt's era. In the Wapiti Valley, cottonwoods line the riverbanks, and the road cuts through gorges surrounded by yellow and pink mesas, buttes, and bluffs. This is the landscape of pioneer treks and movie westerns.

In the **Bighorn National Forest,** which encompasses more than a million acres in north-central Wyoming near the Montana border, the activities are as great as all outdoors: fishing; hiking, camping, and exploring the backcountry. As some areas restrict vehicles, park the car and hike in to sample this forest.

GETTING THERE

To Cody

From Yellowstone the easiest way to reach Cody is to drive east for 52 miles along U.S. 14/16/20. (See What to See and Do). The **Yellowstone Regional Airport,** Cody, serves the Big Horn Basin and is serviced by **Sky West/Delta Connection** and **Mesa Airlines/United Express. The Jackson Hole Airport,** 1250 East Airport Road, Jackson (307–733–7682), is serviced by **Delta, SkyWest, American Airlines, Continental Express,** and **United Express.** From the Jackson Hole Airport, which is located near the southern end of the **Grand Teton National Park,** Yellowstone is about a two-hour drive, or much more if you go leisurely and plan to sightsee. Head north along Highway 287/191/89 from the Grand Teton National Park to the Yellowstone's south entrance. Rental car companies are located at the airports.

To the Big Horn National Forest

The closest regional airport is the **Yellowstone Regional Airport.** The most common way to see the **Big Horn National Forest** is by car. From Cody continue east. The road splits into 14 and 14A (alternate). Along 14 you drive through canyon and forest. The cliffs along the roadside may seem intimidating, but this is the most manageable road, especially for trailers or during winter weather. Highway 14A is a more open, alpine route with great overlooks, but the 10-percent grade makes this road difficult for some vehicles and drivers.

GETTING AROUND

A car is really a necessity, especially if you are continuing from Yellowstone to **Cody** to the **Big Horn National Forest.** A handy booklet is *Wyoming Loop Tour,* available from the Chamber of Commerce, which outlines routes to and through such scenic sites as the Big Horn Mountain Scenic Byway, the Black Hills, Thermopolis and Hot Springs State Park, Sheridan, and Buffalo.

WHAT TO SEE AND DO

Cody

Spending the night in Cody gives you ample time to enjoy the drive to town as well as time to savor two of the town's very different must-sees. The first one you'll come to is **Historic Trail Town,** Highway 14/16/20, 2 miles west of the Buffalo Bill Historical Center (307)-587–5302), open Mid-May to mid-September. Set on a strip of land just off the main drag, Historic Trail Town looks like a cowboy movie set, but this is the real thing. On this site near where western-legend Buffalo Bill Cody and friends first surveyed "Cody City," archaeologist Bob Edgar has collected and placed twenty-six authentic nineteenth-century log buildings that face each other on two sides of a "street." Scores of wagons and wheels line the middle.

The weathered wood and simple furnishings create a haunting feel, evoking the West as it really was. The structures offer up such legends as the Hole in the Wall Cabin where Butch Cassidy and the Sundance Kid plotted, a saloon with bullet holes in the door, and Trail Town Cemetery, where, among others, Jeremiah "Liver Eating" Johnston, a mountain man, hunter, and trapper whose life became a movie legend, lies buried. As you peer in these fragile-looking homes and feel the wind in your face, you can imagine the toughness of pioneer living.

Plan to spend several hours at the **Buffalo Bill Historical Center,** P.O. Box 1000, Cody 82414; (307) 587–4771 or (800) 553–3838. It's aptly labeled the "Smithsonian of the West." Spend an afternoon at this facility's four museums, and you'll come away with an enhanced sense of both western myth and reality. From the artifacts of showman Buffalo Bill Cody and his Wild West Show, you understand the larger-than-life panache of mountain men, rodeo riders, and sharpshooters such as Annie Oakley.

The extensive holdings of the **Cody Firearms Museum** include muskets dating to 1590, as well as eighteenth-century Flintlock rifles, Civil War pistols, and nineteenth-century percussion revolvers. Browse the Whitney Gallery of Western Art to see the land and its people, sometimes idealized, through the eyes of such artists as Frederic Remington, Charles Russell, and Albert Bierstadt.

The **Plains Indian Museum** presents the clothing, religious objects, and daily artifacts of the Sioux, Crow, and twenty-five other tribes who lived from the Mississippi River to the Rocky Mountains, and from Texas to mid-Canada. Children delight in the intricately beaded moccasins, shirts, and dresses. Take time to sit in a real tepee with your kids and discuss its symbolism and practicality, and experience the world from this vantage point.

The Cody Nite Rodeo is the event that has earned Cody its nickname "Rodeo Capital of the World." After dinner follow the crowds to the rodeo grounds, P.O. Box 1327–A, Cody; (307) 587–5155. Every evening from June through August cowboys rope calves, race barrels, and ride broncos. Purchase tickets in advance at the ticket booth wagon, City Park, from the Cody Country Chamber of Commerce, 836 Sheridan Avenue (307–587–2297), or at the gate after 7:00 P.M.

WHERE TO STAY

Cody

The historic **Irma Hotel,** 1192 Sheridan (307-587-4221), a town grande dame that has lost a bit of her "glow," offers forty original rooms in the historic hotel, plus annex rooms in a motel. The **Historic Buffalo Bill Village Resort,** Seventeenth and Sheridan Avenue (800-527-5544), is a complex of three hotels: a Holiday Inn, a Comfort Inn, and the Village, plus a camper village. There's a pool as well. Cody Country offers a combination of ranch activities plus trekking, backpacking, sailing, and rock climbing. For a free vacation guide, call (307) 587-2297.

For a listing of eighty bed and breakfasts in the Wyoming area, contact Bed & Breakfast Western Adventure, P.O. Box 20972, Billings, Montana 59104; (406) 259-7993.

In Cody dine at the **Buffalo Bill Bar** and the **Irma Restaurant,** the Irma Hotel, 1192 Sheridan (307-587-4221), a hotel built in 1902 by Buffalo Bill Cody, and named for his daughter. Belly up to the elaborate cherrywood back bar, a gift to Cody from an appreciative Queen Victoria, who delighted in Buffalo Bill's Wild West Show. Despite the tin ceiling and ornate bar, this place is far from fancy. Locals with muddy boots and dusty chaps come here for the prime rib.

The Sunset House Family Restaurant, Sunset Motor Inn (307-587-2257), serves three meals daily and has take-out lunches. Kids like the piano music. **Franca's Italian Dining,** 1421 Rumsey Avenue (307-587-5354), requires reservations. Try the house specialty, *Tortelloni Verdi al Mascarpone,* prepared by Franca herself. For a free dining guide, call (307) 587-2297.

Special Tours

For a different but delightful perspective on the area's canyon and rivers, sign on for a family-friendly raft trip through the Shoshone National Forest. Most of the trips combine easy paddling with just enough rapids for some thrills, but always ask about the suitability given the ages of your children. With **Wyoming River Trips,** P.O. Box 1541C, Cody 82414 (307-587-6661), excursions range from ninety-minute floats through scenic red-rock canyons to half-day (to five hours) wildlife viewing trips where the rapids and the wildlife add excitement. **River Runners,** 1491 Sheridan Avenue, Cody 82414 (307-527-RAFT), **Cody Boys River Trips,** P.O. Box 1446, Cody 82414 (307-587-4208), and **Red Canyon River Trips,** 1220 Sheridan Avenue, Cody 82414 (307-587-6988), have a similar range of excursions.

WHAT TO SEE AND DO

Bighorn National Forest

On the way to the **Bighorn National Forest,** 23 miles east of Cody on Alternate Route 14, is **Powell,** in the heart of the Shoshone reclamation area. An agricultural center, Powell grew green as a result of the Buffalo Bill Reservoir irrigation project. Look west for a glimpse of **Heart Mountain**—a geological phenomenon, as this mountain's top is older than its base.

Scenic Drives and Hikes

Just beyond Lovell, which is at the junction of U.S. 14A and 789/310, stop by the **Bighorn Canyon National Recreational Area Visitor Center,** U.S. 14A; (307) 548-2251. It's open daily in summer, and on Saturdays and Sundays other times. Ask about summer guided hikes, and nature talks, and obtain a copy of *Canyon Echoes,* the forest newsletter. For more western canyons and wildlife, turn north on Route 37 just before the visitors center for views of **Bighorn Canyon** and the **Pryor Mountain Wild Horse Range,** where more than 120 wild horses roam free. About 17 miles from the turnoff, enjoy the viewed from the **Devils Canyon Overlook** of Bighorn Lake below and the many-hued canyon walls.

While hiking, you might see bighorn sheep and black bear, although the latter are rarely seen by tourists. No grizzlies reside in the Big Horn.

Medicine Wheel, 27 miles east of Lovell, is a controversial attraction within Big Horn National Forest. This prehistoric 74-foot stone circle, with twenty-eight spokes radiating from a central cairn, is said to be a sacred place of worship for Native Americans. Although tourists are not supposed to enter the area, non—Native Americans often park in a nearby lot and hike the mile to the observation area. As the trail is strenuous, a shuttle is available in summer to transport people who may have difficulty making the climb. The information booth provides literature about the significance of this area to Native Americans.

Continue on 14A to **Burgess Junction,** where this road joins U.S. 14. About 5 miles south of this junction, take Forest Road 26 to the **Big Goose Falls Ranger Station.** From here continue on route 296 to **Big Moose Falls.** This 5-mile one-way hike from the ranger station crosses the East Fork four times, providing wonderful views, plunge pools, and water-sculpted rocks. But beware: This 10-mile round-trip may be best for older children and teens who are hearty hikers (parents, too, should be in shape). As always, bring plenty of water, food, and appropriate clothing—T-shirts, sweatshirts, and rain gear.

An easy hike is the 2.4-mile **Blue Creek Loop Trail.** The trailhead begins at Sibley Lake, Highway 14, near the campground. Follow the creek and, if you like, venture onto another loop, the **Deadhorse Park Loop.** While the terrain remains easy, the two loops together amount to 6 miles. Bring your camera for some photographs of the often-seen moose, deer, and elk in the meadows and the lodgepole pines.

On Route 14, the **Shell Falls Trail** in the Paintrock district offers some more easy hiking. Walk through the forest on a path that treats you to some wonderful views of the falls. Spend time at the novelty shop you'll pass, managed by a couple who give a singing/talking introduction to the falls. After hearing the stories and fun facts, the falls are even more fun. Look around for the bighorn sheep, who like the steep cliffs and fresh water.

WHERE TO STAY

Camping areas within the forest are divided into five districts: Buffalo, Tensleep, Paintrock, Medicine Wheel, and Tongue. Each has picnic grounds, grocery facilities, cabins or motels, and restaurants. **Bear Lodge** on 14A (write 1643 Seventeenth Street, Sheridan 82801; 307-655-2444) and **Arrowhead Lodge** (P.O. Box 267, Dayton 82836; 307-655-2388) are two good picks. Both offer modern motel units and rustic cabins. (Be sure to specify which type of lodging you prefer.) Bear Lodge has a stock pond for fishing, and snowmobiling in winter. Arrowhead has nearby rivers and streams for fishing, as well as snowmobiling and skiing in the winter.

WHERE TO EAT

In the Bighorn National Forest

Most cabin lodging comes with meals for guests. A few, such as Arrowhead, have a cafe that may be open to walk-ins depending on the hour and the season. Call ahead. Day trippers should buy ample provisions, including water and food, in Cody before heading out to hike.

SPECIAL EVENTS

January: International Rocky Mountain Stage Stop Sled Dog Race.

February: Buffalo Bill Birthday Ball, Cody.

April: Cowboy Songs and Range Ballads, Buffalo Bill Historical Center.

June: At the Plains Indian Powwow, one of the nation's largest gatherings of Plains tribes from the United States and Canada, members sing and dance in competition wearing tribal dress, Buffalo Bill Historical Center; Frontier Festival.

July: Cody Stampede, which draws crowds for the rodeos, parades, street dances, fireworks, and western entertainment.

July: The Yellowstone Jazz Festival stages outdoor concerts in Yellowstone National Park as well as in Cody and Powell.

August: The Buffalo Bill Festival celebrates the end of summer with a craft fair, chili cookoff, rodeo, and major entertainers in concert.

More Day Trips

Include time in your Yellowstone vacation to explore nearby, and often less crowded, **Grand Teton National Park,** Wyoming. While it's possible to sample the park in a day, try to at least spend one overnight. In season the Jackson area, the southern gateway to Yellowstone, offers good skiing with short lift lines on relatively uncrowded slopes. (See the chapter Grand Teton National Park and Jackson, Wyoming.)

Combining a Yellowstone tour with a dude-ranch stay is sure to be a family favorite. Whether you're a greenhorn beginner or a saddle savvy wrangler, **Paradise Guest Ranch,** P.O. Box 790, Buffalo, Wyoming

82834 (307–684–7876), has a ride to suit you. This ranch offers custom rides twice daily for adults and kids six and older. Feel free to choose a scenic, slow-paced trail ride through the woods, a trot across a ridge top, or an adventuresome all-day trek that has you jumping ravines and galloping across high mountain meadows. Unlike many other guest ranches, Paradise allows you to ride with your kids or send them on with their own group. When not on horseback, kids six and older and preschoolers ages three to five enjoy nature-oriented children's programs from 8:00 A.M. to 5:00 P.M. Nonriders (and the saddle-sore) can join a guided mountain walk, fish for trout, or soak in a hot tub. Evening activities bring the family together at talent shows, chuckwagon barbecues, and square dances. The accommodations are first-rate in modern cabins with kitchen, fireplace, and laundry facilities.

FOR MORE INFORMATION

Yellowstone Information

For park camping, dining, lodging, and tour information, contact AMFAC (307–344–7311). The Grant Village Visitor Center (307–344–7381, ext. 6602). The Yellowstone Association, P.O. Box 117, Yellowstone National Park 82190. For information for the physically challenged: Handicapped Access, Yellowstone National Park, Wyoming 82190; (307) 344–7381, ext. 2108. Log on to the National Parks Internet site: http://www.nps.gov.

Handy publications about Yellowstone include *Yellowstone Today* and the *Yellowstone Guide*. For information about surrounding cities, contact the Wyoming Division of Tourism, I-25 at College Drive, Cheyenne 82002; (307) 777–7777 or (800) 225–5996.

Shoshone National Forest

Contact the Wapiti Ranger District, Shoshone National Forest, 203A Yellowstone Avenue, P.O. Box 1840, Cody 82414; (307) 578–1202. Shoshone National Forest, P.O. Box 2140, 888 Meadow Lane, Cody 82414; (307) 527–6241.

Cody. Cody Country Chamber of Commerce, Visitor Information Center, P.O. Box 2777, 836 Sheridan Avenue, Cody 82414; (307) 587–2297.

Bighorn National Forest

Bighorn National Forest, 1969 South Sheridan Avenue, Sheridan 82801; (307) 672-0751. Big Horn Mountain Sports, 334 North Main, Sheridan 82801 (307-672-6866) and the U.S.D.A. Forest Service, Tongue District, Bighorn National Forest, offer a pamphlet on area day hikes.

General

Wyoming Division of Tourism, I-25 at College Drive, Cheyenne 82002; (307) 777-7777 or (800) 225-5996.

Emergency Numbers

Yellowstone and Cody

Ambulance, fire, police: 911

For rangers in Yellowstone; (307) 344-7381

Hospital, emergency room, and pharmacy: In Yellowstone National Park, Yellowstone Medical Services offers twenty-four-hour emergency room and ambulance service from the end of May through mid-September at Lake Clinic, in Lake, on Yellowstone Lake; (307) 242-7241. Other medical facilities are located at Old Faithful Clinic, Old Faithful area (307-545-7345), from the end of May through mid-October and at Mammoth Family Clinic, Mammoth Hot Springs (307-344-7965), year-round, Monday through Friday. West Park Hospital, 708 Sheriden Avenue, Cody; (800) 654-9447 or (307) 527-7501 in Cody.

Pharmacy: Cody Drug, Eastgate Shopping Center, 1813 Seventeenth Street (307-587-2283), provides an after-hours emergency pharmacy and has delivery service.

Poison Control: (800) 442-2702

17 🎿 Utah

ARCHES NATIONAL PARK AND CANYONLANDS NATIONAL PARK

Arches National Park, just 5 miles north of Moab, features the world's largest concentration of natural red and golden sandstone arches. This is a sight your children will long remember. More than 2,000 majestic arches plus red-rock canyons, fins, spires, and balancing rocks give this landscape an extraterrestrial aura. The fascinating formations were created from the erosion of the Entrada Sandstone and Navajo Sandstone, thick layers of rock deposited as sand some 150 million years ago.

The park comprises 73,000 acres; you could easily get an "eyeful" after a few hours, but plan to spend at least a day, hopefully more, exploring. The early morning and early evening light are dramatic times to view the arches' red desert, with the peaks of the La Sal Mountains in the background. Open year-round, the park has a high season from mid-March to October. **Canyonlands National Park** is quite close, and certainly worth a visit, although it's more rugged and not as accessible for families, particularly those with young children. (In fact, it's the state's least visited national park, albeit the largest.)

GETTING THERE

Canyonlands Field Airport, 18 miles northwest of Moab on Highway 191 (801–259–7421), offers regular commuter service from

Salt Lake City via **Alpine Aviation** (801-575-2839). The nearest major airport is **Walker Field** in Grand Junction, Colorado, two hours east (970-244-9100), which is served by **Mesa** (a United Express connection), **SkyWest** (a Delta connection), **America West,** and **Air 21.** Major car rental companies are located at the airport.

The nearest **Amtrak** (800-USA-RAIL) is in the town of Thompson, 45 miles north. By car, the park is 5 miles north of Moab off U.S. 191.

GETTING AROUND

A car is a necessity. Rental cars and jeeps are available in the area. A 41-mile (round-trip) paved road in the park leads to the major sights. There are also unpaved roads for four-wheel-drive vehicles.

WHAT TO SEE AND DO

The **visitor center,** just inside the park entrance, is open year-round and features exhibits and a slide program detailing the arch formations. Obtain a trail guide here that shows the distances for hiking and the approximate times to allow.

Follow the paved road from the visitor center. While you can see a few of the major arches from the road, short trails (as well as more strenuous hikes) lead to many others. *Best Hikes with Children in Utah* by Maureen Keilty (The Mountaineers) details several trails in Arches, Canyonlands, and other Utah parks, and tells how to stimulate your kids' imaginations as you proceed. On your hike, take the opportunity to teach your children to respect the area's ecology, and remind them not to walk on the cryptobiotic crust, an important feature of the Colorado Plateau. This black, knobby surface frequently seen growing on the soil is composed of organisms that have an important function in the desert; they hold moisture, prevent erosion, and contribute nitrogen and carbon to the soil. They are easily recognized and shouldn't be stepped on or driven on. Stay on the trails and the roads.

Note: In the summer, temperatures can climb to 110 degrees, so it's best to do your hiking early in the day or in the evening; carry plenty of water, wear wide-brimmed hats, and use sunscreen.

Arches National Park at a Glance

- Nature at its most dramatic and rugged

- 2,000 majestic arches plus red-rock canyons, fins, spires, and balancing rocks

- Prehistoric Indian ruins and petroglyphs

- Mill Canyon Dinosaur Trail

- Arches National Park, (801) 259-8161; Canyonlands National Park, (801) 259-7164

Two miles from the visitor center, the paved road passes the **Park Avenue Viewpoint,** where you can follow a moderate 1-mile hike (best with older kids) that starts at **South Park Avenue** and follows a red-rock canyon bottom to **North Park Avenue**—about ninety minutes away. The high vertical walls resemble a city skyline.

Back in the car, follow the road for 10 miles along the foot of the salmon-colored **Great Wall. The Balanced Rock,** approximately at the center of the park, fascinates kids: This massive 50-foot boulder appears to be precariously balanced atop a slim 75-foot pedestal. The .4-mile loop that leads to the rock takes about fifteen minutes and is an easy hike.

East of here, off the main paved road, a spur road leads to the **"Windows** section." An easy .9-mile trail loop to **North** and **South Windows** and **Turret Arch** takes about forty-five minutes.

After continuing your drive on the main road for several miles, you will come to another spur that leads to **Wolfe Ranch,** an 1888 homesteader's creation, with an old log cabin and corral. This serves as the trailhead for a 3-mile round-trip to a park landmark, **Delicate Arch.** The hike takes about three and one-half hours and is moderately strenuous. The trail climbs up slick rock to the arch—making it unsuitable for very young kids and definitely challenging for older siblings. The suspension bridge that crosses **Salt Wash** at .1 mile may intimidate younger kids; if so, you can turn around. If you cross the bridge (older kids will be right in their element), look for petroglyphs on the left cliff. Once you reach the arch, don't walk under it because it's quite steep. You also can see the arch from a viewpoint a half mile to the southeast.

The main road ends at **The Devil's Garden** area, where there about a dozen significant arches, some without names. The only one visible from the road is **Skyline Arch,** which can also be accessed by an easy .5-mile hike that leads to the base. Hopefully, your kids will have the stamina for the easy 2-mile hike to **Landscape Arch,** the largest natural arch in the world at 288 feet high and 306 feet across. If you must limit your hikes, this is a good one to take.

Ranger-led programs take place from mid-March until mid-October. Check the **visitor's center** for current schedules. There are no programs specifically for children.

Pack Creek Ranch, Mountain Loop Road, Moab (801-259-5505), operates two-hour horseback trips on the outskirts of the park from mid-March to the end of October. Kids under five can't ride alone; if doubled-up with a parent, then the pair can go out for a one-hour ride. Depending on the season, there are other off-road rides. The ranch also has room for guests in units with kitchenettes; and, for added convenience, enjoy the restaurant and pool.

See **Adventures,** following the Canyonlands listing, for other outfitters and activities in and around Arches.

SPECIAL EVENTS

The communities around Arches and Canyonlands offer a variety of year-round activities. Contact the **Utah Canyonlands Region** (801-259-8825 or 800-635-6622) for more information.

January: Winter Festival, Monticello.

February: Quarter Horse Show, Moab.

March: Canyonlands Half Marathon, Moab; U.S. Mail Trail Ride equestrian event, Green River.

April: Easter Jeep Safari; Bicycle Stage Race; Quarter Horse Show—all in Moab. Jeep Jamboree, Blanding.

May: Annual Arts Festival, Moab.

June: Rodeo; Butch Cassidy Days, Moab.

The Druid Arch is just one of the magnificent formations located in Canyonlands National Park. (Photo by Jim Marie/courtesy Utah Travel Council)

July: Frontier Days, Blanding; Pioneer Days celebrations, Moab/Monticello; Little Buckaroo Rodeo, Green River.

August: County Fairs, Moab/Monticello; Rodeo, Monticello; Dead Horse Point Square Dance Festival, Moab; Hispanic Folk Festival, Monticello.

September: Whit Mesa Annual Ute Indian Bear Dance, Blanding; Melon Days, Green River; Utah Navajo Fair, Bluff; Moab Music Festival.

October: Canyonlands Fat Tire Bike Festival; Rock, Gem, and Mineral Show, Moab; Jeep Jamboree, Blanding.

November: "Day of the Dead," community art show, Moab.

December: 10K Winter Sun Run, Moab; Canyonlands Christmas Festival, Moab.

WHERE TO STAY

The park's **Devil's Garden** campground is open on a first-come, first-served basis, with water available from mid-March to mid-October.

Facilities include tables, grills, and flush toilets. Because the campground is normally full by late morning or early afternoon during peak season, plan to arrive early. The park begins supplying campground permits at 7:30 A.M. Often, in spring, the campground is full within an hour. In summer and fall, the permits are usually all snatched by noon.

Area accommodations are listed in the brochure *Utah's Canyonlands*, available from **Canyonlands Travel Region** at the visitor centers in Moab and Monticello, or call (800) 574-4386, and in the *Utah Travel Guide*, available from the Utah Travel Council (see For More Information). Lodging includes a variety of motels and several bed and breakfasts. One possibility is **Comfort Suites,** 800 South Main (801-259-5252 or 800-228-5150), with seventy-five rooms, a pool, hot tub, and kitchens. **Cottonwood Condos,** 338 East 100 South, is in a residential area right off Main Street; (801) 259-8897 or (800) 447-4106. This former apartment house has eight one-bedroom units that come with stocked kitchens and a queen-sized sofa in the living room. Linens and towels are provided.

WHERE TO EAT

There is no food served or sold in the park. **Moab** is where you'll satisfy your appetite. **The Moab Information Center** supplies a restaurant guide. **Bar-M Chuckwagon,** 541 South Mulberry Lane (801-259-2276), serves hearty cowboy-type vittles, followed by a one-hour Western show with a live band, Native American dancers, and more. It's held every night except Sunday from June through September in an outdoor tent with a retractable canopy top. The restaurant is open Fridays and Saturdays, April through May.

Some local favorites include **The Rio-Colorado Restaurant and Bar,** 2 South 100 West (801-259-6666), which serves Southwestern cuisine, some Mexican, special desserts, and Sunday brunch with full buffet. "Come Taste the West" at the **Branding Iron,** 2971 South Highway 191 (801-259-6275). Open daily, this lounge offers Tex-Mex items such as tacos, chili, grits, and burgers. Culture is served on Friday nights with karaoke.

Golden Stake Restaurant, 540 South Main (801-259-7000), is a family-style restaurant that serves steaks, hamburgers, and home-style meals.

DAY TRIPS

Canyonlands

Canyonlands is an immense 527-square-mile wilderness composed of three very different areas. The northern Island in the Sky district is a towering, level mesa between the Green and Colorado rivers. The Needles district, southeast of the river's confluence, has the densest concentration of arches, rock spires, canyons, potholes, prehistoric Indian ruins, and petroglyphs—plus the Needles, enormous rock pinnacles of red and white. The Maze district, southwest of the rivers, is wild, remote, and accessible by 4x4 only, with canyons, tall standing rocks, and colorful sandstone fins. Part of the Maze is **Horseshoe Canyon,** which is decorated by Native American rock art. Dating back to 1700 B.C. to A.D. 500, the intricate designs and life-size figures are perhaps the most famous prehistoric rock art in the United States.

Popular seasons in this park are from March to May and August to October. Services are very limited: You won't find food, gasoline, stores, lodging, or drinking water (except seasonally in the **Squaw Flat Campground** in the Needles). **Needles Outpost,** just outside the Needles park boundaries, off U.S. 211, has gasoline, food, and limited supplies available spring through fall.

From Moab, the **Island in the Sky Visitors Center** (801-259-4712) is 32 miles southwest, while the **Needles Visitors Center** (801-259-4711) is 76 miles away. Both are open seven days a week, with reduced winter hours. Rangers offer information, maps, brochures, and, during the summer, guided walks and evening campfire programs.

You can explore the park in several ways. Drive on paved and two-wheel-drive roads to the **Needles** and **Island in the Sky** districts, which lead to overlooks, trailheads, picnic areas, and developed campgrounds. There are also rugged four-wheel-drive trails throughout the park. These are steep and rocky sometimes, and in the park's own words, "tortuous."

Short walks and long hikes lead to some of the park's most outstanding features. Certain trails have wayside exhibits or brochures, available at trailheads or visitors centers. Because this is a desert area, *the park advises taking a number of precautions:* Carry a gallon of water per person per day (active people may require more); drink water frequently; protect yourself from intense sun by wearing a hat, sunglasses, sunscreen, long pants, and a long-sleeved shirt. Save strenuous activity for early morning or late afternoon. Be wary of climbing slick rock because it's often easy to climb up but impossible to climb down. Use special caution near cliff edges, and keep younger children in hand and older children in sight at all times.

Families who have visited **Arches National Park,** but would like to spend at least a half day exploring **Canyonlands,** should head straight to **The Island** district, where they will find "possibly the world's greatest exposure of red-rock canyons." This area is particularly suited to families with younger kids and/or those with limited time. It features short walks and spectacular overlooks of the **White Rim** below, **the Needles,** and **the Maze.** If you have just a half day to spend, drive the 12 miles from the visitors center to **Grand View Point Overlook,** making stops at **Shafer Canyon** and **Buck Canyon overlooks.** You can also take the 1.5-mile dirt road to **Green River Overlook.** All provide different vantage points and superb vistas, which might include such wildlife as bighorn sheep, coyotes, or foxes on the ledges below.

Then drive 6 miles to **Upheaval Dome**—one of the island's most spectacular formations, a 2-mile-wide crater filled with various colored spires and boulders. The **Crater View Trail,** or **Upheaval Dome Trail,** offers an easy-to-moderate hike for kids. The trail starts at a picnic area, and offers two options: a 500- yard (one-way) walk up slick rock to an (unfenced) view of the crater—good for young and/or beginning hikers—or a more challenging 0.8-mile (one-way) hike to a second, fenced-in vantage point.

The Needles District, 49 miles northwest of the town of Monticello, can be accessed by U.S. 191. **Newspaper Rock BLM Recreation Site,** 13 miles off U.S. 191 on Scenic Byway U-211, displays petroglyphs spanning 1,000 years. Although a paved access road in the Needles area leads to number of viewpoints, some hiking or four-wheeling is required to see the area attractions. The main road ends at **Big Spring Canyon Overlook,** where there is a large assortment of mushroom-shaped hoodoos.

Adventures

Moab, the only city in the state on the **Colorado River,** is the headquarters for a number of jeep, raft, canoe, jet boat, and airplane tours of the region. The **visitor's office** (see For More Information) provides a list of outfitters as well as lots of other area information. There are miles and miles of scenic federal lands around Moab that actually have fewer restrictions than the national parkland. Therefore, many of the outfitters, even those licensed to operate in the parks, take advantage of the surrounding areas to schedule adventure activities. Here are some possibilities.

Sheri Griffith Expeditions, 2231 South Highway 191, Moab; (801) 259–8229 or (800) 332–2439. They offer a number of trips on the Green and Colorado rivers, including three specialty trips each summer for families. A recent offering, The Family Goes to Camp—Expedition Style is a five-day/four-night journey to the majestic canyons of the Green River, with hiking, bouldering, water games, playing in the sand, and camping on sandy beaches. The trip is recommended for kids as young as five.

Tag-A-Long Expeditions, 452 North Main, Moab (801–259–8946 or 800–453–3292), offers a variety of adventures. Rafting trips range from a one-day Colorado River trip north of Moab to three to four days through Canyonlands (minimum age six). Canoe 120 miles down the Green River, then take a jet-boat trip back on the Colorado. Enjoy four-wheel-drive trips through Canyonlands and the miles of jeep trails around Moab. The company stresses that the four-wheel trips, though they do cover rugged terrain and can be bumpy, are not meant to be "high adventure," but rather entertaining, narrated guided trips that include short walks. The company has taken kids as young as four, although usually ages ten and up enjoy the trips most. In winter, the company runs combination trips featuring Nordic skiing in the La Sal Mountains and one- or two-day land trips in or around the national parks.

Canyonlands Field Institute (CFI), P.O. Box 68, Moab; (801) 259–7750 or (800) 860–5262. This nonprofit organization explores the ecology, geology, and archaeology of Arches and Canyonlands National Park, the canyons of the Green and Colorado rivers, and the wilderness of the Colorado Plateau. CFI is a licensed river outfitter in Utah and Colorado, and they run a variety of **Eco-River Trips,** many of which provide educational experiences for families. Among their trips led by naturalist instructors: a two-day/one-night Colorado River journey to the **Westwater Canyon,** on the Colorado-Utah state line near Moab. You can spot bald and golden eagles as you float in an open canyon bounded by red sandstone cliffs. Westwater contains one of the three largest sets of rapids on the Colorado River. CFI is also known for its in-depth weekend field seminars that detail natural and cultural history. Several are family oriented. CFI also arranges a variety of programs custom-made for families. These last a half day to one week or more. You choose the place and focus. Sample programs include Arches National Park and/or BLM Wilderness Study Areas near Moab, and one-day naturalist-guided explorations. CFI offers discounted rates for those under sixteen.

Dinosaur Discovery Expeditions, 550 Jurassic Court, Fruita, Colorado; (800) DIG-DINO. They sponsor a **Dinosaur Diamond Safari** for nondiggers (children must be sixteen years), touring significant dinosaur sites in Grand Junction, Colorado, and Moab, Price, and Vernal, Utah—cities that form **"The Dinosaur Diamond."** The trip, held in late September, includes museum visits, dinosaur locations, and national monuments in these fossil-rich areas, including a stop at Arches National Park. In summer, Dinosaur Discovery Expeditions offers a variety of family-oriented educational trips about dinosaurs.

The Moab area is also a favorite of mountain bikers. There's a popular half-day route, the **Slickrock Bike Trail,** which starts about 3 miles east of town and follows an extremely challenging, clearly marked 10-mile loop. This is not for beginners—and be sure to pack plenty of water. Bike shops that offer daily rentals and guided tours include **Rim Tours,** 1233 South Highway 191 (801-259-5223 or 800-626-7335), which also rents camping gear. The tours have no strict age limits and include three- to six-day spring and fall outings to Canyonlands National Park. Call for a brochure, which also details summer trips to western Colorado and northern Arizona.

DAY TRIPS

Take some time to explore Moab, a pleasant town with some interesting attractions.

Dan O'Laurie Museum, 118 East Center Street; (801) 259-7985 (closed Sundays). Archaeological, geological, and historical exhibits detail the area's history from the prehistoric Ute Indian days to the uranium boom of the 1950s.

Mill Canyon Dinosaur Trail, 13 miles northwest of Moab on U.S. 191, is an outdoor paleontological museum. Imbedded in the landscape along this hour-long hike are dinosaur bones and fossils. Only a short distance from the trail are the remains of the **Halfway Stage Station,** a public rest area used from 1883 to 1904.

The Moab area has been a popular filming location since 1949. The visitors center provides you with a movie location guide. Locations are accessible with a two-wheel-drive vehicle. Inside **Arches National Park,** for instance, scenes for *Indiana Jones and the Last Crusade* were shot in **South Park Avenue** and **Windows** areas; the scene where Thelma and Louise of that movie lock an officer in his patrol-car trunk was shot at **The Courthouse Towers** area.

The small town of **Monticello,** 54 miles south of Moab on U.S. 191, close to the turnoff for the Needles section of Canyonlands, has a cinema, a strip of inexpensive motels, and several eateries. Situated on the edge of the **Abajo** or **Blue Mountains** at 7,050 feet, the town provides superb panoramas of the surrounding countryside. The **San Juan County Multi-Agency Visitor Center,** with information about all of southeast Utah, is at Highway 191 and 100 South. Represented here are the National Park Service, U.S. Forest Service, and Bureau of Land Management. For example, pamphlets about the many **Anasazi** sites in southeastern Utah may be obtained from the **visitor's center,** 117 South Main (800-574-4386); the **National Park Service,** (801-587-2737); or the **Bureau of Land Management (BLM)** (801-587-2141).

FOR MORE INFORMATION

National Parks: **Arches National Park,** 2282 Southwest Resource Boulevard, Moab 84532 (801-259-8161); **Canyonlands National Park,** 2282 Southwest Resource Boulevard, Moab 84532 (801-259-7164). Log on to the National Parks Internet site: http://www.nps.gov.

Area Tourist Information: **Grand County Travel Council** (Moab Information Center), corner of Main and Center, Moab (801-259-8825 or

800–635–6622); **San Juan County Travel Council** 117 South Main,
Monticello (800–574–4386); **Utah Travel Council,** Council Hall/
Capitol Hill, Salt Lake City, Utah 84114–1396 (801–538–1030).

Emergency Numbers

The only phones are at the visitor center. The park has qualified
emergency medical personnel who can help the injured or can
transport them to **San Juan Hospital,** 364 West 100 North,
Monticello (801–587–2116).

City Market Pharmacy, 425 South Main, Moab (801–259–
8971), is open from 9:00 A.M. to 7:00 P.M. Monday through Friday, until 6:00 P.M. Saturday, and from noon to 4:00 P.M. Sunday; on most holidays it's open from 9:00 A.M. to 4:00 P.M.

San Juan Pharmacy, 148 South Main Street, Monticello (801–
587–2302), is open 9:00 A.M. to 7:00 P.M. Monday through Saturday. Closed Sundays.

Poison Control: (800) 456–7707

SALT LAKE CITY

Salt Lake City, the capital of Utah, takes its name from the 80-mile-long Great Salt Lake, 15 miles west of town. The lake features white-sand beaches, beautiful pink-streaked sunsets, and many species of migratory birds. The sprawling city, surrounded by the Wasatch Mountains in the east and north and the Oquirrh Mountains to the west, is a safe area where families can enjoy a relaxed vacation at a slower pace than in most other cities. The city is world headquarters of the Mormon religion, whose first settlers arrived in the valley in 1847. Today more than half of the city's population are members of the Church of Jesus Christ of Latter Day Saints (LDS). The city's Mexican American, Greek, and Japanese communities add some cultural diversity to this clean, inviting city. Currently, the city is preparing to host the 2002 Winter Olympics.

GETTING THERE

Salt Lake City International Airport, 776 North Terminal Drive (801-575-2400), serves most major airlines and is ten minutes west of downtown. Car rentals, cabs, city bus #50 (with hourly departures), and courtesy vans from some of the better hotels provide transportation into the city.

The **Amtrak** station (800-USA-RAIL) is at 320 South Rio Grande. **Greyhound** is at 160 West South Temple; (801) 355-9589 or (800) 231-2222. Interstates 15 and 80 intersect in Salt Lake City.

GETTING AROUND

A car isn't absolutely necessary, thanks to the public transportation system and the fact that most of the main tourist activities cluster right in the heart of town. The streets run at right angles to each other, numbered in a grid scale starting at the center point of Temple Square.

The **Utah Transit Authority's** bus system (801–287–4636) is extensive and runs throughout the valley. A free-fare zone helps visitors tour the downtown area. Call the transit authority for information. An old-fashioned trolley, with pickup points at Trolley Square and Temple Square, circles downtown and major hotels.

Among the taxicab companies: **City Cab** (801–363–5550), **Ute Cab** (801–359–7788), and **Yellow Cab** (801–521–2100).

WHAT TO SEE AND DO

Historical Sites

The center of the city, and the heart of the Mormon religion, historic **Temple Square,** 50 West North Temple, encompasses ten acres enclosed within a 15-foot wall. Inside are the six-spired **Mormon Temple,** the **Tabernacle** (which is the concert hall), **Assembly Hall,** gardens, monuments, and information centers; (801) 240–2534. Several types of free guided tours are given throughout the day.

Completed in the 1890s, the Temple, constructed from granite and hardwood, took Mormon pioneers forty years to construct. It rises more than 200 feet above ground at its highest point. Only faithful Mormons may enter the Temple, but millions of visitors are allowed in the adjacent Tabernacle.

The **Tabernacle's** unusual design catches attention with its domed roof and red sandstone piers. The building's acoustics are amazing; kids, seated in the rear, "ooh" and "aah" when they hear the "cling" of a pin as it hits the floor near the front podium. Public organ recitals take place daily. The public may attend Thursday-evening rehearsals of the world famous **Mormon Tabernacle Choir** and their Sunday morning performances at 9:30 A.M. Visitors also are invited to the Tuesday- and Wednesday-evening miniconcerts by the Mormon Youth Choir and Symphony.

At the **Joseph Smith Memorial Building,** just east of Temple Square, 15 East South Temple (801–240–1266), sit down at one of the 150 family research stations and find out about your ancestors by accessing the computer base. It's open Monday through Saturday from 8:00 A.M. to 10:00 P.M. For more in-depth research, head a block west to the **Family History Museum,** 35 North West Temple; (801) 240–2331.

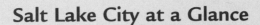

Salt Lake City at a Glance

- Kid-friendly cultural activities at a relaxed pace

- Historical sites, including the Mormon Tabernacle

- Family History Museum, the world's largest collection of genealogical informationl

- Swimming in the Great Salt Lake, skiing in nearby resorts

- Salt Lake Convention and Visitors Bureau, (801) 521–2686 or (800) 541–4955

It has the world's largest collection of genealogical information, including registers, passenger lists, local histories, and much more. You do not need to be a Mormon to access these records or find them useful. The archives cover information on many generations of individuals in more than fifty countries.

Beehive House, 67 East South Temple, a block east of Temple Square; (801) 240–2671. Here, city-founder Brigham Young made his home in the mid-1800s. See how pioneers conducted their daily lives through displays that include hand-stitched quilts and rugs, butter churns, and iceboxes. Free twenty-minute tours take place regularly throughout the day. The beehive, a symbol of the Mormon's work ethic, is on the building's small tower and is also part of the Utah state seal.

The **State Capitol,** North State Street and Capitol Hill (801–538–3000), is quite impressive, with an ornate interior and great views from Capitol Hill. Admission is free.

Museums

While not exactly teeming with museums, Salt Lake City has some kid-friendly places the whole family will enjoy.

At the **Hansen Planetarium,** 15 South State Street (801–538–2098), you can see not only stars, but also 3-D shows with laser beams that dance in sync with popular music, three floors of exhibits, including a rock brought back from the moon, and educational science presentations. Kids spin in the Gyro Rings, and make their hair stand on end by touching the Van de Graaf generator. In the domed theater, participate in the frequent star-identification lectures and shows that allow you to push buttons and decide which journey through the starry skies you embark upon.

Utah Museum of Fine Arts, 1530 East South Campus Drive; (801) 581-7332). This collection includes works by such masters as Peter Paul Rubens, as well as period furniture and seventeenth-century tapestries.

The Pioneer Memorial Museum, 300 North Main Street (801-538-1050), has an extensive collection of pioneer artifacts. Step back in time to prairie days as you peruse old-fashioned dolls, wooden clocks, and hand-stitched clothing of the period. In the Carriage House is the covered wagon used by Brigham Young to cross the plains as well as a mule-drawn streetcar. There's also a blacksmith shop.

The Children's Museum Utah, 840 North 300 West; (801) 328-3383. Here kids have a chance to play surgeon and implant an artificial heart, experience what it's like to get around in a wheelchair, and be a TV anchor or a 747 jet pilot. Regularly scheduled seminars and workshops explain things from how to make a clay pot to how a cow produces milk.

Utah Museum of Natural History, University of Utah campus, Wasatch Drive; (801) 581-4303. *Jurassic Park* fans will be impressed by the almost-complete dinosaur skeletons unearthed in the state. Other worthy collections, such as the Hall of Minerals, also intrigue kids.

Great Salt Lake

The 80-mile-long **Great Salt Lake** is quite marshy and somewhat sticky. Kids are fascinated by the tiny brine shrimp that live in the lake and the "thick" water, which has a salinity rate as high as 27 percent, though the salt concentration is not as high as it used to be. Floating in the lake is still a unique experience. Warning to kids: Don't get a mouthful of this water because it tastes terrible. And if you get water in your eyes, you'll wish you hadn't. The water stings. Be sure to wear eye goggles when swimming.

Salt Lake City's Trolley Square holds much in store for visitors.
(Courtesy Salt Lake City Convention and Visitor Bureau)

Catch a rare sight each November on the park's **Antelope Island.** Modern cowboys employ jeeps and helicopters to round up herds of bison. As the name implies, there are antelope and elk on the island, but these herds were introduced after the original animals died off.

One of the most accessible points on the lake is **Saltair Beach State Park,** 16 miles west of the city on I-80; (801) 250-4400. Here you'll find white-sand beaches, picnic areas, paddleboats, food concessions, and a parking lot. At the **Saltair Pavilion,** summer concerts take place.

Amusement Parks

Cool off in the huge freshwater pools and nineteen water slides of **Raging Waters,** 1700 South 1200 West; (801) 977-8300. Among the popular attractions is the H_2O Roller Coaster and the Acapulco Cliff Dive.

Lagoon Amusement Park and Pioneer Village, 17 miles north on

I-15 in Farmington (801-451-8000), is the largest amusement park between Kansas City and the West Coast. Get an all-day passport for access to 125 rides, ice show, pioneer village, music, games, food courts, and the water park. There's an adjacent campground and RV park.

The Utah Fun Dome, off 700 West; (801) 263-2987. This entertainment mall has an 80-foot bungee tower (but we don't recommend jumping; just watch if you must), bowling, video games, roller skating, and a food court with lots of choices.

Parks and Zoos

Hogle Zoo, 2600 Sunnyside Avenue (801-582-1631), is home to more than 1,200 furry, feathered, and scaly creatures from around the world. Those with special kid-appeal: The Great Apes exhibit, the African Savannah, and the tropical rain forest. Don't miss the hands-on Discovery Land, where kids experience what it feels like to be an animal, sliding down the middle of a hollow tree or "burrowing" under the earth. Tiny tots might like to touch the critters at the Small Wonders Barn.

Stroll through fifteen acres of gardens at the **Red Butte Garden and Arboretum,** the University of Utah, off South Campus Drive on the eastern edge of Fort Douglas; (801) 581-5322 or (801) 581-IRIS for recorded information. This is a pastoral, take-a-break place with duck ponds, water lilies, abundant floral displays, and rare plants. Free tours are offered, or guide yourself through the well-labeled gardens. Outside the main garden, another one hundred acres remain in their natural state, except for the easy hiking trails that are open to visitors. On summer Saturday mornings, a Canyon Kids Concert might include Scottish or Greek dancing and a demonstration of symphony instruments. Sunday-evening summer concerts bring top local and national talent. Entrance to the gardens, open year-round from 9:00 A.M. to sunset, is free.

Located on sixteen wooded acres in the southwest corner of Liberty Park is **Tracy Aviary,** 59 East 1300 South; (801) 596-8500. A leader in nature education and the oldest public aviary in the world, it features more than 1,000 bird species, from vultures to eagles to tropical varieties. Free bird shows held twice daily (except Monday) delight all. **Liberty Park,** 1000 South and East streets (801-972-7800), has kiddie rides and boat rides on a pond.

Place State Park, 2600 East Sunnyside Avenue (801-584-8391), below the mouth of Emigration Canyon on the east side of the city, marks the end of the Mormon Trail, used for twenty-two years by 68,000 pioneers migrating from Illinois. Facilities include a re-created pioneer town where costumed hosts greet visitors in buildings (some reconstructions, most relocated original dwellings) with authentic furnishings. At the visitor's center, a mural and audio presentations detail the migration of the Mormon pioneers. The park is also the site of **This is the Place Monument,** 2601 Sunnyside Avenue, commemorating the site where Brigham Young first explained, "This is the place," referring to a safe refuge for Mormons. From here, enjoy a breathtaking view of the valley.

Go country at **Wheeler Farm,** 6351 South Ninth East; (801) 264-2212. At this horse-powered seventy-five-acre dairy, visitors can help milk cows, feed chickens, and gather eggs each afternoon. Nature walks, fishing, wagon rides, farming and weaving demonstrations, songs, and pioneer stories are part of the fun. December brings Christmas on the Farm, with wagon rides, Santa, a nativity play, and homemade decorations.

Special Tours

Old Salty (801-359-8677 or 800-826-5844) is a two-hour summer tour of Salt Lake's main attractions aboard canopied open-air rail cars that leave from Temple Square. Just because of the vehicle, these tours have more kid appeal than the city bus tours provided by companies such as **Gray Line Tours,** 353 West 100 South; (801) 521-7060.

Theater, Music, and the Arts

Salt Lake City Visitors Bureau provides information on cultural attractions, or consult the morning *Salt Lake City Tribune* or evening *Deseret News.* The city hosts several theaters, including the **Pioneer Theater Company** at the University of Utah (801-581-6961 or 581-5682), a well-respected regional theater with equity actors in leading roles. **Salt Lake Repertory Theater** (City Rep), 148 South Main Street (801-532-6000), stages musical comedies. There is also the **Promised Valley Playhouse,** 132 South State Street; (801) 364-5696.

Ballet West (801-393-9318), **Ririe-Woodbury Modern Dance Company** (801-328-1062), and **University of Utah's Repertory**

Dance Theater (801–581–6702) all perform at the Capitol Theater, 50 West 200 South (801–534–4364), as does the **Utah Opera Company** (801–355–ARAS).

The **Utah Symphony** gives concerts year-round at Symphony Hall, 123 West South Temple; (802) 533–6407 or 533–5626.

Sports

Salt Lake Buzz minor league baseball team plays from mid-June to Labor Day at Franklin Quest Field, 77 West 1300 South; (801) 485–3800 (tickets: 325–BASE). The popular NBA **Utah Jazz** basketball games are held at Delta Center, 301 West South Temple (801–325–SEAT or 800–358–SEAT), where the **Grizzlies Hockey** games also take place.

Shopping

Trolley Square, 600 South 700 East, is a complex of fashionable shops, eateries, and theaters in buildings that used to house the town's electric trolleys. Just south of Temple Square, you'll find two enormous downtown shopping malls—**Crossroads Plaza,** 50 South Main (801–531–1799), with four floors of shops and restaurants; and **ZCMI Center Uptown,** 36 South State (801–321–8743), with two floors of stores, including the ZCMI Department Store and a food court.

Gardner Historic Village, 1095 West 7800 South, West Jordan; (801) 566–8903. The village features old-style shops and the 1877 Gardner Mill, converted into a country store. In the village, **Archibald's Restaurant** (801–566–6940), a former grain silo, serves up teriyaki chicken, fish, salads, and other dishes. The builder of the silo, Archibald Gardner, was a Mormon during the time when polygamy was still accepted. Each booth has a portrait portraying one of Gardner's eight wives, along with a brief history of her life.

SPECIAL EVENTS

Contact the Salt Lake Visitors Bureau for more information on the following events.

March: Music in the Mountains offers a variety of musical talents.

June: Utah Arts Festival with performing artists, crafts, children's art yard, and environmental exhibitions.

July: The Days of '47 Celebration honors the arrival of the pioneers in 1847, with square dancing, fireworks, rodeos, and one of the biggest parades in the U.S.A.

August: Belly Dancing Festival, with Middle Eastern food and festivities; Nature Fair at Tracy Aviary.

September: Utah State Fair; Greek Festival, three days of dancing, performances, and plenty of baklava.

November: Historic Temple Square Christmas Lighting Ceremony electrifies 250,000 lights that decorate the square; a Dickens Festival with Christmas shops and entertainment operates from late November to mid-December at the Utah State Fair Park; Buffalo Round-up, Antelope Island in Great Salt Lake.

December: Candlelight Christmas Tour, Pioneer Trail State Park, features caroling and costumed pioneer families who welcome visitors to their period-decorated homes and share stories and cookies.

WHERE TO STAY

The *Salt Lake Visitors Guide* has a comprehensive listing of lodgings, including several bed and breakfasts. Because tourism is Utah's number-one industry, expect a wide choice of reasonably priced accommodations. If you plan to visit in April or October, when Mormons from other regions congregate here, be sure to reserve well in advance.

Downtown: **Peery,** 110 West 300 South Street; (801)521–4300 or (800) 331–0073. The city's oldest lodging is an elegant, renovated seventy-seven-room hotel with in-room movies, free breakfast, free cribs, and two restaurants. **Red Lion Hotel,** 255 South West Temple (801–328–2000) is large and modern, with 495 rooms and nineteen suites (some with refrigerators), a pool, free airport shuttle, restaurant, and coffee shop. **The Quality Inn City Center,** 154 West Sixth Street (801–521–2930 or 800–4–CHOICE), offers well-priced, comfortable accommodations.

Elsewhere: **The Residence Inn by Marriott,** 765 East 400 South (801–532–5511 or 800–331–3131), is 8 blocks from downtown and 1 block from Trolley Square. Suites sleep up to six, and there's an outdoor pool, complimentary continental breakfast, and free airport shuttles. **Embassy Suites Hotel,** 600 South West Temple (801–359–7800 or

800–362–2779), offers another suite option for families, plus an indoor pool.

Budget accommodations are available at **Travelodge,** 524 South West Street (801–531–7100 or 800–255–3050), and the **Shilo Inn,** 206 South West Temple (801–521–9500 or 800–222–2244). Both are near numerous restaurants, and the Shilo Inn has a pool.

WHERE TO EAT

Salt Lake Visitor's Guide has a restaurant section with maps and descriptions. Here are some good family choices.

Ruth's Diner, 2100 Emigration Canyon Road; (801) 582–5807. About ten minutes from downtown, the diner is known for its great breakfasts (lunch and dinner also served) presented amidst 1940s decor. Right next door is the **Santa Fe Restaurant,** 2100 Emigration Canyon Road; (801–582–5888), which has a romantic Southwest lodge setting and serves a Sunday brunch buffet, plus daily lunch and dinner.

The Cafe Pierpont, 122 West Pierpont Avenue; (801) 364–1222. Located in a renovated school, this restaurant welcomes families with Mexican fajitas, enchiladas, fresh tortillas, and nachos. **Brackman Brothers Bagels,** 147 South Main (801–537–5033), the best place for New York-style bagels, also sells sandwiches and snacks.

Check out the elaborate setting, as well as the Mexican and American food at **Totem's Club and Cafe,** 538 South Redwood Road; (801) 975–0401. Wooden pillars, wagon wheels, spouting fountains, and live entertainment add to the western-lodge feel. Because the restaurant is a bit out of the way, many of the downtown hotels provide shuttle service.

DAY TRIPS

Salt Lake City is the gateway to nine ski resorts, all located within an hour of downtown. This is a skier's paradise, as the season runs from November until May or June. The UTA (801-BUS-INFO) provides daily buses to Alta, Brighton, Solitude, and Snowbird. (See the Wasatch chapter for additional information on Utah ski areas as well as the recreational opportunities of the **Wasatch National Forest.)**

In summer, these slopes offer families great hikes and a variety of recreational opportunities. Snowbird (801-521-6040) and Solitude (801-534-1400) offer weekend mountain-bike clinics for all levels. In addition, in summer take the aerial tram to the summit of Hidden Peak for splendid views of Heber Valley and the canyons of the Wasatch Mountains. Two trails lead back to the base, about a two-hour hike. Guided hiking tours can be arranged.

Kennecott's Bingham Canyon Mine, U-48, Copperton; (801) 322-7300. Located 22 miles west of Salt Lake City, the canyon is the largest man-made excavation on earth—2½ miles from rim to rim. A visitors center houses an exhibit explaining the pit's geology and open-pit copper-mining operations. A theater features a twelve-minute video on the mine. The center provides a bird's-eye view into the huge open pit where trucks and shovels appear to be toy sized. Open April to October, it's worth seeing.

Adventure

A number of Salt Lake outfitters offer rafting trips on the Green, Colorado, San Juan, and other rivers from May to September. Try **Holiday River Expeditions,** 544 East 3900 South (801-266-2087 or 800-624-6323), which also heads to the Yampa River in Dinosaur State Park. Another option is **Moki Mac River Expeditions,** 1821 East Fort Union Boulevard; (801) 268-6667 or (800) 284-7280. Minimum ages vary with the trips, which range from one day to two weeks.

Salt Lake City is a good starting point for heading to the state's five national parks, all a day's drive away: Arches and Canyonlands (see the Arches chapter), Capitol Reef, Bryce Canyon, and Zion. Contact the Utah Travel Council for more information.

Originally constructed for the U.S. Ski Team, the **Utah Winter Sports Park** has opened for public use—becoming the nation's only public ski-jumping facility. Certified instructors will teach thrill seekers aged three to eighty-three.

FOR MORE INFORMATION

Salt Lake Convention and Visitors Bureau, 180 South West Temple; (800) 541-4955 or (801) 521-2686; http://www.saltlake.org.

Utah State Travel Council, 300 North State Street, Capitol Hill Council Hall, Salt Lake City 84114; (801) 538-1030 or (800) 222-UTAH. **Visitor Information Center,** Temple Square at South Temple Street (801-240-2534), has information on the Mormon church.

Emergency Numbers
Ambulance, fire, police: 911

Hospitals: Holy Cross Hospital, 1045 East 100 South; (801) 350-4111.

Primary Children's Medical Center, 100 North Medical Drive; (801) 588-2233; main number 588-2000

Poison Control twenty-four-hour hotline: (801) 581-2151 or (800) 456-7707

A twenty-four-hour pharmacy is located inside the grocery store **Harmon's,** 3200 South 1300 East; (801) 487-5461.

WASATCH-CACHE NATIONAL FOREST AND SKI VACATIONS

The **Wasatch-Cache National Forest**—more than a million acres of lakes, forests, canyons, and mountains located north, east, and southeast of Salt Lake City—provides families with a variety of year-round vacation possibilities. The Wasatch Mountains, part of the Rocky Mountain range, are home to several ski areas, some considered among the best in the country, with slopes for every age and ability. Many ski resorts stay open all year, offering hiking, mountain biking, and other fair weather recreation.

GETTING THERE

Salt Lake International Airport, 776 North Terminal Drive (801–575–2400), is served by most major airlines. Car rentals are available. Salt Lake City's **Amtrak** is at 320 South Rio Grande; (800) USA-RAIL. **Greyhound** is at 160 West South Temple; (800) 231–2222.

GETTING AROUND

On a ski vacation, you may not need a car if you plan to spend most of your time at the resort or on the slopes. Shuttle buses transport skiers from the airport and downtown Salt Lake City to the ski resorts. Call **Canyon Transportation** at (801) 225–1841 or (800) 255–1841. **Lewis Brothers Stages** (801–359–8677 or 800–826–5849) operates buses from the airport and downtown, plus **Canyon Jumper** buses from Park City to Alta, Snowbird, Solitude, and Sundance. **Share-A-Ride Van Services** is available upon request from the airport or downtown to all locations along the Wasatch Front. There's also **Park City Transportation,** 1555 Lower Ironhorse Loop, Park City 84060; (801) 649-8567 or (800) 637-3803. **Utah Transit Authority's Ski Bus** (801-262-4636) operates to and from most downtown hotels, with several stops around the valley.

WHAT TO SEE AND DO

Skiing

The Wasatch Mountains, with an average of 460 inches of light and fluffy snow each year, feature some of the country's best skiing. The following ski areas, all located within an hour of downtown Salt Lake City, promise an exhilarating experience for the whole family. (Distances are from downtown Salt Lake City.)

Big Cottonwood Canyon. **Brighton** is 31 miles southeast on Star Route 152; (801) 532-4731 or 943-8309—recording—or (800) 873-5512. Known as "the place where Salt Lake learns to ski," this is a great place for beginners. KinderSki classes lasting one hour and forty five minutes are offered to ages four to six three times daily. Ages seven and up take group lessons and can opt for a new program that allows beginners to stay all day for additional instruction. Two children up to ten years ski free with one paying adult. A cafeteria and restaurant-pub are on premises.

Solitude Ski Resort is 23 miles southeast on Star Route 152; (801) 534-1400 or (800) 748-4754. Rated as one of the top forty North American ski resorts, Solitude has a Moonbeam Learning Center offering instruction and full-day supervised skiing for ages four to seven, and Quad Squad for ages eight to twelve. Solitude's Nordic Center offers 11 miles of groomed trails through the canyons, forests, and fields. Solitude not only permits snowboarding but also offers instruction for all ages.

Snowbird adjoins Alta on Utah 210; (801) 742-2222 for snow report, or (800) 453-3000 for reservations. Although Snowbird has been known for its steep and rugged trails, nearly half of the mountain is designated beginner and intermediate, which makes the resort

Wasatch-Cache at a Glance

- Lakes, forests, canyons, and mountains offer year-round family vacations

- 460 inches of light, fluffy snow each year

- Rails to Trails path for nature walks and biking in nearby Park City

- Wasatch-Cache National Forest main office, (801) 523–5030; Utah Country Travel Council, (800) 222–UTAH

appealing for families. Snowbird features child care for ages six weeks to three years, as well as Camp Snowbird, a state-licensed facility, for toilet-trained kids three to twelve. The camp provides day care, outdoor play, crafts, and movies, either hourly or by the half and full day. The Children's Ski School starts its Chickadee Program with ages three to four, who have ninety-minute lessons. Child/Teen Super Classes for ages five to fifteen are organized by age and ability. Half days are available for beginners; full days include lunch. Also offered for teens is Wings, a six-hour mountain adventure for skiers and boarders, which provides coaching in ski and riding techniques. Snowbird's Kids Ski Free Program allows up to two children (twelve and younger) to ski all chair trails free with each paying adult.

Little Cottonwood Canyon. **Alta** is 25 miles southeast on Utah 210; for lodging, call (801) 742–3333 or 942–0404. Known as a superb expert slope, Alta also has terrain for beginners and intermediates. **Alta Children's Center** (801–742–3042) provides child care for ages three months to twelve years. The Ski School (801–742–2600) features two-hour group lessons twice daily for ages four to twelve, as well as half- and full-day programs including lunch and day care, if needed.

Alta has more similarities to a European ski hideaway than it does to other local resorts. It also holds the honor of having North America's second-oldest lift service—in operation since 1939. With 500 inches of powder annually, this resort is heaven for many destination skiers. There are many expert trails and several blue and green trails for skiers of lesser ability. An advantage for families is that lift tickets are about half the price of those at nearby rivals Park City and Deer Valley. Alta's state-licensed Children's Center handles kids from three months to ten years. A variety of options for ages four through twelve is offered by the Children's Ski School. Private lessons are suggested for those under four. Mini-Adventures is a group program for four to six-year-olds that includes two hours of skiing, lunch, and an afternoon of day care. Mountain Explorers, which includes skiing and specialized instruction, is offered for children ages seven through twelve.

Provo Canyon

Laid back, environmentally conscious, and just plain beautiful, **Sundance,** RR3, Box A-1, Sundance, Utah 84604 (800–892–1600 or 801–225–4107), is on 5,000 acres of protected wilderness at the base of Utah's mighty 12,000-foot Mount Timpanogos. This relatively small resort offers 450 acres of downhill skiing and 14 kilometers of cross-country trails. About an hour from Salt Lake City's airport, this retreat was created by Robert Redford in 1969. The property features eighty-two cottages and ten mountain homes tastefully accented with Native American crafts and western hand-hewn furniture. Inquire about a supervised kids' ski school for ages six and older.

Park City. Located about forty-five minutes east of Salt Lake on I-80 and U-224, the former mining town of Park City is now home to trendy restaurants and boutiques. It also sports three resorts that offer something for every level of ability. Salt Lake City won its bid to host the 2002 Winter Olympic Games, and the area will be the site of a number of competitions, including bobsled/luge, ski jump, and freestyle events. A new $35-million Winter Sports Park in Bear Hollow, 4 miles west of Park City on Route 224 (801–649–5447), has four Nordic jumps, a freestyle jump, and a snowboard half-pipe, open to the public.

The Park City Ski Area, 1345 Lowell Avenue (Highway 224); (801) 649–8111, (800) 227–2745 for ski school reservations, or (800) 222–PARK. This is Utah's largest ski area, featuring eighty-three designated trails, 650 acres of open-bowl skiing, and a mixture of beginner,

The scenery in Wasatch National Forest's Logan Canyon is nothing short of spectacular.
(Courtesy Utah Travel Council)

intermediate, and expert terrain. Kids ages seven to thirteen take full- or half-day (afternoons only) group lessons, Kinderschule, for age three to six (toilet-trained), includes snack, lunch, and lessons. A Youth School provides group lessons tailored for kids seven to thirteen years old. Mountain Adventure and Mountain Experience classes draw many pre-teens and teens. Park City now opens trails to snowboarders. For après-ski fun the Resort Center has an outdoor ice skating rink.

Wolf Mountain, 4000 Park West Drive (Highway 92); (801) 649-5400. This resort starts them young with a Skiers in Diapers program for ages three or younger. Experienced instructors work with babies on skis—with bottles and stuffed animals along for the ride. Kids Central also offers half- and full-day state-licensed day care for eighteen months up to about twelve years. A variety of packages include day care and group lessons for various ages. The resort has a snowboard park and offers evening sleigh rides.

Deer Valley, 2250 Deer Valley Drive South, Highway 224; (801) 649-1000 or (800) 424-3337. Deer Valley's philosophy is to be a first-class resort attached to a ski mountain. Don't be surprised when someone removes your skis and luggage from your trunk, as ski valets are some of the upscale amenities and services that attract the rich and famous as well as real people. Olympians of several events will also head to the resort in 2002. Deer Valley is known mostly for its intermediate trails. The resort offers half- and full-day care to infants two to twenty-four months and children two to twelve years. Reservations are recommended for full days during holidays. Children's Ski School offers a variety of programs, including group lessons to kids in first grade through twelve years, a full-day Reindeer Club skiing program for ages four and one half through kindergarten, and a full-day Bambi Special for ages three to five with lessons, snow play, and indoor activities. A Kids' Club is available for children five through twelve during holiday and peak periods. For three hours every evening, kids enjoy games and movies after a "kid-approved" dinner. Teen Equipe workshops for ages thirteen to eighteen feature a full day of challenging skiing. Note that snowboarders are still banned from the resort's trails.

Nonskiing activities in Deer Valley include **The Norwegian School of Natural Life** (801–649–5322 or 800–649–5322), which guides snowshoe tours, and **Snowest Snowmobile Tours** (801–645–7669 or 800–499–7600, ext. 2001), which rents snowmobiles. Dogsledding, sleigh rides, and hot-air-balloon rides are available through **ABC Reservations Central** (801–649–ABCD, ext. 2223, or 800–820–ABCD, ext. 2223). The **Park City Silvermine Adventure** (801–649–8011) sends visitors 1,500 feet underground to explore mining tunnels. At aboveground hands-on exhibits, you can listen to old miners' tales, learn how to search for gems, and see the tools of the trade.

Summer Slopeside

Several of these area resorts also offer warm-weather pleasures.

Snowbird's aerial tram stops at the top of Hidden Peak, offering mountain bikers a spectacular 11,000-foot view of canyons and valleys. The tramway is open daily year-round except in May and from late October to late November. Snowbird's summer sizzles for kids with Camp Snowbird Day Camp for ages four to twelve, featuring activities such as panning for gold, hiking, tennis, nature studies, movies, and crafts. The camp operates weekdays from early June through the Friday before

Labor Day. Overnight camps and workshops for older kids, held on selected dates, include swimming, tram rides, nature studies, and more. For further information and reservations, call (801) 521-6040, ext. 5026.

At **Sundance** summer's bonuses include hillsides of wildflowers, horseback trail rides and day trips, guided hikes, hot-air-balloon flights, fly fishing forays, hayride dinners, waterskiing clinics, outdoor theater, free movies, and low lodging rates. The Sundance Kids Day Camp, complimentary from 9:00 A.M. to 4:00 P.M., Monday through Saturday for ages six to twelve, features Native American myths and crafts, hiking and horseback riding, and a theater workshop. Deluxe rooms come with a kitchenette, and summer rates include breakfast and the kids' program, which operates with a minimum of four children.

Strap your mountain bikes to the chairs of **Solitude's Moonbeam Lift** for the ride that leads to 25 miles of trails for all levels of cycling. Ed Chaunder, author of the book *Mountain Bike Techniques,* offers weekend clinics here and at Snowbird. Bike and accessory rentals are also available. Call Snowbird or Solitude for more information.

Deer Valley's Sterling Lift near Silver Lake Lodge carries mountain bikers up to thirteen trails totaling 20 miles for beginner to advanced rides (more terrain planned soon). Open Wednesday through Friday afternoons, with extended hours weekends and holidays, the lifts can be accessed with an all-day pass. Bike and helmet rentals are available at the Silver Lake ticket office at the base; call (801) 645-6733 for more information. Children must be accompanied by a paid adult eighteen or older. The resort also has a 4.8-mile primarily single-track course—the former site of World Cup mountain bike action. More summer fun: a swim and tennis club open Memorial through Labor days, where everyone is welcome; call (801) 649-1000 for information. Deer Valley hosts summer-long outdoor Utah Symphony Orchestra performances, as well as several pop music concerts and a Bluegrass Festival.

Guided meal or trail horseback rides provided by Park City Stables leave from both **Deer Valley** and **Park City** resorts. For reservations and information, call Rocky Mountain Recreation (801) 645-7256. (This company operates fishing and pack trips and winter snowmobile tours; minimum age is six for all trips.) The horseback rides are offered from Memorial Day through mid-October. **Park City**

Resort also has a pony corral for younger kids, an Alpine Slide (younger kids slide down with a parent), a Little Miners Theme Park, with scaled-down rides for ages six and under, and a terrific miniature golf course.

The town of **Park City** is part of a nationwide Rails to Trails program that converts abandoned rail lines for multi-use recreation. The town's 20-mile rail trail is great for biking as well as easy nature walks. To find out more about bike rentals from local shops and hotels, or to get a free *Park City Bike Guide,* call the Chamber Bureau at (801) 649–6100 or (800) 453–1360.

ABC Reservations Central, Park City (801–649–2223 or 800–523–0666), books a number of area adventures including hot air ballooning, historic tours, glider flights, and backcountry snowmobile tours; they also book lodging and transportation.

Aside from ski resort trials, the Wasatch Mountains have fat-tire trails, some as close as ten minutes from Salt Lake. The Wasatch Crest Trail, for instance, branches off Millcreek Canyon (3800 South and Wasatch Boulevard). This experts-only challenging trail features spectacular alpine views, steep climbs, stream crossings, and rocky stretches. Call the Salt Lake Ranger District, 6944 South 3000 East (801–943–1794) for maps and tips if planning a fat-tire trek through the Wasatch.

Backcountry Adventures

Wasatch-Cache National Forest also offers unlimited opportunities for family excursions. A great deal of planning should go into a backcountry outing. Even the forests get crowded on holidays and in summer. Wasatch-Cache is one of the country's most heavily used forests for recreation. To avoid crowds and temperature extremes, visit in autumn and spring. Contact a National Forest Service Office (see For More Information) for specific advice and information.

Logan District

Logan, home of Utah State University and about 90 miles north of Salt Lake, is just southwest of **Logan Canyon Highway,** U.S. 89, a National Scenic Byway, most of it traveling primarily through the forest's Logan Ranger District. The byway, just over 39 miles long, runs from the mouth of Logan Canyon to Bear Lake.

This scenic byway tour starts at the **Logan District Ranger Office,** where you'll find information, rest rooms, picnic tables, and pleasant canyon views. Some highlight of the drive include the following.

Logan Wind Cave, 5 miles from Ranger Office, can be found high above Logan Canyon. A 1.5-mile trail, moderately difficult for kids, leads to the cave. Spring visitors are treated to clusters of blooming wildflowers, while fall brings spectacular autumn foliage. The cave is part of the rock formation you'll pass midway up the canyon wall, called the China Wall. *Best Hikes with Children in Utah* by Maureen Keilty (The Mountaineers) details this and other hikes in the Wasatch National Forest. On this hike Keilty advises that you watch out for rattlers.

At **Wood Camp Campground** and **Jardine Juniper Trail,** 10.3 miles from Lady Bird, campers find only seven individual family units with no water. The big attraction here is west of the campground, where the Jardine Juniper trailhead is located. This moderately strenuous and long (5 miles one-way) trail climbs more than 2,000 vertical feet through glacier-carved moraines and green forests. With older, hardy kids, it's worth the hike to the end to see the tree thought to be more than 2,000 years old—and one of the largest living junipers anywhere.

Accessed by a paved but winding 7-mile road that climbs 2,300 feet to the lake, at 8,100 feet elevation, is a popular thirty-nine-unit campground, **Tony Grove Lake Area,** 19.2 miles from the Ranger Office, usually open July 4 to October 1. From here try a self-guided nature trail around the perimeter of the lake, which passes ancient glacial deposits and fields of wildflowers. Spruce and fir trees stand in the wetter areas of the shore and spread into a thick forest beyond. See fauna such as mountain chickadees, ground squirrels, yellow-bellied sapsuckers, and muskrats. As for flora, the lake is home to gooseberry shrubs, pink coral bells, tangled willows, and mountain sunflowers.

Beaver Mountain Ski Road Junction, 24.2 miles from the Ranger Office, leads to the ski resort (801-753-0921), via Road 243. From late November to mid-April, the resort has three chair lifts and a day lodge. The road leads to camping spots in the Sink Hollow and Beaver Creek areas.

The Limber Pine Nature Trail, 30.0 miles from LB, is an excellent spot for a family hike. The 1¼-mile loop, which starts from a picnic spot, is easy for kids and takes about an hour to complete. A guide available at the trailhead points out the geological history and different wildlife species. You'll hear (and maybe even see) the nuthatches, woodpeckers, and mountain chickadees that fly through the treetops, and you'll witness the quaking aspen trees, bent over in arches by heavy snows.

The scenic byway ends at **Bear Lake,** 20 miles long and from 4 to 8 miles wide, one of the state's most popular spots for water recreation. Half of the lake is in Utah, the other half in Idaho. Year-round fishing from shore is excellent on the east side. (Legend has it that the lake is home to the mythological Bear Lake Monster.) Raspberries grow wild all around the lake, and several small stands sell raspberry milk shakes.

Bear Lake State Park (801-946-3346), the final stop, comprises three state-operated facilities: **Bear Lake Marina,** 2 miles north of Garden City; **Rendezvous Beach,** which has a sandy beach and is 2 miles west of Laketown; and **Eastside,** 20 miles north of Laketown.

For a brochure detailing things to see and do on this scenic byway, contact Logan Ranger District, 860 North 1200 East, Logan, Utah 84321; (801) 755-3620. For more information you can also contact Bridgerland Travel Region, 160 North Main, Logan; (801) 752-2161 or (800) 882-4433. More than forty hiking trails are listed in the book *Cache Trails,* available at area sporting-good stores.

The Ogden District

A scenic byway, U-39, starts in **Ogden,** some 30 miles north of Salt Lake, and stretches for 44 miles through the narrow **Ogden Canyon.** The road climbs through the Wasatch-Cache National Forest to some of northern Utah's most breathtaking vistas. Along the way you may catch glimpses of wildlife such as mule deer, ground squirrels, and marmots. If you venture onto back roads that lead away from the traveled route, you find breathtaking overlooks, picnic areas, fishing, and campgrounds.

The byway also leads to a highlight of this district, the **Pineview Reservoir,** a popular summer recreation area with two designated swim areas with lifeguards, two campgrounds, two boat ramps, and two trailheads, including the 22-mile **Skyline Trail** (also open to mountain and motor bikes). This is a part of the **Great Western Trail,** which, once completed, will stretch from Canada to Mexico, incorporating various hiking, biking, horseback, and vehicle trails.

This region features twelve developed campgrounds. For more on this area, contact the **Union Station Information Center,** 2501 Wall Avenue, Ogden; (801) 625-5306/TDD (801) 625-5644. It has detailed recreation maps showing roads, trails, and campgrounds. Information is also available from Ogden Ranger District, 507 Twenty-fifth Street, Ogden, Utah 84401; (801) 625-5112.

Wasatch Mountain State Park

About 45 miles east of Salt Lake City, 2 miles northwest of Midway, and 22 miles from Park City, Wasatch Mountain State Park is a popular destination; (801) 654-1791. It features a twenty-seven-hole golf course, more than 135 camping/picnicking areas, modern rest rooms, hot showers, utility hookups, and plenty of recreation areas. Nature trails are used by cross-country skiers and snowmobilers (rentals available in the park) in the winter, and by hikers in the summer. This is Utah's most developed state park, and, as you might expect, summers are crowded—and hot.

SPECIAL EVENTS

See the Salt Lake City chapter for more festivities. For more information on the following, contact one of the visitor's bureaus listed under For More Information, or the individual ski area.

January: Treats await as you ski from station to station at Solitude Ski Resort's Chocolate Lover's Tour and Chocolate Tasting Extravaganza.

March: Winterfest Snow Sculpture; Music in the Mountains, both in Park City.

April: Easter Egg Hunt, Park City Ski Area.

June: Savour the Summit, Park City's food festival, features samples from more than thirty area restaurants.

July: The nation's best cowboys take part in the Oakley Rodeo.

August: Park City Art Festival; Summit County Fair, Coalville Fair Grounds.

September: Autumn Aloft, thirty hot air balloons ascend from Park City: Miner's Day Celebration, with parade down Main Street, fun, and games, Park City.

October: Oktoberfest at Snowbird Mountain features polka dancing, German beer, and live entertainers.

November: America's Opening, Main Street, Park City, kicks off ski season with Men's World Cup Ski Races, fireworks, on-snow parades, music, food, and more.

December: On Christmas and New Year's eves, many ski resorts have visits from Santa complete with on-slope parades and more.

WHERE TO STAY

The Utah Travel Guide, published by the Utah Travel Council, is a helpful reference, which includes lodging and other state information.

A wide variety of accommodations exist in and around the **Salt Lake City** and **Park City** areas. Most of the major ski resorts mentioned previously offer their own lodging and/or chalet arrangements; ask for reservations when you call. *The Utah Winter Vacation Planner,* available from the **Utah Travel Council,** lists ski-area lodging. There are several reservation services that book entire packages, including **Park City Ski Holidays** (801–649–0493 or 800–222–PARK), representing more than 3,000 units in town including private homes and condos.

Moderately priced family lodging is available in Park City. Try **Best Western Landmark Inn,** 6560 North Landmark Drive; (801) 649–7300 or (800) 548–8824. It features rooms with refrigerators, a twenty-four-hour restaurant, free shuttle to the slopes, and a convenient location just minutes from the mountain and next to a factory mall. You will find moderate rates at the **Chamonix Lodge,** 1450 Empire, only 150 yards from Park City Ski Area; (801) 649–8443 or (800) 443–8630. Rooms have small refrigerators and coffee makers. Third and fourth persons in room cost an additional $10 each. The **Edelweiss Haus,** 1482 Empire Avenue (801–649–9342 or 800–438–3855), offers moderate motel-style rooms, some of which are suites with kitchenettes.

The ten-room, renovated, 1893 former miners' boardinghouse, the **Old Miners' Lodge,** 615 Woodside Avenue (801–645–8068 or 800–648–8068), is fun. Families are welcome, and cribs are $5.00 extra. The **Prospector Square Hotel,** 2200 Sidewinder Drive (801–649–7100 or 800–453–3812), offers one- and two-bedroom condominiums, an indoor pool, and free shuttle service to the ski area. See the Salt Lake City chapter for accommodations in the city.

The Cliff Lodge is Snowbird's flagship property. This upscale ski-in/ski-out hotel features a child-care facility, a spa with a rooftop pool, and a wide range of pampering treatments. Three condominium properties—**The Lodge at Snowbird, The Inn,** and the **Iron Blossom Lodge**—let efficiencies and one-bedroom units with a loft, all of which have kitchenettes. Some even have fireplaces. Access to swimming pools, saunas, and exercise facilities is included in the room rates. Call (800) 453-3000.

Alta Lodge (801-742-3333) has an easygoing atmosphere. Its fifty-seven rooms are dorm-style, with bathroom-in-the hall accommodations. Others have fireplaces and glass walls that overlook the canyon. Meals are a great opportunity to meet other guests, as tables seat eight to ten. **Blackjack Condominiums** (800-343-0347), which provides transportation to Alta and Snowbird, lets studio and one-bedroom condos.

Near Deer Valley, **Stein Eriksen Lodge** (801-534-0563) is a splurge. Before dismissing this option based on its price, consider that this four-star hotel is consistently rated among the top ski lodges in the United States.

Shadow Ridge Resort Hotel and Conference Center (800-451-3031) has hotel rooms and one- to three-bedroom condos located at the base of Park City. A shuttle bus is run to Deer Valley and Park City from the **Radisson Inn Park City** (800-333-3333). The hotel also features a kids-eat-free program for those twelve and under, and an indoor-outdoor pool. **Marriott's Summit Watch Resort** (800-210-8200), just off Main Street, Park City, offers two-bedroom villas with kitchens.

For lodging in the **Ogden area,** contact the **Ogden/Weber Convention and Visitors Bureau,** 2501 Wall Avenue, Ogden; (801) 225-8824 or (800) ALL-UTAH. For the Logan area, contact **Cache Chamber of Commerce,** 160 North Main; (801) 752-2161 or (800) 657-5353.

Some of the **National Forest** campgrounds can be reserved by calling (800) 280-2267/TDD (800) 879-4496. Other sites book on a first-come basis. The most popular (read "crowded") camping areas are in Ogden and near Salt Lake City. A few choices: **Perception Park,** on the shore of the Ogden River, features about fifty sites, lots of nature trails, and good fishing. It's also one of the few campgrounds equipped with flushing toilets, and it's handicapped accessible. **The Spruces,** in the mountains east of Salt Lake City off I-215, is an expansive camping area with rest rooms.

WHERE TO EAT

In **Logan,** typical American-style eats are served up at the **Blue Bird Cafe,** 19 North Main; (801) 752-3155. Kids love the almost 20-foot-long counter where the cafe's famous chocolates are displayed.

People come from miles around to the town of **Perry,** about 20 miles north of Ogden, to eat steak, prime ribs, BBQ, and other tasty dishes at the five-star **Maddox Ranch House Restaurant,** 1980 South Highway 89; (801) 723-8545 or (800) 544-5474.

In Odgen, dinner (steak, shrimp, prime ribs) is an experience at the **Prairie Schooner,** 445 Park Boulevard; (801) 392-2712. Eat inside a covered wagon, with a campfire and howling coyote sounds.

Enjoy a local specialty, freshly harvested peach milk shakes, at the **Peach City Drive-In,** 306 North Main; (801) 723-3923. Located north of Ogden in **Brigham City,** this eatery also offers chicken baskets, steak sandwiches, and cheeseburgers.

Park City has more than fifty restaurants serving everything from continental cuisine to hearty western fare. **Baja Cantina** (801-649-BAJA) has a children's menu and perennial favorites such as tacos and burritos. **Ziggy's** features a moderately priced pizza, pasta, sandwiches, and calzones. For award-winning Southwestern fare, head to the **Barking Frog Grill,** Main Street; (801-649-6222).

Around Snowbird, the **Forklift** (801-742-2222, ext. 4100) serves breakfast and lunch. **Pier 49 San Francisco Sourdough Pizza** bakes gourmet pizza on a sourdough crust. Less fancy varieties are available for finicky eaters. Contact the **Chamber/Bureau** at (801) 649-6100 or (800) 453-1360 for dining information.

DAY TRIPS

The booklet *Utah's Scenic Byways and Backways* contains descriptions of popular touring routes in the state, including several in and around the Wasatch area. Obtain the guide from the chamber of commerce and regional travel offices listed under For More Information. The drives last from forty-five minutes to several hours, and the routes are also denoted by rainbow-colored signs throughout the state. Included is one of the most popular mountain routes in the state, **the Mirror Lake Scenic Byway,** U-150 from Kamas through the Wasatch-Cache National Forest to the Utah/Wyoming border. Scenic viewpoints, picnic areas, lakes, meadows, and rugged peaks and cliffs can be accessed from this high mount byway, much of which parallels the Provo River.

For more day trip ideas, see the chapters on Arches and Canyonlands, near Moab, and Salt Lake City.

FOR MORE INFORMATION

Visitor Information: **Salt Lake Convention and Visitors Bureau,** 180 South West Temple; (801) 521-2868. **Utah Travel Council,** 300 North State Street, Capitol Hill Council Hall, Salt Lake City 84114; (801) 538-1030. **The Utah County Travel Council,** 51 South University, Suite 111; (801) 370-8393 or (800) 222-UTAH. The Utah Travel Guide Internet site is http://www.netpub.com/utah/w. For a copy of the *Ski Utah Winter Vacation Planner,* contact **Ski Utah,** 150 West 500 South, Salt Lake City, Utah 84101; (800) SKI-UTAH or http://www.skiutah.com.

Forest Service and Ranger Districts: The USDA Forest Service (800-322-4100; TDD 801-524-6762) distributes a pamphlet called *Leave No Trace! An Outdoor Ethic,* which provides helpful advice and rules of the forest. The main office of the **Wasatch-Cache National Forest** is located at 8226 Federal Building, 125 South State, Room 8103, Salt Lake City 84138; (801) 523-5030. You may also contact individual district offices, some of them listed above.

Contact the **Wasatch-Cache National Forest's** main office for information on handicapped-accessible campgrounds and trails. **The Ogden Ranger District** (801-625-5112), for one, has an accessibility program that encourages the disabled to be involved in an outdoor experience.

Emergency Numbers

Ambulance, police, fire: 911

Hospitals: Salt Lake City—**Holy Cross Hospital,** 1045 East 100 South (801-350-4111); **Primary Children's Medical Center,** 100 North Medical Drive (801-588-2000). Ogden—**McKay-Dee Hospital,** 3939 Harrison Boulevard; (801) 627-2800. Park City—**Park City Family Health and Emergency Center,** 1665 Bonanza Drive; (801) 649-7640. Logan—**Logan Regional Hospital,** 1400 North 500 East; (801) 752-2050.

Poison Control twenty-four-hour hotline: (800) 456-7707 or (801) 581-2151

Smith's has twenty-four-hour pharmacies in locations including 442 North 175 East in Logan (801-753-6570) and 4275 Harrison Boulevard in Ogden (801-479-0700). In Park City a twenty-four-hour pharmacy is located inside **Albertson's Food Store,** 1800 Park Avenue; (801) 649-6134. In Salt Lake there's a pharmacy open until midnight inside a grocery store, **Harmon's,** 3200 South 1300 East; (801) 487-5461.

BOISE

Families feel welcome in Boise, Idaho, a small, friendly metropolis in the foothills of the Rocky Mountains. Boise, the state's capital and largest city, appears like a green oasis in the middle of the surrounding brown hills, earning it the nickname the City of Trees. The Boise River cuts through the center of town, and the Greenbelt bicycle and pedestrian path that follows the river offers year-round recreation. Boise also is a convenient gateway to fun and adventure: An abundance of whitewater rivers, mountain slopes and lakes, forest trails, and dramatic desert landscapes offer families a variety of ways to enjoy the great outdoors.

GETTING THERE

Boise Municipal Airport (208–383–3110), 8 mile southwest of downtown off I-84, is served by several airlines, including **Delta, Northwest, Horizon, Alaska, Sky West,** and **United.** Car rentals are available at the terminal.

Amtrak (800–USA–RAIL) is at 2601 Eastover Terrace. For bus transportation, **Greyhound's** station is at 1212 West Bannock Street; (208) 343–3681 or (800) 231–2222. By car, Boise is reached by I-84.

GETTING AROUND

A car is really a necessity to explore Boise and the surrounding area. **Boise Urban Stages** (208–336–1010) offers public bus transportation around town, with schedules available at City Hall or by calling the company.

Spring trough fall, the **Boise Tour Train,** a narrated tour aboard a replica of an 1890s locomotive, departs from Tour Train depot in **Julia Davis Park** between Myrtle Street and the Boise River (208–342–4796 or 800–999–5993) and travels to the city's historical sights.

WHAT TO SEE AND DO

Museums

Julia Davis Park (208-384-4240), in the heart of town between Myrtle Street and the Boise river, contains museums, the zoo, botanical gardens, and more (see Parks, Zoos, and Gardens).

Idaho Historical Museum, 610 Julia Davis Drive; (208) 334-2120. Two floors of exhibits reveal the colorful history of Idaho and the Pacific Northwest. Among the reconstructed interiors are a Chinese apothecary shop, an Old West saloon, a blacksmith forge, and a vintage kitchen. Among the period pieces on display are beaded moccasins and Native American clothing.

The ten galleries of the **Boise Art Museum,** 670 Julia Davis Drive (208-345-8330), feature works by notable artists. Permanent exhibits revolve around an extensive collection of American Realist art on loan from Sun Valley collector Glenn C. Janss. Kids should have no trouble picking out things they like from the watercolors, drawings, and other media portraying animals, urban scenes, flowers, and portraits by such artists as Georgia O'Keeffe, Red Grooms, and Edward Hopper. Because the collection is so large, exhibits change seasonally. Sign up for one of the twice-weekly tours or browse on your own. Be sure to visit the Museum Store, which has a good selection of jewelry and books.

Visit the **Discovery Center,** 131 Myrtle Street (208-343-9895), on the end of the park. Here you can play with magnetic sand, see your shadow on the wall, and create giant bubbles. These are some of the more than one-hundred hands-on exhibits that teach kids about science. An echo tube and after image, for example, explain about delayed perception. A sun tracker brings a beam of sunlight into the museum for solar experiments.

Elsewhere in town is **The Basque Museum,** 607 and 611 Grove Street (208-343-2671), at the Cyrus Jacobs-Uberuaga House (the oldest brick house in Boise, built in 1864). The building—the only Basque museum in the U.S.A.—served as a boardinghouse for newly arrived immigrants from northern Spain during the 1900s who came to central Idaho's rocky terrain to work as sheepherders. Black-and-white photographs collected from local families and original furniture create

Boise at a Glance

- A small, friendly metropolis offering year-round recreation

- Old Idaho Territorial Penitentiary, an Old West jail

- Incubated eggs hatch into peregrine falcons at the World Center for Birds of Prey

- Skiing at Sun Valley, Ketchum, and other resorts

- Boise Convention and Visitors Bureau, (208) 344-7777 or (800) 635-5240

the era, as do the traditional dance nights held throughout the year and upon request.

The State Capitol, Jefferson Street and Capitol Boulevard (208–334-2470), constructed of Idaho sandstone and marble from Vermont, Alaska, and Georgia, offers free self-guided tours and exhibits on gems and timber products. Several statues may interest kids: a replica of the *Winged Victory of Samothrace,* a gift from Paris; *The Patriot,* a tribute to a 1972 disaster in which many miners died; and a dignified commemorative depicting George Washington atop a horse.

The **Old Idaho Territorial Penitentiary** is at 2445 Old Penitentiary Road (1½ miles east on Warm Springs Avenue, then left); (208) 334-2844. The jail grew from a single-cell building in 1870 into an Old West complex that served as a regional prison until 1973. A tour of the museum reveals portraits of famous inmates and lawmen, as well as captured contraband weapons and artifacts. An eighteen-minute slide show tells about this penitentiary's colorful past. Inside the compound, view the effects of a riot, see several cell houses, a punishment area nicknamed Siberia, the Women's Ward, Death Row, and the Gallows. A former dormitory houses several history of electricity hands-on exhibits. A former prison shirt factory now sports a transportation display of a 1903 steam fire pumper, buggies, and other vehicles.

Parks, Zoos, and Gardens

Along with museums, **Julia Davis Park,** spanning more than ninety acres, features playgrounds, tennis courts, boat rentals, picnic facilities, a rose garden, free summer entertainment at the band shell, and kid-pleasing attractions.

Visit **Zoo Boise,** 355 North Julia Davis Drive; (208) 384-4260. It's noted for the Northwest's largest display of birds of prey, such as bald and golden eagles and hawks. Idaho's native elk, deer, and bighorn sheep delight kids, as does the petting zoo. The zoo is only one of five in North America to feature a moose habitat.

Ever expanding, the **Idaho Botanical Garden,** 2355 Penitentiary Road (208-343-8649), is a living museum of plants. Among ten theme gardens: the children's, Basque, Chinese and meditation, and native plant gardens.

Boise's **Greenbelt** links a network of five parks along the Boise River. **Ann Morrison Park,** between Americana Boulevard and the river, is the city's largest, with 40 miles of trails. The park's 153 acres include playgrounds, picnic areas, and tennis courts. You can rent skates and bicycles at Shoreline Park, on the west end. For further information on the city's parks, call the Park System (208-384-4240).

Morrison-Knudsen Nature Center (208-334-2225), a 4½-acre habitat between Warm Springs Avenue and the river, has outdoor viewing windows where visitors observe different facets of the underwater life of a mountain stream. An interpretive center features hands-on exhibits revolving around wildlife and the flow of the river. The facility has an indoor aquarium, an outdoor lagoon with sturgeon, bass, and rainbow trout, an outdoor nesting ground for ducks and geese, and a beaver pond.

The **World Center for Birds of Prey** is off I-84 on South Cole Road, on the outskirts of town; (208) 362-8687. This endangered species center has an interpretive center with a number of hands-on activities. At the Tropical Raptor Building, see such birds as the giant harpy eagle, whose wing span nears 7 feet. In spring, watch, via one-way mirrors, as incubated eggs hatch into young peregrine falcons. Enrap-

Boise's famous family-oriented festivals hold something special in store for everyone.
(Courtesy Boise Convention & Visitors Bureau)

tured and want more? Visit the **Prey National Conservation Area,** another raptor center; (208-384-3300). It's one hour from Boise near San Falls Dam off Highway 69, south of Kuna. This area boasts the world's largest concentration of nesting eagles, hawks, and prairie falcon. Access to the area is gained via some fairly rough gravel roads. Although you can see the area on your own, the best way to tour is via guided boat trips (see Outfitters).

Adventures

Beyond Boise, there's the great outdoors: snow-packed mountains, raging rivers, lush forests, and rugged canyons. Some of the following make perfect day trips, while others, farther afield, are suitable for a weekend (or longer) jaunt.

Mountain Pleasures

Bogus Basin, 2405 Bogus Basin Road, 16 miles north; (208) 332-5100 or (800) 367-4397. Sister mountains, Deer Point and Shafer

Butte, offer 2,000 skiable acres, eight chair lifts, and extensive night skiing. Day care is available for infants and up (no strict age limit). There are Mogul Mouse ski lesson for ages three to five, Mogul Mites for ages six to eight, and Junior Beginners for ages eight and up. Snowboarding is available for ages eight and older. Nordic skiing bounds along trails that glide through some breathtaking scenery.

Sun Valley, a mile north of Ketchum on Sun Valley Road, is a year-round resort 154 miles (about three hours) northeast of Boise (or thirty minutes by air from Boise to Hailey, 12 miles south of the resort). In winter, Bald Mountain's 3,400-foot vertical drop is inviting to experts, while kids and beginners favor Dollar/Elkhorn, where the Sun Valley Ski School is located. Kids seventeen and under (one per parent) ski free during selected periods. Non-Alpine devotees enjoy cross-country skiing, snowboarding, and sleigh rides, as well as ice skating. When the snow melts, the area offers tennis, golf, hiking, biking, and white-water rafting. Accommodations range from condos to hotels to resorts to bed-and-breakfast cabins.

The **Elkhorn Youth Activities Center,** P.O. Box 6009, Sun Valley 83353 (208) 622-4511, ext. 1014), provides both full- and half-day child care for ages six months to three years, as well as ages three to ten. It may also be possible to arrange for nighttime babysitting. The **Sun Valley Resort Playschool,** Sun Valley Mall behind the Post Office (208-622-2133), offers full-day child care for ages six months to six years. Check with the care givers about after-hours babysitting.

Call the **Sun Valley-Ketchum Chamber Central Reservations** for lodging and activities throughout the area; (208) 726-3423 or (800) 634-3347.

Summer visitors to Sun Valley often head 7 miles north to the **Sawtooth National Recreation Area** in the state's Central Rockies, for the alpine lakes, dense forests, and nearly 600 campsites. If you come from Boise, access the area via the Ponderosa Scenic Byway, State Highway 21. At mile #125, stop to see the spectacular views of Stanley Lake Overlook. You'll soon come to the point where this scenic highway converges with State Highway 75 (Sawtooth Scenic Byway) at the town of **Stanley,** headquarters for several Salmon River outfitters. If you stop at the **Stanley Ranger Station** (208-774-3681), pick up a cassette and player that tells you about the sites as you travel south. The tape and recorder may be returned at the **Sawtooth Visitor Information Centre** (208-726-8291), just north of Ketchum and Sun Valley on Highway 75 (or pick up the tape at Sawtooth and drop it off at Stanley if you're coming from Sun Valley). The Visitor Center has year-round information on camping, hiking, biking, and campfire programs.

Closer to Boise, the verdant forests surrounding the city of **Cascade** and the **Payette River,** 1½ hours north of Boise via Highway 55 (Payette River Scenic Route), offer more recreation. Outfitters take you down three forks of the Payette River, a popular white-water destination (see Outfitters), on half-, full-, or three-day outings.

Desert Dunes

At **Bruneau Dunes State Park,** one hour south of Boise on Highway 51 (208-366-7919), you'll find North America's tallest dune, 470 feet. A 5-mile, self-guided nature trail explains the desert habitat. Stroll in the early morning or late evening, the best times for observing the desert wildlife, and you might see a rabbit dart by or an eagle soar. Get your camera ready; sunrises and sunsets are spectacular. There's a campground and environmental education center with area wildlife and natural history displays.

Hell's Canyon

In a class by itself, **Hell's Canyon National Recreation Area** encompasses more than 650,000 acres. Straddling the Snake River in Idaho and Oregon (two to three hours north of Boise), Hell's Canyon features rugged outdoor river country. The gorge is more than a mile deep in some locations, making it the deepest river gorge on the continent. This is an area of desert slopes, rugged mountain peaks, cool lakes, and clean streams. Cougars, bobcats, elk, deer, mountain goats, and bighorn sheep live within the forests and ridges. The more than 1,000 miles of trails range from easy to difficult, though access roads to trailheads are often narrow, steep, and rocky.

Most people concur that **Heavens Gates Overlook** offers the best view into the canyon from Idaho. To reach this spot, drive a half-day from the south end of Riggins via an extremely steep and winding gravel road, Forest Road 517. A strenuous ½-mile trail, open from July to September, provides an access to the overlook. A better and easier way to explore the canyon is via an aluminum jet boat or a float trip. More than thirty outfitters offer various trips (see Outfitters), many of them center on a 1-mile stretch in Riggins, located in a steep canyon at the confluence of the Salmon and Little Salmon rivers. For more information, contact the **Hells Canyon National Recreation Area,** P.O. Box 832, Riggins 83549; (208) 628-3916.

Outfitters

Idaho has literally hundreds of outfitters that offer adventurous excursions, some of them offering combination trips. For a free directory, contact the **Outfitters and Guides Association,** P.O. Box 95, Boise, Idaho 83701 (208-342-1438) or **Idaho Tourism** (800) VISI-TID. Here's a sampling:

Boise Tours, P.O. Box 5723, Boise; (208) 342-4796 or (800) 999-5993. They offer jet boat trips to Hell's Canyon and overland trips to Prey National Conservation Area.

Two companies that cover Idaho rivers offer special family expeditions along the Lower Salmon: **River Odysseys West (ROW),** P.O. Box 579, Coeur d'Alene (800-451-6034), and **Outdoor Adventure River Specialists (OARS),** P.O. Box 67, Angels Camp, California (800-346-6277). Programs are flexible and allow ample time for exploring such shore findings as caves, mines, and waterfalls. Lower Salmon runs glide by otters, eagles, and bighorn sheep. Camp out on sandy beaches where kids can wade in shallow water. Age limits vary, though generally the trips are best with ages five and older.

Rocky Mountain River Tours, Dave and Sheila Mills, P.O. Box 2552, Boise, 83701; (208) 345-2400; in summer (208) 756-4808. They offer four-, five-, and six-day white-water raft trips on the Middle Fork of the Salmon River. This river cuts through scenic and rugged areas. The Mills welcome families. When the water is high in early season, the trips are better suited to experienced rafters and teens.

Another family-operated outfitter is **Wilderness River Outfitters,** P.O. Box 871, Salmon; (208) 756-3959. In addition to guiding trips down the Salmon, Owyhee, and Bruneau rivers, they offer biking and backpacking tours.

Theater, Music, and the Arts

In season, **Ballet Idaho** (208-343-0556) performs at the Morrison Center of Boise State University (BSU), 1901 University Drive. Look for classic holiday performances such as *The Nutcracker*. **The Boise Philharmonic** (208-344-7849) also plays at the Morrison Center, sometimes accompanied by **Boise Master Chorale** (208-344-7901), which also presents a series of their own concerts. **The Idaho Shakespeare Festival** performs a full summer season, including one contemporary play, in an open-air amphitheater along the Boise River at ParkCenter; call (208) 336-9221 for tickets and information. The Oinkari Basque Dancers, an internationally known troupe, perform several times during the year in celebration of their culture.

Sports

Boise Hawks semiprofessional baseball team plays mid-June through early September at Memorial Stadium, 5600 Glenwood, at the edge of the Fairgrounds; (208) 322-5020.

Shopping

Boise Towne Square Mall, on the west edge of the city, I-84 at Franklin and Cole roads (208-378-4400), has more than 185 specialty shops, larger stores such as J.C. Penney and Sears, plus a fast-food court. At **Made in Idaho USA** (208-378-1188), at the mall, browse a majority of products made or grown in Idaho. Downtown shops include **Toycrafters World,** 276 North Eighth Street (208-345-2971), featuring handcrafted toys from around the world, with an emphasis on those made of wood.

SPECIAL EVENTS

Contact the Boise Convention and Visitors Bureau (800-635-5240) for information on the following.

January: Winter Carnival Week, Sun Valley.

February: Winter Carnival, McCall (about 100 miles north of Boise), nationally acclaimed week-long event with giant ice sculptures and races.

March: Drag racing season at Boise's Firebird Raceway.

May: Wednesday entertainment, food, and music at Alive After Five, The Grove, downtown pedestrian mall.

June: Idaho Shakespeare Festival through August, Boise. Boise River Festival, four-day event includes Nite-Lite Parade with lighted floats and music, Hot Air Balloon Rally, food, concert, fireworks finale, and Women's Challenge Bicycle Race. Old Time Fiddlers' Contest, third full week of June, Weiser, about ninety minutes west of Boise; call (800) 437-1280 for tickets.

July: Fourth celebrations throughout the city parks; Liberty Parade downtown in the evening and fireworks at the Fairgrounds at dusk.

August: Western Idaho Fair, Boise, ten-day event.

September: Julia Davis Park Art in the Park displays arts and crafts.

November: Festival of the Trees, Boise Convention Center, four- or five-day event; volunteers decorate then auction of trees, and sell crafts.

December: Fantasy of Lights, Holiday Lights Tour.

WHERE TO STAY

The Boise Visitors Guide has a lodging listing, including several bed-and-breakfast inns. Here are a few choices for families.

The Owyhee Plaza Hotel, 1109 Main Street; (208) 343-4611, (800) 821-7500—ID, or (800) 233-4611. The hotel has a convenient downtown location, one hundred guest rooms, plus a courtyard swimming pool. Airport shuttle is free.

Residence Inn Marriott, 1401 Lusk Avenue; (208) 344-1200 or (800) 333-3131. It has penthouses with a bedroom and bath on the second floor, a full kitchen, and complimentary breakfast buffet.

Red Lion Inn Downtowner, 1800 Fairview Avenue, and **Red Lion Inn Riverside,** 2900 Chinden Boulevard; (800) 547-8010. Both have outdoor pools, coffee shops, and laundry service.

Idaho Heritage Inn, 109 West Idaho; (208) 342-8066. This five-room bed and breakfast close to downtown offers complimentary newspapers, in-room breakfast, plus bicycles.

Families staying in **Sun Valley** might try the **Idaho Country Inn,** 134 Latigo Lane, Sun Valley 82340; (208) 762-1019. This log-and-rock lodge offers such modern amenities as a Jacuzzi and rooms with TVs and refrigerators.

WHERE TO EAT

The *Boise Visitors Guide* features a dining guide.

The **Brick Oven Beanery,** Eighth and Main Street on the Grove (208-342-3456), serves up roasted chicken and crusty bread. **Red Robin Burger and Spirits Emporium,** 267 North Milwaukee (208-323-0023), gets Boise's vote for the best burgers. There's also one on the lake at Park-Center, east on Beacon off Broadway; (208) 344-7471. Parents appreciate the children's menu and outdoor patio. For deep-dish pizza, pasta, sandwiches, and salads—kid pleasers, all—try **Chicago Connection Pizza,** at two locations: 7070 Fairview (208-377-5551) and 3931 Overland (208-344-6838). Sample the Basque cuisine at **Onati,** 3544 Chinden Boulevard (208-343-6464), where specialties include lamb and seafood dishes. For tasty lunches and yummy desserts, try **Cristina's Bakery & Coffee Bar,** corner of Fifth and Main streets; (208) 385-0133. Pastries, breads, and gourmet coffees are among the treats offered by this local favorite.

DAY TRIPS

In addition to the adventurous possibilities above, there are some shorter, tamer side trips, many of them accessible via the state-designated Scenic Byways. A popular swimming area with Boise residents is **Lucky Peak Reservoir,** 10 miles northeast on Highway 21 (208-344-0240), comprising Sandy Point, a swimming beach with lifeguards, located below the dam, and a picnicking and marina area. Continue on Highway 21 northeast to **Idaho City** (about 45 miles from Boise), a well-preserved gold rush town with many structures from the 1860s. Walk along the planked boardwalks that lead past the old jail where criminals carved their names on the wooden walls; Boise Basin Museum, with a collection of gold rush artifacts; an old schoolhouse; the Idaho World building; The Boise Basin Mercantile, the state's oldest general store; and other landmarks. Visit the Greater Idaho City Chamber of Commerce, 215 Montgomery Street, just off I–21, or call (208) 392–4290 for more information One-and-one-half miles away is **Warm Springs Resort,** where you can swim in geothermally heated pools.

The entire Boise Basin is surrounded by **Boise National Forest** (208–364–4100), encompassing more than 2½ million acres including 900 miles of hiking trails, the headwaters of the Boise and Payette rivers, ghost towns, and abandoned mines. Big game roam through large areas of the forest in the summer. Cross-country skiing and snowmobiling are popular winter activities.

FOR MORE INFORMATION

For Boise travel information: **Boise Convention & Visitors Bureau/Southwest Idaho Travel Association,** 168 North Ninth Street, Suite 200; (208) 344–7777 or (800) 635–5240; http://www.boisecub. org. Visit Idaho's Internet site: http://www.doc.state.id.us.

Emergency Numbers
Ambulance, fire, police: 911
Hospital: St. Luke's Regional Medical Center, 190 East Bannock, (208) 381–2222, twenty-four-hour emergency service
Twenty-four-hour pharmacy: The pharmacy in the twenty-four-hour **Albertson's Grocery Store** (208–344–8660), 1650 West State, has the latest hours in town (open until 10;00 P.M.)
Poison Control Hotline: (800) 860–0620

NORTHERN IDAHO'S PANHANDLE

Northern Idaho, or Idaho's "panhandle," is a region of dense forests, lakes, meadows, and mountains covered with huge cedar and fir trees—a green, pristine slice of "God's country." Coeur D'Alene, in the southern part of the panhandle about 16 miles from the Washington state border, is a major resort area. For thousands of years Schee-Chu-Umsh Indians called the territory in what became Idaho's northern panhandle their home. During the early nineteenth century, as French explorers and fur traders moved through the region, the tribe came to be knows as *Coeur d'Alêne,* French for "heart of an awl." Some speculate the Indians acquired this new name on account of their shrewd and tough trading practices. Later in the century prospectors found gold in the Coeur d'Alene Mountains. But the region earned its mark on the map with silver, a discovery that made Coeur d'Alene once the hub of one of the richest mining districts in the world.

Coeur d'Alene at present names a lake, a river, a mountain range, a mining district, a forest, and a city, and the area is regarded as the "Playground of the Northwest." Sixty lakes can be found within a 60-mile radius of the city, making the region a popular summer destination. Winter brings snowmobiling, skiing, and hundreds of miles of cross-country trails.

GETTING THERE

Coeur d'Alene is 35 miles east of Spokane, Washington, on I-90. Though Coeur d'Alene Airport at Hayden Lake provides service for small jets, most people find access more convenient through Spokane International, which is located approximately 45 minutes west of

Coeur d'Alene. Vans, taxis, rental cars, and shuttles are available from both airports. **Brooks Sea Plane Service** (208-664-2842 or 208-772-9059) offers seaplane service to Coeur d'Alene.

GETTING AROUND

Unless you plan on staying in one place, a car is a necessity, as there is no public transportation. **Dollar Rent A Car,** First and Sherman streets (208-664-0682), is located in Coeur d'Alene across from the Coeur d'Alene Resort. **OmniBus,** 2315 Monte Visa Drive, Coeur d'Alene (208-667-6664), runs group tour buses to northern Idaho attractions; it provides shuttles to and from the airports as well.

WHAT TO SEE AND DO

Coeur d'Alene

The major attraction is **Lake Coeur d'Alene,** a big, blue expanse stretching for 25 miles, covering 25,100 acres, and featuring 135 miles of shoreline. The **Coeur d'Alene Resort,** Second and Front (208-765-4000 or 800-826-2390), is the town's premier resort property. (See Where to Stay.) Kids like walking on the resort's 3,300-foot floating boardwalk, reputedly the world's largest. The path leads by the dock, restaurants, and boat, canoe, and kayak rental shops. A kid-pleaser is a tour of the lake. **Lake Coeur d'Alene Cruises,** Independence Road (208-765-4000), offers narrated one-hour tours of the lake.

Canoes, kayaks, paddleboats, and jet skis can be rented from the **City Dock** on Independence Point. **Coeur d'Alene City Park,** Lakeside Drive and First Street, has a public beach. This sandy area stretches west, joining the **North Idaho College Beach,** which offers views of the lake and the Spokane River. Along these sandy shores the Coeur d'Alene Native Americans used to camp and enjoy salmon bakes.

Tubbs Hill, Third Street and the Lake, Adjacent to the City Dock, provides a scenic lookout. A 136-acre city park on land homesteaded in 1882 by German immigrant Tony Tubbs, this undeveloped bit of shoreline in Coeur d'Alene has the **Tubbs Hill Historical Nature**

Walk, a 2-mile loop that affords scenic views of the lake. A trail guide is available from the Coeur d'Alene Parks Department, 221 South Fifth Street; (208) 769-2252.

Museums and Historic Sites

Though they are not major attractions, **Fort Sherman** and the **Museum of North Idaho** offer places to visit when your kids want something to do off the lake. Fort Sherman, North Idaho College Campus (208-664-3448), has two of Idaho's oldest structures. Construction on this frontier fort began in 1878. Built to maintain peace in this once remote, yet rapidly growing, region, Fort Sherman's mission was to help establish settlements, to watch the nearby Canadian border, and to protect railroad and telegraph crews. Only three of the fort's original fifty-two buildings remain intact. Walking tours lead through an ammunition depot, officer's quarters, and a chapel.

The Museum of North Idaho, 115 Northwest Boulevard (208-664-3448), open April 1 to October 31, exhibits items and life-styles from frontier life. A blacksmith shop, an old-time kitchen, logging equipment, mineral samples, and photographs of steamships, and mining and Indian culture are displayed.

Four miles north of Coeur d'Alene is **Farragut State Park,** 13400 East Ranger Road, Athol; (208-683-2425). During World War II this area served as the second largest naval training station in the world. Its 43-mile-long, 1,255-foot-deep Lake Pond Oreille was used for submarine testing. On the grounds today is a model airplane flying field, as well as a museum that relates the area's history.

OTHER ATTRACTIONS

Fourteen miles north of Coeur d'Alene is the **Silverwood Theme Park,** North 26225 Highway 95; (208-772-0515). Themed as a Victorian-era mining town, Silverwood offers train rides, carnival rides, an air show at selected times and days, and the Grizzly, the park's wooden roller coaster. Silverwood Theme Park is open daily June through September.

Idaho's oldest public building is the **Museum of the Sacred Heart;** (208-682-3814). Located 35 miles east of Coeur d'Alene at

---

Northern Idaho at a Glance

- The "Playground of the Northwest" with year-round sports

- 3,300-foot floating boardwalk at Lake Coeur d'Alene Resort

- Living-history demonstrations at Museum of the Sacred Heart

- Silver mining in Wallace

- Visitors Plus, (208) 664-3194

---

exit 39 off I-90, this structure was assembled without any nails. Craftspeople used only woven straw, adobe mud, and pegs to secure the foot-thick walls and ceiling. Check the schedule for the living-history demonstrations.

Go Kart Family Fun, West 3585 Seltice (208–667–3919), keeps your kids on the fast track. Near I-90, this amusement park offers go-carts, laser tag, miniature golf, bumper boats, and an arcade. For a more serene afternoon, take a hike on some of the area's trails.

Shopping

Twenty-eight miles east of Spokane, **Post Falls Factory Outlets,** exit 2 off I-90 (208–773–4555), is worth a stop. Merchants include Levi's Osh Kosh, London Fog, Fieldcrest, and Farberware. The sixty-store mall is open daily.

Downtown Coeur d'Alene encompasses more than 350 businesses. **Harvey's Coeur d'Alene Pendleton,** Sherman and Third, sells men's and women's apparel as well as Pendleton wool blankets. **Wiggett Mall and Marketplace** comprises 21,000 square feet of shops spread across four stories. Antiques, collectibles, artisan work, and jewelry are sold here. Even if you aren't buying, the ambience of creaking wood floors and the aromas of popcorn and coffee make window shopping an experience. **Journey's,** Fourth and Front, features a selection of Native American goods from forty cultures. Beads, baskets, pottery, moccasins, and jewelry are sold. Spark your child's imagination with the toys at the **Purple Dragon Toy Store.** This shop arranges its displays by age, and none of the items are run on batteries, only on children's creativity.

Coeur d'Alene also offers the **Plaza Shops,** 210 Sherman Avenue; (208) 664-1111. The prices at these jewelry and clothing shops reflect their association with the Coeur d'Alene Resort.

Kellogg and Wallace

East of Coeur d'Alene on I-90 are Kellogg and Wallace. **Kellogg** is best known for the **Silver Mountain** ski area; (208) 783-1111. With a 3.1-mile gondola trip, Silver Mountain bills itself as "the world's longest single cable ride." The area's two peaks, Kellogg and Wardner, reach 6,300 and 6,200 feet respectively. In summer and fall the gondola ride offers scenic vistas. On a clear day you can see Montana to the east and Canada to the north. Have little ones and others unnerved by the incline ride in the seats facing the mountain.

In winter Silver Mountain offers SKIwee classes for ages five to twelve. MINIrider is a program for seven- to twelve-year-olds who want to learn how to snowboard. Ages two through six can either play in day care, receive lessons, or combine both in the Minor's Camp.

About 50 miles from Coeur d'Alene, **Wallace,** the "Silver Capital of the World," is listed on the National Historic Register because some of its buildings are more than one hundred years old. Many feature their original cast-iron cornices, pilasters, and decorative glass. Just such features, as well as its mountain background, made Wallace the place where the movie *Dante's Peak* was shot. Remember the main street that is blasted apart by the volcano's force? That scene was shot in downtown Wallace.

During the nineteenth century Wallace served as a Panhandle hub of mining and railroading. **The Wallace District Mining Museum,** 509 Bank Street (208-753-7151), is housed in an old bakery. Displayed are mine lighting devices ranging from stearic candles and oil lamps to more modern electric lamps as well as other tools and artifacts.

A twenty-minute video, *North Idaho's Silver Legacy*, screened in the forty-person theater, shows the toil of mining.

One-half block west is the ticket office for the **Sierra Silver Mine Tour,** 420 Fifth Street; (208-752-5151). If you've never been underground in a mine, don a hard hat for this one-hour guided walking tour through a mine tunnel. The guide points out such early twentieth-century equipment as the Diamond Drill machine, which drills for a core sample, and the "slusher," which brings the rock out and dumps it. The best part is the blasting board demonstration. The guide explains how the five-hole burn method was employed to ignite the dynamite that blasted through these rock walls. Special effects create the flash and boom of the blast. Buy your tickets in town and take the trolley to and from the mine. A taped narration during the trip highlights mining history and talks about historic sites in town.

The **Northern Pacific Railroad Museum,** Sixth and Pine Street, Wallace (208-752-0111), focuses on the importance of railroads to this region. Most kids will find the static displays boring. The first floor re-creates the interior of a train station complete with ticket window, a telegrapher's desk, and heavy oak waiting benches. Upstairs exhibits depict the route of the North Coast Limited. The museum has a rare, 13-foot glass map of the Northern Pacific Railroad. Kids giggle at the early 1900s high tank flush toilet.

Avoid the **Oasis Rooms Bordello Museum,** 605 Cedar Street, Wallace; (208) 753-0801. The twenty- to thirty-minute guided tour through one of Wallace's most famous brothels simply features peeks at several 1950s tacky bedrooms. The gift shop downstairs, along with some revealing lingerie, has a collection of interesting books about strong women pioneers and trail-blazers in the west.

Dude Ranch

Hidden Creek Ranch, 7600 East Blue Lake Road, Harrison; (208) 689-3209 or (800) 446-DUDE. Bookings are also available through American Wilderness Experience; (800) 444-DUDE. The aroma of sage, cedar, and mint from the pipe ceremony made the night air smell sweet outside the tipi setup in a grassy meadow by a pond. A steady stream of whirling smoke spun skyward as the stars began to pop and glow in the northern Idaho night sky. Inside, the

Historic Treaty Rock in Post Falls. (Courtesy Coeur d'Alene Post Falls Convention and Visitors Bureau)

heated lava rocks took on the reds and oranges of a fiery sunset, and the drummer beat an ancient pattern as we called upon the four directions to carry our prayers and thoughts outward into the corners of our planet.

This sweat lodge is just part of what makes **Hidden Creek Ranch** special. In its brochure Hidden Creek indicates the ranch's commitment "to being one with nature ... In the spirit of this Native American philosophy, we help our guests to reconnect themselves with the earth and also to awaken their awareness for a means to save Mother Earth." There are also medicine trail hikes, sacred circle dances, yoga, and massages as well as trap shooting, fishing, and pontoon boat rides.

To an overlay of Native American philosophy and a core program of good riding instruction, Hidden Creek adds such cushy vacation accouterments as maid service, comfortable lodge rooms in modern log cabins, waiters, and an evening cocktail hour. This place is no rough-'n'-rustic, down-and-dirty ranch for wanna-be wranglers who think mud, dust, and discomfort get them closer to the real West. This dude ranch appeals to die-hard riders, sometime saddle bosses, absolute greenhorns, as well as those who want nothing more physically challenging than a rocking chair and a good book.

Hidden Creek is also a place for families. From mid-June through August, a kids' program operates for ages three through early teens. Preschoolers keep busy with storytelling, nature awareness walks, arts and crafts, visits to the petting corral, and pony rides. Ages six and older go out on kids' trail rides, and families play together at afternoon ropin' sessions, evening campfires, and hay wagon rides. The six-day program has a kids' overnight in Native American tipis. There are always cookies in the lodge cookie jar along with juice, tea, coffee, hot chocolate, and milk.

With a capacity of forty to fifty guests, including children, Hidden Creek is large enough to hire experienced wranglers and small enough to pay particular attention to its guests. But the key to fitting in here is to make sure your family feels at ease with the ranch rhythms, which sometimes require strict adherence to a predetermined schedule. Rules are emphasized, and that's good for maintaining safety requirements and smooth ranch operations, but sometimes the frequent reminders made us feel uncomfortable, as if somehow we were fifth graders who needed a hall pass and a mini-lecture instead of a family on a vacation—and we're not a rowdy bunch.

The riding instructor is very good. We won't soon forget head wrangler Elaine Mitchell's centered riding dictum that "the horse is the mirror of the rider." Elaine reminded us to think what our body language conveyed to the horse. Creating such awareness is the goal of centered riding. "This sensitivity to the horse allows for a true partnership," Mitchell states. "It enables you to become one with the horse instead of trying to dominate the horse."

With afternoon rides ending at 4:00 P.M. and dinner beginning promptly at 6:00 P.M., there was little time for napping or relaxing after a hard day on the trail. We often felt rushed. Billed as "gourmet," the food is average—except for the last night's seven-course dinner—and most of the meals offer little choice.

The typical program is six days. Depending on availability there may be stays as short as three days. The nearest major airport is Spokane, Washington, 40 miles west of Coeur d'Alene, Idaho, on I-90. From Coeur d'Alene, Hidden Creek Ranch is 30 miles south of I-90 along I-95.

SPECIAL EVENTS

May: American Heritage Days; Huck Finn River Fest.
July: Bayview Daze lighted boat show; Historic Skills Fair.
August: International Water Fight Competition; Festival of the Falls; Northern Idaho Fair and Rodeo.
September: Paul Bunyan Days.

WHERE TO STAY

Coeur d'Alene Resort, Second and Front (208-765-4000 or 800-826-2390), is the area's most well known and upscale property. Built in 1986, this 338-room hotel added upscale accommodations to a resort area previously dominated by quaint, yet charming, bed and breakfasts and the ubiquitous chain motels. The resort's facilities include two swimming pools, a fitness center, a spa, tennis courts, and a watersports center. An eighteen-hole golf course—with the world's only floating green—is shared with its adjacent sister resort. Both welcome families.

While there are more than a dozen cozy B&Bs in the area, few will permit children younger than twelve. **O'Neils Bed and Breakfast,** 1221 Coeur d'Alene Avenue (208-664-5356), has only a handful of rooms, but it is one of the few that welcomes children. Rooms are wall-papered with sheet music, and each comes with vinyl records and record players. The suite has a separate kitchen and sitting area with cable TV. There is a dog kennel beyond the house for pets.

In Hayden a family-friendly bed and breakfast inn is the **Clark House on Hayden Lake,** East 4550 South Hayden Lake Road; (208-772-3470 or (800) 765-4593). Among the more than a dozen camp-grounds is **Coeur d'Alene KOA Kampgrounds,** East 10700 Wolf

Lodge Bay Road; (208) 664-4471. Facilities include Kamping Kabins and Teepee, terraced sites, and separate tenting areas. There is a heated pool, a hot tub for adults, miniature golf, a playground, a game room, and bike rentals.

WHERE TO EAT

Visitors Plus+, the Coeur d'Alene Chamber of Commerce, provides a restaurant guide. Some suggestions include **Heathcliff,** 301 East Lakeside; (208-667-0269), a deli making soups, salads, hot and cold sandwiches, and desserts. Try their Grubsteak Chili, a one-hundred-year-old recipe passed down from Aunt Tillie, who moved into the region with her husband Gus in the 1800s. Another good sandwich shop is **Java,** 324 Sherman Avenue (208) 667-0010. It serves cereal, eggs, and baked goods for breakfast. Hot and cold sandwiches, soup, and pizza top its lunch menu. **Applebee's,** 280 West Appleway (208-762-1000), is open brunch through dinner. Signature items include Bourbon Street steak, low-fat veggie quesadilla, and blackened chicken salad. Hamburgers, sandwiches, and fajitas are also on the menu. **IHOP,** 2301 North Fourth Street (208-765-5032), **Pizza Hut,** 212 West Appleway (208-765-5032), and **Kentucky Fried Chicken,** 218 Appleway (208-664-3838), are among the fast-food standbys.

In Wallace you can rustle up some cheap, kid-pleasing fare at the **Pizza Factory,** Bank Street; (208) 753-9003. Along with pizzas you can get pasta, sandwiches, calzone, and kids' plates. Adjacent is **Mrs. Dean's Old-Fashioned Ice Cream Parlor.** Not only do children like the sundaes, but kids like sitting on the high stools. The **Historic Jameson Saloon,** Pine and Sixth streets (208-556-1554), looks like a turn-of-the-century western saloon, with its ceiling fans and brass-trimmed wooden banquettes. The moderately priced burgers, salads, chicken fingers, and pasta make this a good family pick.

DAY TRIPS

Spokane, 35 miles west of Coeur d'Alene, offers several family-friendly attractions. Many consider **Waterfront Park** to be the city's centerpiece. This one-hundred-acre tract of paths, cut through by the river, features amusement rides, mini-golf, an ice rink, and an IMAX theater. But the best known attraction in the park is the still operational **Looff Carousel,** a 1909 antique carousel with fifty-four hand-carved horses. The **Centennial Trail** follows the Spokane River from Riverside Park to Coeur d'Alene, Idaho.

Cheney Cowles Museum and Historic Campbell House, 2316 West First Avenue; (509) 456-3931. The museum displays exhibits concerning the development of the Northwest region and local Indian cultures. Changing shows include traditional and contemporary arts and historical and current issues exhibitions. Adjacent to the museum is the 1898 **Campbell House,** a National Register historic landmark. The beautifully restored house portrays the life-style of a mining tycoon during Spokane's Age of Elegance. The museum is open Tuesday through Saturday.

Don't miss **Cat Tales Zoological Training Center,** North 17020 Newport Highway, Mead; (509) 238-4126 or http:www.spokane.net/ cattales. On this four-acre preserve north of Spokane, paths weave through natural habitats dedicated to big cats. Residents include bobcats, Bengal tigers, leopards, panthers, and mountain lions. Arrive late in the afternoon just before feeding time to catch the educational demonstration and feeding time, when the cats are most active.

Manito Park & Gardens, 4 West Twenty-first Avenue (509-625-6622), is an enchanting urban landscape that comprises five major gardens. Duncan Garden is a formal garden, with roots dating back to ancient Egypt, Persia, and Rome. Annual plantings begin in May and peak from mid-July through early October. Rose Hill blooms with 1,500 roses. There are also beds of antique and miniature roses. Joel E. Ferris Perennial Garden displays perennials native to the Northwest. Spokane/ Nishinomiya Japanese Garden is a serene place, whose design is meant to soothe. Gaiser Conservatory couples tropical foliage with floral displays.

North of Spokane Highway 20, **Gardner Cave,** part of Crawford State Park (509-446-4065 or 800-562-0990), is the second largest limestone cave in Washington. The chambers were created about 70 million years ago, when rock collapsed as mountains were forming.

Walks through the stalagmites and stalactites are guided by park staff.

For more information contact the Spokane Convention and Visitors Bureau, 926 West Sprague Street 180, Spokane, WA 99204; (509) 624–1341; http://www.spokane-areacvb.org.

FOR MORE INFORMATION

Visitors Plus+, P.O. Box 850, Coeur d'Alene, 83816; (208) 664–3194

Kellogg Chamber of Commerce, 608 Bunker Avenue, Kellogg, 83837; (208) 784–0821

Post Falls Chamber of Commerce, 510 East Sixth, Post Falls, 83854; (208) 773–5016

Wallace Chamber of Commerce, P.O. Box 1167, Wallace, 83873; (208) 753–7151

Idaho's Internet site: http://www.doc.state.id.us.

Emergency Numbers

Police, fire, and medical emergencies: 911

Coeur d'Alene Police Department: (208) 769–2320

Coeur d'Alene Fire Department: (208) 765–1112.

Kootenai Medical Center: 2003 Lincoln Way, Coeur d'Alene; (208) 666–2000 or (208) 664–3000

BANFF

Banff, Canada's first National Park, is a breathtaking four-season resort in the heart of Alberta's Canadian Rockies. The town of Banff and the tiny village of Lake Louise, forty minutes west, are the park's civilized centers. Banff (the town) is surrounded by a ring of majestic mountains and exudes the atmosphere of a European resort—but don't be surprised to see an elk walking Banff Avenue. Beyond "civilization" is truly spectacular scenery: 2,564 square miles of varied terrain where wildlife roam free among towering peaks, lush forests, alpine valleys, rivers, glaciers, hot springs, and lakes, including Lake Louise, one of the region's most popular destinations. This splendid setting provides countless recreational opportunities for families, from winter skiing to fair-weather pursuits: boating, hiking, horseback riding, cycling, and more.

GETTING THERE

The nearest airport is **Calgary International;** (403) 292–8400. You can rent a car here or take a bus to the town of Banff, ninety minutes to the west. Lake Louise is forty minutes farther west.

Via Rail no longer serves Banff. **Rocky Mountaineer Railtours** (800-665-7245) runs two-day east and/or westbound rail tours between Vancouver, Banff, and Calgary from May to early October, with an overnight stay in Kamloops, British Columbia. Add-on hotel and sightseeing packages and car rentals in Banff can also be arranged.

Bus service is provided by the following companies. **Greyhound of Canada** (800-661-8747—Canada/800-332-1016—Alberta) serves Banff from various points in Canada, including Calgary. **Laidlaw Transportation** (403-762-9210), on the arrivals level of Calgary Airport, transports passengers anywhere in the park. **Brewster Transportation** (800-661-1152) also offers scheduled bus service from the airport to Banff and Lake Louise.

TransCanada Highway 1 from Calgary leads to Banff and Lake Louise. From Banff, Lake Louise also can be accessed by a slower but more scenic route, the Bow River Parkway, which runs parallel to Highway 1 on the other side of the river and has interpretive signs, scenic viewpoints, and picnic sites.

GETTING AROUND

If you're driving, a map is helpful within the park, since few of the drives connect directly to the TransCanada Highway. The town of Banff is located 10 miles inside the park's entrance. The Banff Information Center, 224 Banff Avenue (403-762-0270), shared by the Tourism Bureau and the Canadian Parks Department, is open daily year-round. A brochure titled *Banff and Vicinity Drives and Walks* lists drives and attractions, with maps indicating their locations.

WHAT TO SEE AND DO

How you spend your days will depend on whether you visit in summer or in winter, when the area becomes a skier's dream. Spring and fall (when the foliage is outstanding) offer some of the activities available to winter and summer visitors, at lower prices and with fewer crowds.

Note: Even in the middle of town, you may come within an arm's length of animals. Although some may appear tame, they are not, and the park urges visitors to keep their distance: Never feed them or get too close. Remember: Banff is not a game farm. During mating season the elk that stroll nearby can become quite territorial and aggressive. Park visitors are asked to report any aggressive animals to the warden's offices (see For More Information.)

Here are some sensational sights your family shouldn't miss.

Banff Area

Sulphur Mountain Gondola, open daily from December 26 to mid-November, south on Banff Avenue to Mountain Avenue, then 1½ miles to the gondola's lower terminal; (403) 762-2523. This is an eight-

Banff at a Glance

- Four-season resort in Alberta's Canadian Rockies

- Spectacular views from the Lake Louise Summer Mountain Lift

- Costumes, hunting equipment, and dioramas of Native American life at the Luxton Museum

- Top-notch skiing mid-November to late May

- Banff/Lake Louise Tourist Bureau, (403) 762-8421

minute journey aboard four-passenger, glass-enclosed gondolas to the mountain top, where observation decks offer spectacular views of Banff and the Bow Valley. For more views try the short, easy hiking trails along the mountain ridges. The Summit Restaurant has seating in the round, so all diners have a superb panorama. Breakfast and dinner specials are offered seasonally.

Cave and Basin National Historic Site, 311 Cave Street; (403) 761-1566. The discovery of natural hot springs here in 1883 led to the creation o Canada's first National Park two years later to preserve the springs and encourage visitors. You step through a tunnel to see the cave's hot springs and bathhouse, though the sulphur smell (reminiscent of rotten eggs) may be too strong for some kids. The site shows videos and exhibits year-round that tell the story of the discovery. Take a short, self-guided or guided interpretive walk (free) along the boardwalk on the hillside above the site.

Another boardwalk follows a marsh trail, which shows how the heated mineral water from the hillside has resulted in lush vegetation. Telescopes and benches are provided along the way along with interpretive signs. Because of lack of funding, the warm outdoor mineral-water swimming pool may not be open.

Up the hill, less than a mile west on Mountain Avenue (next to Sulphur Mountain Gondola), **Upper Hot Springs** offers an outdoor soaking pool of hot water that bubbles up from Sulphur Mountain. Once considered therapeutic, the waters are now appreciated for their relaxing effect. Children ages three and up are allowed, but the temperature (about 104 degrees) the strong sulphur smell, and the twenty-minute-maximum stay may annoy most kids. You can rent bathing suits and towels for a small fee. Massages are also offered by appointment only; call (403) 762-1515 for information. The pool is open all year (though closed periodically for maintenance); skiers find the waters soothing for their sore limbs.

Buffalo Paddock, 0.6 miles west of the Banff interchange, just off the TransCanada Highway, is a free drive-through enclosure open between May and October. Visit in the morning or evening for the best chance to see a small herd of bison.

Lake Louise

This turquoise lake edged by Whitehorn Mountain is truly stunning. Stop by the Lake Louise Information Centre, Samson Mall, (403) 522-3833, for tourist information. The new, architecturally striking building shows a multimedia presentation, *The Building of the Canadian Rockies,* and has exhibits on the area's natural and human history.

The Château Lake Louise Resort, the only resort on the lake, hugs the lake's eastern shore. Canoes can be rented at the boathouse on the left side of the resort; call (403) 522-3511. A popular stroll (best for kids because it's level) starts in front of the château and follows the lake's northwest shore for about 1½ miles. You walk below the high cliffs at the far end of the lake, where rock climbers can often be observed. At the muddy delta, just beyond the cliffs, the paved walk ends—and this is where families with young children will want to stop. Hardy, fit families accustomed to hiking may turn this stroll into a day trip by continuing on the somewhat strenuous trail (now called the Plain of the Six Glaciers), which climbs about 2½ miles over a rocky creek, gravel fields, and, ultimately, to icy glaciers. Mountain goats can often be seen on the slopes of the glaciated peaks surrounding the area. You'll end up at the rustic **Plains of the Six Glaciers** teahouse, where beverages, light lunches, and snacks are served during the summer. Prices are a bit steep because food is brought in via helicopter or packhorses.

If all this sounds like too much work, consider taking the **Lake Louise Summer Mountain Lift,** a twenty-minute ride atop White-horn Mountain. The lift is located across the valley from the Château Lake Louise resort. Although there are open-air chairs, families can take an enclosed gondola car or a covered "bubble" chair. Bring a picnic lunch to eat on the mountain slopes. Call (403) 522-3555 for information; open June to September.

Museums

The following museums, all in the town of Banff, are worth a visit.

Banff Park Museum, 92 Banff Avenue (403-762-1558), houses a taxidermy collection of animals, from birds to grizzly bears, indigenous to the park. Built in 1903, this is the oldest natural history museum in Canada, and the building, an unusual type of architecture known as "railroad pagoda," is a Canadian Historic Site. Admission is free; open year-round.

Banff Natural History Museum, Clock Tower Mall; (403) 762-4747. The museum displays the geological evolution of the Rockies via dioramas, models, fossils, and a twenty-minute audiovisual show on the eruption of Mt. St. Helens. It's open year-round.

The Whyte Museum of the Canadian Rockies, 111 Bear Street; (403) 762-2291. Everything in the museum portrays the cultural heritage of the Canadian Rockies. The art gallery has changing exhibits that feature historical paintings as well as modern sculpture, and the heritage gallery displays changing artifacts and photos. Summer programs for children and families are frequently offered. It is open daily in the summer, with abbreviated winter hours.

Luxton Museum, 1 Birch Ave., (403) 762-2388. Kids enjoy the exhibits here, honoring the heritage of the Indians of the Northern Plains and Canadian Rockies. Displays include costumes, hunting equipment, and dioramas of native and pioneer life. The building that houses the museum is an old fortlike structure overlooking the Bow River. The museum is operated by the Buffalo Nations Cultural Society, representing Stoney, Blackfoot, Blood, Sarcee, and Peigan tribes. It's open daily year-round.

Interpretive programs, utilizing slides, nature talks and strolls, and dramatizations are offered from late June to early September. Pro-

The opulent Banff Springs Hotel is one of many first-class accommodations in this exciting area. (Courtesy Alberta Economic Development and Tourism)

grams are usually held nightly at the theater at the **Banff Visitors Center,** and on weekends at some of the campgrounds, including Lake Louise, Tunnel Mountain, and Johnson Canyon. Although there are no programs especially for children, topics are chosen to appeal to the widest variety of ages, and, if there are many children in the audience, the program will be aimed at them. Check the posted program schedules at campground kiosks, or at the Canadian Parks Service Visitors Centre, 224 Banff Avenue (403-762-1550), and at the Lake Louise Visitor Reception Centre, Samson Mall (403-522-3833).

Adventures

Here are some ways for active families to enjoy the best that Banff has to offer.

Boating: **Lake Minnewonka,** about 15 miles northeast of the town of Banff, off the TransCanada Highway, is the park's largest lake and the only one on which power boats are allowed. You can rent 16-

foot boats with outboard motors from mid-May to Labor Day from Lake Minnewonka Tours (their office is on the dock) or take one of their guided tours to the end of the lake; (403) 762-3473. They also provide fishing licenses, which are required in the park, and fishing equipment rentals. The lake, noted for its trout, splake, and Rocky Mountain whitefish, is the park's most popular fishing spot.

Cycling: The Banff Visitors Centre has a list of rental shops and a trail-bike pamphlet. Beware of traffic and wildlife while you ride. Because of the bike's speed and relatively quiet approach (compared with hikers), trail cyclists are vulnerable to sudden bear encounters. So make noise; put bear bells on your pedaling shoes.

Dogsled Racing: The season runs from about November 1 to April 1. Experienced mushers pick you up at the Banff Springs Hotel; afterwards, you're welcome to take photos and visit with the friendly Siberian Huskies. Two adults fit comfortably in the sleds, plus a child or two, depending on size (babies are welcome). Reserve at least several days in advance from Mountain Mushers Dog Sled Company, P.O. Box 1721, Banff T0L 0C0; (403) 762-3647.

Horseback Riding: There are several stables and outfitters in the area. **Warner Guiding and Outfitting Ltd.,** 132 Banff Avenue (office above Trail Rider store), has trail rides that run from one hour to a full day, generally from mid-April to mid-November; (403) 762-4551. While no strict age limits apply, nine years is the recommended age for the backcountry trips that operate from July 1 to the end of September. These range up to six days; but a good ride with children is the 10-mile route along Bow River to Sundance Lodge on Brewster Creek for a two-day stay.

The **Brewster Lake Louise Stables,** located to the right of the Château Lake Louise (403-762-5454), specializes in guided half-day trail rides around the lake and up to the **Plain of Six Glaciers** or all-day trips farther afield. There is no strict age limit; a small child may be allowed to ride with a parent. During the winter horse-drawn sleigh rides follow the lakeside trail.

River Rafting: **Rocky Mountain Raft Tours** offers float trips along the Bow River (follow Wolf Street to the river). Trips are either one or three hours in length; children's rates are available; no age minimum, but use common sense. Inquire about whether the trip is a float or white-water journey. Call (403) 762-3632.

SKIING

Ski season generally operated from mid-November to late May. There are three resorts within the park, linked with one interchangeable ski/shuttle bus pass, available from **Ski Banff/Lake Louise,** Box 1085, Banff; (403) 762-4561 or (800) 661-1431—western Canada. The company also offers vacation packages and other ski services. For extreme skiers, heli-skiing trips are coordinated by **R.K. Heli-Ski Panorama** (800-661-6060). A note of caution: This type of excursion can be dangerous and may not be appropriate for children.

Banff Mount Norquay (403-762-4421), ten minutes northwest of downtown Banff, is the closest major ski resort to town. It is also the region's oldest. Famous for its beginner and expert terrain, the resort also has intermediate runs. Twenty-five groomed trails are currently offered. Norquay also features night skiing and a snowboard park. The visitor's service complex has a restaurant/lounge, cafeteria, day-care services for ages nineteen months to six years (two-hour minimum; ski lessons available, if desired), ski rentals, and retail shops. Ages six to twelve can take two-hour lessons (lunch not included). The three-day Camp Adventures couple the same instructor and kids daily. Snowboarding group camps are also offered.

Lake Louise; (403) 256-8473 or (800) 258-SNOW—Alberta, September to April (800) 567-6262—Western Canada/Pacific Northwest, October to April. This ski area is 35 miles west of Banff and 115 miles west of Calgary. Situated in Banff National Park, it offers four distinct mountain faces and a variety of runs that range from gentle novice—green runs are accessible from every lift—to challenging expert terrain. There are 1,500-foot black-diamond descents. Destination skiers are also drawn to Lake Louise for its small-town hospitality and big-city elegance. Saturn Play Station, a fully-licensed program, offers day care for infants eighteen days to eighteen months and toddlers nineteen months to six years, either hourly (minimum three hours) or daily. Older kids can attend half- or full-day programs. Ages three to six have supervised indoor and outdoor play. Ages seven to twelve can take a Kids Ski program.

Sunshine Village; (403) 762-6500. For one thing, Sunshine Village has the only ski-in—ski-out accommodations in the Banff National Park. You get to the Sunshine Inn; (800) 372-9583—Alberta/(800) 372-

9583—Canada/(800) 661-1363—U.S. Sunshine receives more than 30 feet of snow per year, enough to keep the runs going with 100 percent natural snow. More than half the terrain of Sunshine's three mountains is for intermediates. There is unrestricted glade skiing as well as double-black-diamond runs. For beginners there are treeless trails. The Sun-Rype Kids Kampus day care center is offered for ages nineteen months to six years. For three- to six-year-olds, there is the Day Care Ski and Play. Young Devils features six levels of classes for kids six to twelve.

Whistler/Blackcomb (604-932-3928 or 800-944-7853) has repeatedly won acclaim from skiers. This dual ski area is big, to say the least. It offers more than 200 marked runs plus eight alpine bowls, and the longest season in North America. The area is also a hotspot for snowboarders, providing one of the most comprehensive programs of snowboarding instruction anywhere. There is also a Free Ski and Snowboard Tip Area set up at Blackcomb, enabling potential riders to meet the instructional staff and get free advice. For those who don't ski or for skiers who need a break, there is a movie theater, a bowling alley, a billiard hall, and an amusement arcade. For kids there is day care and programs.

Whistler expanded its Children's Learning Center, located at Olympic Station. The Ski Scamps children's programs can now accommodate 500 children. Ski and snowboard lessons are offered for several ability levels.

At Blackcomb kids' lessons start at age five. Also offered is the Junior Instruction Program, designed for kids ages fourteen to seventeen who want to become instructors.

Cross-country Skiing: There are thousands of beautiful trails within the park. A map available from the parks department for a nominal fee lists the trails and their difficulty.

Theater, Music, and the Arts

The **Banff Centre School for Fine Arts,** St. Julien Road (403-762-6100), is the site of year-round cultural events, including ballet, opera, jazz, dance, theater, and free recitals and concerts. It's also headquarters for the annual **Banff Festival of the Arts,** running from the end of May through the third week of August, with plays, dance, opera, concerts, visual-arts exhibitions, and more. For ticket information call the box office at (403) 762-6300.

Shopping

Cascade Plaza, 317 Banff Avenue and Wolf Street, offers upscale shops (Polo Ralph Lauren, Esprit, Timberland, Godiva Chocolates) as well as those that sell Canadian art and artifacts. There's a food court on the concourse level. The shops along **Banff Avenue** sell Canadian-made goods and souvenirs, British woolens, and Irish linens.

SPECIAL EVENTS

Annual events, fairs, and festivals include the following.

January: Banff/Lake Louise Winter Festival—ten days of ski races, skating parties, barn dances, and wine tastings; Ice Magic International Sculpture Competition and Exhibition—ice sculpture teams design magnificent creations, which are displayed through February.

February: Banff/Lake Louise Winter Festival.

April: Banff/Lake Louise Cowboy Jubilee—a tribute to Canada's western heritage.

June: Banff Television Festival, a conference of TV producers, writers, and actors who meet to sell TV shows, which are shown to the public for free.

July: Banff International Street Performers Festival, with clowns, musicians, jugglers, and fire eaters.

August: Buffalo Nation Days includes parade and native dancing.

September: Melissa's Mini-Marathon is a popular event.

November: Banff Festival of Films—a weekend of lectures, demonstrations, and adventure shows surrounding a festival of mountaineering films. Banff Springs Christmas Bazaar—this weekend kicks off a season of activities celebrating winter and the holidays with food, entertainment such as jugglers, buskers, and children's games, and arts and crafts shows. Santa Claus Parade.

WHERE TO STAY

An accommodations guide and a bed-and-breakfast directory are available from the **Banff/Lake Louise Tourist Bureau;** (403) 762-8421. The bureau can also give you information on the fifteen campgrounds within the park; three have electricity, and four have showers.

The bureau advises summer visitors, particularly those arriving on weekends, to make reservations at least one day in advance. There have been days, particularly in August, when every park lodging was filled by noon; visitors were sent to Calgary and Lake Louise.

Summit Vacations owns and operates the computerized central reservations for hotels in Banff, Lake Louise, and Jasper National Park; (403) 762-5561/(800) 661-1676/(800) 372-9593—Alberta. Despite the splendid winter skiing, summer (early June to early October) is the high season in Banff, with higher prices.

Banff

Families have excellent lodging options in Banff. Here are a few that are family-friendly.

Banff Springs, Spray Avenue; (403) 762-2211/(800) 441-1414—Canada/(800) 828-7447—U.S. This majestic Canadian Pacific hotel is elegant and opulent, a historic landmark styled after the baronial castles of Scotland. Even if you aren't staying here, come to see the sumptuous surroundings. On property are a twenty-seven hole golf course and a mini-golf course, fifty shops, tennis courts, a bowling alley, indoor and outdoor pools, and fourteen restaurants. A European-style spa was added in 1995. An enchanting Festival of Christmas starts in November and runs through January 1, with organized activities such as hayrides, skating parties, scavenger hunts, evening stories by the fire, and a nightly Lighting Ceremony.

Douglas Fir Resort, Tunnel Mountain Road; (800) 661-9267. The resort has one- and two-bedroom condos with full kitchens, perfect for families. The convenience store, coin laundry, and barbecues come in handy, too. So does the complex, with two indoor water slides, a children's pool, and a video games room (open to nonguests for a fee and free to guests). Ski packages are available in winter.

Lake Louise

Château Lake Louise is 2½ miles southeast off TransCanada Highway 1; (403) 522-3511/(800) 268-9411—Canada/(800) 828-7447—U.S. This large lakeside resort offers a pool, six restaurants, and a shopping arcade on site. Some suites are available. During ski season a supervised playroom is open for ages two and up.

Two other options are the **Rimrock Resort Hotel** in Banff (800–661–1587) and the **Post Hotel** (800–661–1586.) Rimrock features good cuisine, including a children's menu, a pool, an exercise facility, and good mountain views. It is also located next to the sulfur hot springs and the Banff gondola ride. Don't be fooled by the Post Hotel's age. Despite its fifty years, it offers whirlpool tubs, fireplaces, and lodge furnishings. Family-oriented movies are shown on weekends in its conference center.

Whistler/Blackcomb

The chic place to stay at Whistler/Blackcomb is the plush 342-room **Château Whistler.** Other walk-to-the lift properties include the **Delta,** the **Mountainside,** and the **Glacier,** all with kitchen units. For lodging reservations call 800–WHISTLER. These resorts are close to several family attractions. **Whistler Resort's Meadow Park Sports Center** has an indoor pool and a skating rink. At **Kids Kamp** near Blackcomb's Wizard Chair, kids can drive snowmobiles designed for small riders. There is also nighttime tobogganing at Blackcomb.

WHERE TO EAT

A helpful restaurant guide is available from the Banff/Lake Louise Tourist Bureau. You'll find a wide selection of restaurants in the town of Banff, including the ubiquitous **McDonald's,** 116 Banff Avenue (403–762–5232), which also serves pizza. **The Hard Rock Cafe** (403–760–2347), opened in late 1995, is a perpetual favorite. It is located downtown in Banff, and its menu lists the chain's typical meals of burgers, wings, and rock 'n' roll. **Lake Louise Station** (403–522–2386) displays vintage rail cars in a historic log station. **Frankie's Pizza & Pasta** (403–522–3791) serves the best pizza in the Canadian Rockies. **The Caboose,** CP Rail Station, Elk and Lynx streets, offers beef, seafood, and a self-service salad bar amidst railway memorabilia and a rustic decor. A children's menu is available.

Banff Grizzly House, 207 Banff Avenue (403–762–4055), specializes in steak and fondue, though there's also buffalo and rattlesnake on the menu. The kids love the atmosphere, complete with totem poles and Indian crafts. Dine outdoors, if you prefer.

DAY TRIPS

If you have older kids who don't mind a slow, winding car trip, venture out along the **Icefields Parkway** (Highway 93), 78 miles north of Lake Louise to the **Athabasca Glacier.** You see the highest, most rugged mountains in the Canadian Rockies, and you can spot moose, elk, goats, and sheep along the way. Twenty miles north of Lake Louise, stop at **Bow Summit,** the highest point on the parkway. A short access road leads to the **Bow Summit–Peyto Lake viewpoint area.** Peyto Lake, shaped like a grizzly bear, has a distinctive color, ranging from pale green to deep turquoise.

The Columbia Icefield, one of the largest accumulations of ice and snow south of the Arctic Circle, is on the boundary of Banff and Jasper National Parks. Continuous snow accumulations feed eight major glaciers, including the **Athabasca,** 4 miles long and located directly across from the **Columbia Icefield Visitors Center;** (403) 852-7030. The center has maps, brochures, and schedules for interpretive events, such as guided hikes and evening programs, given by park naturalists, as well as a scale model of the entire ice fields and an audiovisual presentation on the area.

Kids like the narrated tour of the icy slopes of the glacier aboard a specially designed Brewster "Snowcoach" bus. (Brewster also has round-trip tours from Banff or Lake Louise.) Passengers are allowed to step out onto the slippery glacier. Contact **Columbia Icefield Snowmobile Tours,** P.O. Box 1140, Banff T0L 0C0; (403) 762-6735. Tours are available May 1 to October 10. Children's rates apply for ages six to fifteen; under age six free when sharing a seat with an adult. Reservations aren't required; the busiest time at the ice field is from 11:00 A.M. to 3:00 P.M.

FOR MORE INFORMATION

Banff/Lake Louise Tourism Bureau: 224 Banff Avenue, Banff; (403) 762-8421; http://www.cuug.ab.ca: 8001/VT/banff-town.html; http://www.worldwebcom/parkscanada.banff/parks.htm.
Canadian Parks Service: (403) 762-1500

Visitor Reception Center: Samson Mall; (403) 522-3833
Each center is open seven days, year-round.

The park trails and other facilities are constantly being upgraded to be accessible to the physically challenged. Contact the Tourism Bureau for more information.

Emergency Numbers

Ambulance, fire, police: (403) 762-2000

Lake Louise Fire: (403) 522-2000

Police: Royal Canadian Mounted Police; (403) 762-2226

Warden: To report an aggressive animal, call the Banff Wardens Office (403-762-4506) or the Lake Louise Warden Office (closed Wednesday and Thursday) at (403) 522-2000.

Hospitals: Banff's Mineral Springs Hospital, 301 Lynx Street (403-762-2222); **Lake Louise Medical Clinic,** 200 Hector (403-522-2184)

Pharmacy: Cascade Plaza Drug, Cascade Plaza, Banff Avenue at Wolf; (403) 762-2245. There are no twenty-four-hour pharmacies.

CALGARY

Set in the lovely rolling foothills of the magnificent Canadian Rockies, Calgary achieved international attention when it hosted the 1988 Winter Olympics. Originally an outpost of the North West Mounted Police, the city became a mecca for "Cattle Kings" who built mansions and sprawling ranches when the transcontinental railway reached town in 1892. Later, Calgary thrived as an oil boomtown. Although still one of Canada's major oil centers with a population nearing 770,000 and a downtown sparkling with shiny skyscrapers, the city has managed to retain a small-town feeling. That friendly, Old West atmosphere comes alive during Stampede Week in July, when everyone dons western gear for a "rip roarin'" good time.

The feeling also extends to kids. In mid 1993, Calgary proclaimed itself "child-friendly" and is encouraging businesses to create places for children to play while parents shop, to provide adequate rest rooms, and, in restaurants, to offer more toddler seating and to provide crayons and paper. An advisory committee of kids ages seven to seventeen meet regularly with city administrators to discuss issues concerning the younger set.

GETTING THERE

Calgary International Airport (403-292-8477) is about 3 miles (twenty-minute drive) from the city center. The **Airporter Bus** (403-531-3907) is the most efficient way to get to town. Car rentals and taxi service are available.

VIA Rail no longer serves Calgary. **Greyhound,** 850 Sixteenth Street S.W. (403-265-9111), provides frequent service throughout Canada.

By car, Calgary is on the TransCanada Highway (Route 1), which runs from coast to coast, and on Highway 2 from the border. **Rocky Mountaineer Railtours** (800-665-7245) offers a two-day rail trip through the Rockies from Calgary to Vancouver.

GETTING AROUND

Calgary is divided into quadrants, with Centre Street providing the east-west dividing line, and the Bow River and adjacent Memorial Drive dividing north from south.

Calgary Transit (403-262-1000) operates an excellent public bus and light rail transit (LRT) system known as C-train. Travel within the downtown core (between City Hall and Tenth Street S.W.) is free. Maps and information are available at the Calgary Transit information center, 270 Seventh Avenue S.W. The C-train and most buses are wheelchair accessible.

WHAT TO SEE AND DO

Museums

The **Calgary Science Centre,** 701 Eleventh Street S.W. (403-221-3700), has interactive exhibits in the large Discovery Hall. Activities there usually complement a current, traveling exhibit; for example, a recent one, Marine Monsters, featured robotic sea creatures. A series of mystery plays (such as Agatha Christie's *Murder in the Vicarage)* are held in the facility's Pleiades Mystery Theatre throughout the year.

The **Calgary Chinese Cultural Centre,** 197 First Street S.W.; (403) 262-5071. This facility, by the Bow River in the heart of downtown, is quite an eyeful. The impressive six-story Great Cultural Hall was modeled after the Temple of Heaven in Beijing, which took more than 100,000 man-hours to build. Twenty-two artists from mainland China contributed the hand-painted, gold-foiled paintings on the dome. Supported by four columns representing the four seasons, the dome boasts 561 dragons and forty phoenixes. The museum contains a number of paintings and artifacts from various dynasties, including a full-scale replica of terra cotta soldiers from the First Dynasty and a pot filled with water that, when rubbed with two hands, gives the illusion that the water is dancing. Special concerts and events are fre-

---

Calgary at a Glance

- Sophisticated downtown with small-town feel

- "Child-friendly" shops and restaurants

- Calgary Stampede in July

- Interactive displays at the Energeum

- Calgary Convention and Visitors Bureau, (403) 263–8510 or (800) 661–1678

---

quently held in the auditorium. In addition to the arts-and-crafts shop with goods from mainland China, there is a restaurant, an herb shop, and a snack shop.

Energeum, 640 Fifth Avenue S.W.; (403) 297–4293. Run by the Energy Resources Conservation Board, this free museum devoted to fossil fuel is small but surprisingly interesting. Watch the big-screen video on Alberta's first oil discovery; then try some computer games and interactive displays—including a chance to put your gloved hand into some "black gold." Be sure to see the pink 1958 limited edition Buick in the memorabilia display; it's a beauty.

At **Fort Calgary Historic Park,** 750 Ninth Avenue S.E. (403–290–1875), experience Calgary's history firsthand. Located at the confluence of the Boy and Elbow rivers, at the site of the 1875 North West Mounted Police post, the forty-acre park is within walking distance of downtown. First stop: the interpretive center to see a fifteen-minute video on the area's history that emphasizes the Mounted Police. Next: the Discovery Room where kids (and adults) can, among other things, try on Mounted Police uniforms and have their picture taken next to a stuffed bison. The permanent exhibit room features life-size recreations of important figures from Calgary's past. Step outdoors to enjoy the beautiful surroundings. A short, paved trail leads to the site of the fort, which is being reconstructed. Currently, the northwest corner of the fort has been completed, and in the next few years, the entire fort should be rebuilt. The adjacent 1906 Deane

House, 806 Ninth Avenue S.E. (403–269–7747), serves as a restaurant, offering lunch, afternoon tea, and Murder Mystery dinner theater. The house was built in 1906 for the Mounties' Commanding Officer, Captain R.B. Deane, and is operated as part of the park. The building beside the Deane House is the oldest (1876) in Calgary that is still on its original site. At press time, this house was being restored and will open to the public.

The largest museum in western Canada, **the Glenbow Museum,** 130 Ninth Avenue S.E. (403–268–4100), focuses on the area's settlement and its native peoples. There seems to be something for everyone, including lots of colorful "stuff" that should appeal to kids: Eskimo and Inuit art and artifacts, a Blackfoot tepee, a mineral exhibit, modern art and sculpture, military artifacts that include armor, a large gun collection considered one of the country's best, stamps, coins, and a collection of carriages. Some exhibits incorporate interactive displays. This museum also hosts major traveling exhibits, so check to see what's currently on display.

Heritage Park Historical Village, 1900 Heritage Drive S.W. at Fourteenth Street; (403) 259–1900. This sixty-six-acre park presents life in western Canada prior to 1914. The original buildings were moved here from various locations throughout Alberta. Hop aboard the old steam train that travels throughout the village. Visit a Hudson Bay Company Fort, a one-room schoolhouse, an oil rig, a bakery, an ice-cream parlor, and a working grain mill. Try your luck at the antique midway. The village is on the edge of the Glenmore Reservoir, and for an extra fee you can take a sternwheeler cruise aboard the S.S. *Moyie.* Inquire about the variety of family programs throughout the year. Free breakfast with admission during summer.

Other Attractions

Calaway Park, 6 miles west of Calgary on the TransCanada Highway and Springbank Road; (403) 240–3824. This is western Canada's largest amusement park. Enjoy the rides, a petting farm, mazes, miniature golf, fishing, a driving range, live entertainment, cinema, shopping, and special events. Family passports are available. The park is open daily July and August and on weekends only in May, June, September, and October. There's also an RV park and campground; for reservations call (403) 249–7372.

Calgary Stampede, 1410 Olympic Way S.E.; (403) 261–0101 or (800) 661–1260. This is the big one: Ten days in July of rip-roaring fun

Calgary's Winter Festival draws people from all over the world.
(Courtesy Calgary Convention and Visitors Bureau)

kicks off with a parade and features rodeo events, chuck-wagon races, concerts, shows, an amusement park, agricultural exhibitions, and more. Everybody dresses western style. Plan ahead for a visit: Attendance is more than one million.

Calgary Tower, 101 Ninth Avenue S.W.; (403) 266–7171. Take an elevator ride to the top of the 626-foot tower for spectacular views of prairies and the Rockies from the observation deck or revolving restaurant. On special occasions, the Calgary Olympic Flame that tops the tower is lit.

PARKS, GARDENS, AND ZOOS

Canada Olympic Park, Highway 1 West, 6 miles west of Calgary; (403) 247–5404. This impressive place is where the bobsled, luge, and ski-jumping competitions took place during the 1988 Olympics. Enjoy the guided bus tour open to the public during summer that goes to the top of the 90-meter Ski Jump Tower, the highest point in the city, and along the twisting Bobsleigh/Luge Track. Self-guided tours are also possible. Summer luge rides start from the bottom third of an iced track (for ages ten years and older). At the Olympic Hall of Fame, see displays, films, and videos and ride the Ski Jump and Bobsleigh Simulator. From November to April, the park offers downhill skiing and bobsleigh and luge rides.

Calgary Zoo, Botanical Gardens and Prehistoric Park, 1300 Zoo Road N.E., St. George's Island; (403) 232-9300 or (403) 232-9372 for recorded information. Accessible via a river walkway over the Bow River, this world-renowned facility houses some 1,500 animals who live in indoor and outdoor natural habitats. Popular attractions include the underwater viewing area for sea lions and seals, and the children's petting zoo.

The Aspen Woodlands (opened July 1993) is the first phase of a ten-year Canadian Wilds project to create five unique ecosystems of the Canadian wilds. The Canadian Rockies section is a simulation of high mountain habitats and their inhabitants. The Aspen Woodlands, a transitional habitat where the prairie meets mountains, is the most endangered in Canada. The zoo feels that by highlighting habitats close to home, visitors will become aware of the fragility of these areas. Using only plants and animals native to the area, the zoo has created four acres of rolling hills and valleys filled with wildflowers and aspen. White-tail deer, mule deer, and (in the coming months) elk, graze in the meadows. Native birds fly freely in the aviary.

Explore a human-size magpie nest, travel through a tunnel to view elk from a special blind, and walk through a fox's den to get a peek at these creatures. The colorful graphics appeal to kids. Docents are available to answer questions.

Dinosaur fans delight at the twenty-seven life-size models in Prehistoric Park, an eight-acre area with lakes, badlands, and swamps. The Botanical Gardens, with thousands of plant species, provide a fragrant, relaxing refuge.

Devonian Gardens, Toronto Dominion Square, Seventh Avenue between Second and Third streets S.W.; (403) 268-3830. If the weather's bad, this 2.5-acre indoor park provides a welcome oasis with 16,000 tropical plants and 4,000 local plants, plus waterfalls, fountains, ponds, playgrounds, a reflecting pool, and occasional lunchtime entertainment. Stores and restaurants, located below the gardens, offer another fun refuge.

Olympic Plaza, corner of Macleod Trail and Seventh Avenue S.W (403-268-5203), was created for the medal presentations during the 1988 Winter Olympics. Now this plaza is an outdoor activity center, with skating in the winter and special events year-round. Note: You must bring your own skates; there are no rental facilities here.

Prince's Island Park, Third Street S.W. at the Bow River, is accessible by footbridges from either side of the river. Stop here and enjoy the surroundings, which includes a playground, fitness trails, and a snack bar.

Village Square Leisure Centre, 2623 Fifty-sixth Street N.E. (403-280-9714), Calgary's indoor waterpark attraction. There are five waterslides, a diving tank, kiddies' pool, concessions, and ice skating. Family admission is less than $20.

Theater, Music, and the Arts

The *Calgary Herald* and the *Calgary Sun* are good sources of information on local entertainment. There are also a number of free publications at newsstands, hotels, and other locations around town that list entertainment, including *Where Calgary, Downtown Calgary, CityScope, Vox* (a publication of the University of Calgary), and *Impact* (a health/fitness/life-style magazine).

Theater is alive and well in Calgary, and chances are you will find a play to appeal to the whole family. The Convention and Visitors Bureau can help arrange tickets, or call Ticket Master Alberta at (403) 270-6700. For the little ones, **StoryBook Theatre,** (403-291-2247) offers matinees at the Pumphouse Theatre, 2140 Pumphouse Avenue S.W.

Sports

The hottest team in town is the NHL **Calgary Flames** Hockey Club, (403-261-0475), skating from October to April at the Olympic Saddledome, 1410 Olympic Way S.E. For Flames tickets, call (403) 261-0455. The **Calgary Cannons** Baseball Club (403-284-1111), number one minor league affiliate of the American League Seattle Mariners, has seventy-two home games at Foothills Baseball Stadium, 2255 Crowchild Trail N.W., from April to September. For Cannons tickets, call (403) 270-6200. **Calgary Stampeders** Football Club (403-289-0205 or 800-667-FANS—Canada), a member of the professional Canadian Football League, kicks off at McMahon Stadium, 1817 Crowchild Trail, from July to November 30. For tickets call (403) 289-0258.

Race City Speedway, Sixty-eighth Street and 114 Avenue S.E. (403-264-6515), hosts stock and sports car, truck, motorcycle, and drag racing on three world-class paved tracks weekends from May to September.

Spruce Meadows, south on Macleod Trail, west on Highway 22X (403-254-3200), is a world-famous equestrian facility with three annual jumping tournaments (see Special Events). Visitors are welcome to tour the training facility.

Shopping

The **Eau Claire Market,** Second Avenue and Second Street, S.W., (403-264-6450), downtown on the Bow River, adjacent to Prince's Island Park, is a shopping and entertainment complex. It combines a fresh-food market, specialty retail shops, restaurants, and an IMAX Theater (403-263-IMAX) plus a cinema.

The downtown shopping core runs from First Avenue S.W. on the east to Eighth Street S.W. on the west. Shoppers are protected from the elements by an enclosed-walkway system of bridges at least 15 feet above grade level, known as "Plus 15s."

There are several shopping centers downtown; the largest is the **Toronto Dominion Square 1000,** 333 Seventh Avenue S.W. (403-221-0600 or 403-221-1368), which includes the Devonian Gardens (described earlier) and two anchor department stores: Eaton's and The Bay, plus about one hundred specialty shops.

SPECIAL EVENTS

Contact the Calgary Convention & Visitors Bureau for more information on the following events.

January: PlayRites Annual Festival of New Canadian Plays; Cowboy Festival.

February: Calgary Winter Festival.

March: Rodeo Royal, Stampede Park.

May: International Children's Festival; Lilac Festival.

June: The National equestrian event, Spruce Meadows; CariFest, a Caribbean festival.

July: Calgary Stampede; Calgary Folk Festival; Shakespeare in the Park (evenings); North American Invitational equestrian event, Spruce Meadows.

August: International Native Arts Festival; Alberta Dragon Boat Races; Afrikadey!, a festival of African arts and culture.

September: The Masters equestrian event, Spruce Meadows; Artwalk at various locations throughout town; Old-Time Fall Fair (CQ), Heritage Park: horse-pull competitions, entertainment, displays.

Mid-November—Mid-December weekends: Twelve Days of Christmas, Heritage Park.

December–January: Lions Club Christmas Lights Display, Confederation Park.

WHERE TO STAY

The CCVB offers an accommodations directory that includes several area guest ranches. If you're coming for the Stampede, reserve well in advance. The **Bed and Breakfast Association of Calgary,** Box 1462, Stn. M, Calgary T2P 2L6 (403–531–0065), handles forty rooms in Calgary and the surrounding area.

Several all-suite hotels are located downtown, including **Prince Royal Inn,** 618 Fifth Avenue S.W.; (403) 263–0520 or (800) 661–1592. This hotel has separate, fully equipped kitchens in studios and one- and two-bedroom units, plus offers complimentary continental breakfast and in-room coffee makers. Also on site is a restaurant and coin laundry.

The largest hotel in Calgary is also downtown: the luxurious **Westin Hotel,** 320 Fourth Avenue S.W. (403–266–1611 or 800–228–3000), which offers the Westin Kids Club amenities. These include child-friendly rooms, children's sport bottle or tippy cup upon check-in, as well as a safety kit with a nightlight, Band-Aids, and emergency phone numbers. Rooms feature bath toys and bath products for kids, and parents can request—at no charge—jogging strollers, potty seats, bicycle seats, and step stools. Restaurants and room service also feature children's menus. **Delta Bow Valley,** 209 Fourth Avenue, also features children's programs. Call (800) 877-1133.

A number of reasonably priced motor inns are located outside downtown. In the Northeast section: **Ambassador Motor Inn,** 802 Sixteenth Avenue N.E., (403) 279-2271 or (800) 661-1447—Canada. The Ambassador features family suites with kitchenettes, a restaurant, and an outdoor pool. In the Northwest section: the **Econo Lodge,** 10117 West Valley Road N.W.; (403) 188-4436 or (800) 424-4777. Here you will find family suites, a kids' playground, and an outdoor pool.

WHERE TO EAT

Contact the Calgary Convention & Visitors Bureau (CCVB) for dining information. There's no distinct local cuisine, but plenty of diversity. **Billy McIntyres** and **Buzzards** offer cowboy cuisine; **Treatio, Divino, Mescatero,** and **River Cafe** offer nouvelle cuisine in renovated buildings. **La Caille** offers casual dining. For steak dinners (jackets required for men), try **Hy's Calgary Steak House,** 316 Fourth Avenue S.W. (403-263-2222), where kids' meals are served. **Mother Tucker's,** 345 Tenth Avenue S.W. (403-262-5541), in an informal setting, serves prime rib and features a salad bar, fresh bread, homemade desserts, and a kids' menu.

DAY TRIPS

While it may not be Jurassic Park, the **Royal Tyrell Museum of Paleontology,** 80 miles northeast via Highway 9 in Drumheller (403-294-1992), should elicit some oohs and aahs, as it harbors the world's largest exhibit of complete dinosaur skeletons: thirty-five in all. Watch museum technicians prepare fossils, see a video, and stroll through a prehistoric garden, called a "palaeoconservatory," which houses more than one hundred species of tropical and subtropical plants that once grew in this area. Computer information terminals plus interactive games add to the fun.

Once in Drumheller, you're not far from **Reptile World,** 1222 Highway 9 South, Drumheller (403-823-8623), where among the 150 reptiles are some of the rarest in North America. Hands-on exhibits (do you dare hold a boa?).

The **Head-Smashed-In Buffalo Jump Interpretive Centre** (403–553–2731), 11 miles west of Highway 2 on Highway 85, Fort Macleod, ninety minutes south of Calgary, sounds gruesome, but it is quite an interesting attraction. Several levels of displays built into a cliff re-create the hunting techniques used by Native American tribes. For more than 6,000 years, Plains Indians hunted buffalo by driving them over this cliff to their death. Highly valued, the buffalo provided fresh meat, warmth, tools, and shelter. A film simulates the jump, and guided tours led by members of the Blackfoot Confederation are available. Browse the displays and Indian artifacts, and walk the trails located above and below the cliff. This site is considered the best-preserved buffalo jump site anywhere; it's a visit your family won't soon forget.

Banff and **Banff National Park** are 80 miles west of Calgary on TransCanada Highway 1. Though it's possible to do in a day, we advise setting aside several days for a visit (see Banff chapter).

FOR MORE INFORMATION

The **Calgary Convention & Visitors Bureau,** 237 Eighth Avenue S.E., Alberta T2G 0K8 (403–263–8510 or 800–661–1678), supplies helpful information. Year-round visitors centers are at Calgary Tower, 120 Ninth Avenue S.W. at Centre Street, and at Calgary International Airport, arrivals level. Calgary **Handi-Bus Association** (403–276–1212) provides service to the disabled. Internet: http://www.visitor.calgary.ab.ca.

Emergency Numbers
Ambulance, fire, police: 911
Poison Centre: (403) 670–1414
Hospital: Alberta Children's Hospital, 1820 Richmond Road, S.W.; (403) 229–7211
Twenty-four-hour pharmacy: Shoppers Drug Mart Chinook Centre, 1323 North 6455 Macleod Trail South; (403) 253–2424

EDMONTON

Alberta's cosmopolitan capital has its share of appealing attractions for vacationing families. For starters, there's the West Edmonton Mall, the world's largest, with everything from a wave pool to a roller coaster. But there's more to Edmonton than mall heaven. In summer, add bountiful festivals that offer days of merriment and culture. All year long enjoy the museums, concerts, cultural and sporting events, and the superb natural beauty that includes 8,500 acres of parkland stretching along the lush North Saskatchewan River valley that curves through the city. Don't forget the clean subway system, friendly people, and a fascinating heritage that started with the fur trade and includes a lively past as a Klondike boomtown.

GETTING THERE

A few years ago, all passenger-airline service was consolidated into one airport, Edmonton International Airport, 18 miles south of the city; (403) 890–8382. For shuttle information, contact Sky Shuttle at (403) 465–8515.

Via Rail offers transportation between Edmonton and other major Canadian cities. The station is downtown at 1004 104 Avenue; (403) 422–6032 or (800) 561–8630—Canada.

Greyhound Bus Lines has service from Edmonton to all points in Canada and the United States. The station is downtown at 10324 103 Street: (403) 421–4211. **Red Arrow Express,** 10014 104 Street (403–424–3339), provides motorcoach service between Edmonton, Red Deer, Calgary, and Fort McMurray.

The two major highways that run through Edmonton are the Yellowhead TransCanada Highway (#16), running east and west, and Highway 2, running north and south.

GETTING AROUND

The city street system is on a grid, with streets running north and south, and avenues running east and west. A series of downtown pedestrian walkways (pedways) offer easy access to shopping, hotels, and cultural facilities. Downtown parking information and maps are available at the **Edmonton Visitor Information Centres;** (403) 496-8400 or (800) 463-4667.

The city has both bus and light rail transit (LRT). The **Edmonton Transit Downtown Information Centre** is open weekdays at 100 A Street and Jasper Avenue, or call (403) 496-1611 daily for route and schedule information.

WHAT TO SEE AND DO

Museums and Historical Attractions

Alberta Legislature, 97 Avenue and 107 Street (403-427-7362), is the seat of the province's government. Older kids may enjoy the free guided tours given every half hour of this grand, ornate building, on which construction began in 1907. (When you get to the fifth floor, listen to what seems to be a torrential downpour: actually, it's the echo of the fountain five stories below.) The beautiful grounds—with flowers, fountains, and pools in summer and a skating rink in winter—make this an extremely pleasant place to linger.

Edmonton Space and Science Center, 11211 142 Street; (403) 452-9100 or (403) 451-7722 for recorded information. From the outside, this facility resembles a sleek, modernistic flying saucer, and inside are fascinating exhibits. Most kids head straight to the Challenger Centre, a simulator composed of a mission control and the space station Alpha 7, where kids transform themselves into astronauts. Call ahead to schedule a visit.

The Children's Discovery Land is located in the gallery of the museum. With Lego blocks, a walk-on piano, a jungle gym, and other hands-on activities, it's a good place for children ages two through eight. The Universe Gallery includes a piece of the moon on loan from NASA and a scale that measures what your weight would be on other

---

Edmonton at a Glance

- Superb natural beauty in a culture-rich town

- 33 miles of linked parks on the North Saskatchewan River

- West Edmonton Mall, the world's largest

- For youngsters, live insects in the Bug Room at the Provincial Museum of Alberta

- Visitor Information Centre, (403) 496–8400 or (800) 463–4667

---

planets, such as Pluto. In the rotunda, the audience participates in science demonstrations, and the IMAX theater has a four-story screen. The North Gallery houses the traveling exhibits. The Margaret Zeidler Theatre boasts the largest planetarium dome in Canada. More than 200 computer-controlled projectors, special effects, and a laser system combine with a powerful audio system to offer visitors unforgettable laser light music concerts, live plays, and planetarium shows. If the weather is clear, stop by the public observatory, where attendants show you how their four astronomical telescopes work. For snacks, stop by the Cafe Borealis.

Fort Edmonton Park, Whitemud and Fox drives; (403) 486–8787. Step back in time at this low-key historical theme park located on 158 acres on the south bank of the North Saskatchewan River and home to more than sixty period buildings. The fort is a replica of the 1846 home base of the Hudson's Bay Company fur trading industry. Costumed interpreters grade furs, repair a boat, and bake bread in an outdoor oven. Kid volunteers may get to assist. Three long streets transport visitors to different periods in the city's history. On 1885 Street, a small frontier town, take a horse-drawn wagon ride (small additional charge), browse in quaint shops, visit homesteaders on their farms, and see the blacksmith in action at his forge. On 1905 Street, the city appears as it did in the year it became the provincial capital. On 1920 Street, explore the brickyard and greenhouses, stop by the Ukrainian Bookstore, then have a soda at the old-time soda fountain. Daily special events and programs include visitor participation. A steam engine travels the length of the park (no additional charge). Pony rides are available for an extra fee. This pleasant park, without a lot of glitz, appeals to younger school-age kids. It's especially charming at Christmas when the park can be toured by horse-drawn sleigh or wagon (depending on the snow), and you can see the different street windows elaborately decorated for the Christmas Reflections program.

Combine a visit for Fort Edmonton Park with a stop at the **John Janzen Nature Centre,** at the southwest corner of Quesnell Bridge, adjacent to the park; (403) 496-2939. The place is noted for the displays of the small creatures that inhabit the river valley, such as salamanders, ant colonies, and garter snakes. There are 2.2 miles of marked nature trail. Free admission.

Old Strathcona Model and Toy Museum, 8603 104 Street (Highway 2 south); (403) 433-4512. This free museum is thought to be the only one of its kind—and it certainly is unusual. The more than 400 models on display are made entirely of paper. Included are castles and other historic sites and buildings, boats, planes, trains, space vehicles, dolls, birds, people, and animals. There's also an operating model railroad.

Telephone Historical Centre, 10437 83 Avenue; (403) 441-2077. Kids tend to like this hands-on facility, where they walk through a telephone cable and see an audiovisual show presented by a robot who interacts with the audience.

Provincial Museum of Alberta, 12845 102 Avenue; (403) 453-9100. Devoted to Alberta's human and natural history, this museum focuses on the Ice Age and boasts a gigantic mammoth skeleton. The Bug Room, which has live inhabitants, proved so popular that the temporary exhibit is now a permanent fixture. Preschoolers particularly enjoy the Discovery Room, where they can do lots of hands-on things, such as trying on animal costumes and learning about camouflage.

In September 1997, the museum will open the Canada Aboriginal Peoples Gallery, displaying one of North America's best exhibits of native artifacts.

Parks and Zoos

Muttart Conservatory, 9626 96A Street; (403) 496–8755. The four pyramid-shaped glass pavilions set along the river valley house more than 700 species of flowers, plants, and trees from tropical, arid, and temperate zones. In the show pavilion, displays change frequently. The Conservatory is open year-round—where else would you find bananas growing in January, especially in Canada? For a lovely view of downtown, stand by the reflecting pools at the base of the pyramids.

Valley Zoo, 134 Street and Buena Vista Road; (403) 496–6911. Spend several fun-filled hours at this seventy-acre zoological garden featuring more than 400 animals, including an African veldt and a bird of prey exhibit plus daily elephant and sea lion training demonstrations. The kid's section has a storybook theme. Other attractions include camel, paddleboat, and pony rides; a train; and merry-go-round.

The North Saskatchewan River valley runs through the center of town, providing acres of parkland—the longest stretch of urban parkland North America. There are 33 miles of hiking, biking, jogging, and groomed ski trails, plus golf courses, boat launching sites, picnic areas, nature walks, and skating areas located in a series of linked parks. At **Hawrelak Park,** beside Groat Road on the south side of the river, enjoy a lake stocked with trout, pedal boats, a playground, barbecue grills, and lots of room for kids to romp. Call the **Edmonton Parks and Recreation River Valley Outdoor Centre** (403–496–7275) for information on specific facilities and events within the park system. In summer take tots to the wading pools and older kids to the indoor and outdoor pools. Particularly popular: the Wave Pool at **Mill Woods Recreation Centre,** 7207 28 Avenue and 72 Street; (403) 496–2929.

Other Attractions

The West Edmonton Mall, 8770 170 Street (403–444–5200 or 800–661–8890), is more than just a mall, it's an attraction in itself, even for those who run from malls. With 5,200,000 square feet—the equivalent of forty-eight city blocks—this is the world's largest mall.

You can body surf, swim, suntan, or spin down a water slide at the world's largest indoor water park, located at the West Edmonton Mall. (Courtesy Edmonton Tourism)

There's just about everything for everybody: aviaries with exotic birds; an aquarium with shark tanks; a casino; bottle-nose dolphin shows; a Spanish galleon; an ice-skating rink covered by a glass dome; Deep Sea Adventure submarine rides; miniature golf; World Waterpark, complete with a giant wave pool; and Galaxyland (403–444–5300), the world's largest indoor amusement park, with more than twenty-five rides and attractions, including the world's largest indoor triple-loop roller coaster and a special children's area called Galaxy Kids. And, yes, there are scores and scores of stores as well—more than 800 stores and services, including seven major department stores; 210 women's fashion shops; thirty-five men's wear stores; thirty-two shoe shops; and many toy, souvenir, sports, book, and record stores.

Cruise or enjoy dinner on the North Saskatchewan River aboard the *Edmonton Queen Riverboat,* Rafter's Landing, across from the Convention Center; (403) 424–5015. The cruise lasts an hour and may be better suited to older children.

Theater, Music, and the Arts

For information on the arts, check the city's two daily newspapers, the *Edmonton Journal* and *Edmonton Sun,* or the monthly entertainment publications, *Where* and *Billy's Guide.* TicketMaster outlets (403-451-8000) located throughout the city handle tickets for most events. There are sixteen professional theater companies in town, including **Chinook Theatre,** 83 and 103 streets (403-448-9000), in the heart of historic Old Strathcona, with a variety of story theater, puppetry, music, adapted classics, and modern theater for young people. **The Citadel Theatre,** 9828 101 A Avenue (403-426-4811), offers world-class plays from September to May. The Northern Alberta International Children's Festival (see Special Events) takes place every May in suburban St. Albert. More family entertainment can be found at **The Stage Polaris,** 85 Avenue and 101 Street (403-432-9483), where shows for the very young are performed.

Sporting Events

Edmonton is home to three professional sports teams. The **Edmonton Oilers,** several times Stanley Cup Champions of the National Hockey League, play from October to April in the Edmonton Coliseum, 118 Avenue and 74 Street; tickets are available from TicketMaster. The **Edmonton Eskimos** are members of the Canadian Football League and play from June to November at Commonwealth Stadium, 111 Avenue and Stadium Road; (403) 448-3757. The **Edmonton Trappers,** members of the Pacific Coast League, play baseball from April to September at Telus Field, 96 Avenue and 102 Street. Tickets are available at the gate (403-429-2934), or through TicketMaster.

Arts

The **Edmonton Opera** (403-429-1000), **Edmonton Symphony Orchestra** (403-428-1414), and **Alberta Ballet Company** (403-424-3136) perform in the Northern Alberta Jubilee Auditorium, on the University of Alberta Campus, 87 Avenue and 114 Street (403-427-9622).

Shopping

If you find West Edmonton Mall (described earlier) too daunting, there are several more reasonably sized malls downtown (100 to 103 streets). **The Old Strathcona Historic Area,** extending around 82 Avenue (Whyte Avenue) and 104 Street, is a pleasant place to stroll and shop. Restored buildings in the area date back to 1891, the year the Calgary/ Edmonton railroad arrived. Browse at the trendy boutiques and year-round farmer's market (403-439-1844) that sells crafts and fresh vegetables.

SPECIAL EVENTS

Contact Edmonton Tourism for more information on the following annual festivals.

March: Northlands Farm and Ranch Show; Local Heroes International Screen Festival features films and workshops.

May: International Children's Festival, St. Albert Theatre, a five-day event with music, mime, puppetry, dance, and theater from around the world; Dream Speakers Festival, an international celebration of First Nations art and culture.

June–July: The Works: A Visual Arts Celebration covers the entire spectrum of visual, environmental, wearable, and even edible art; International Jazz City Festival.

July: International Street Performers Festival includes clowns, acrobats, mimes, magicians, and jugglers performing for ten days in more than 900 free shows downtown; Klondike Days, ten days of food, fun, music, costumes, old-time fair, international trade and cultural exhibits, the largest traveling midway.

August: Heritage Festival features music, dance, costumes, arts, and food from around the world; The Fringe, a nine-day theatrical event featuring seventeen theaters, three outdoor stages, and more than 1,200 performers; Folk Music Festival has more than sixty acts, eight stages, workshops, food, handicrafts, and music.

December 31: First Night Festival, more than seventy-five live performances of music, theater, visual arts, and a rooftop fireworks spectacular.

WHERE TO STAY

A lodging listing is available in the *Edmonton Visitors Guide*. For bed-and-breakfast selections, contact **AHHA (Affiliated Holiday Home Agencies, Inc.),** 10808 54 Avenue (404-436-0649), which can arrange stays in cities, towns, villages, farms, ranches, and resort areas. Here are some good hotel choices for families.

Fantasyland Hotel, West Edmonton Mall, 17700 87 Avenue; (403) 444-3000 or (800) 661-6454. Altogether, there are 355 guest rooms, with 158 theme rooms, including Igloo, Victorian Coach, Hollywood, Polynesian, and Arabian themes. Some, such as the Canadian Rail room, have particular appeal to families: The berths of the train cars are perfect for kids. With the giant mall/recreation center right at your doorstep, this could be a family fantasy come true.

The Crowne Plaza-Château Lacombe has been converted to the **Holiday Inn Crowne Plaza,** 101 Street at Bellamy Hill (403-428-6611 or 800-HOLIDAY) features La Ronde, the city's only revolving restaurant. The **Westin Hotel Edmonton,** 10135 100 Street, Edmonton, Alberta T5J 0N7 Canada (403-426-3636 or 800-228-3000), offers the new Westin Kids Club amenities. These include child-friendly rooms, children's sports bottle or tippy cup upon check-in, as well as a safety kit with a night-light, Band-Aids, and emergency phone numbers. Rooms feature bath toys and bath products for kids, and parents can request—at no charge—jogging strollers, potty seats, bicycle seats, and step stools. Restaurants and room service also feature children's menu.

WHERE TO EAT

Edmonton Visitors Guide has a short listing of restaurants, but with more than 2,000 eateries to choose from, it's hard to select a mere handful. Contact Edmonton Tourism; they often have free publications, such as *Where* and *Billy's Guide,* which list restaurants. Ethnic food, particularly Italian, is always a good bet with kids. Two to recommend: **The Old Spaghetti Factory,** 10220 103 Street (403-422-6088), and **Packrat Louie Kitchen and Bar,** 10335 83 Avenue (403-433-0123), which, in addition to pasta, serves pizza cooked in a wood-burning oven and offers a terrific dessert selection. For moderately priced breakfast, lunch, or dinner, search out a **Smitty's Family Restaurant,** where steaks, chicken, burgers, pancakes, and waffles are among the specialties. There's one at the West Edmonton Mall (403-444-1981) and ten other locations citywide. Any Boston Pizza location, such as 9308 34 Avenue (403-436-9086), is also a good bet to

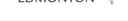

please the taste buds of any age. They serve more than pizza, and Edmonton is where the chain began.

DAY TRIPS

Reymonds-Alberta Museum, 4705 50 Avenue, Wetaskiwin; (403) 352-5855. Located about forty minutes south of Edmonton, this sprawling, sparkling museum is devoted to transportation, agriculture, and industry, and is also the home of Canada's Aircraft Hall of Fame. The museum evolved from the private collection of the Reynolds family, who had started a small local automobile service center in 1910. The exhibits and audiovisual displays of vintage bicycles, cars, aircraft, agricultural and industrial machinery—and their impact on life throughout the province—delight adults and kids alike, especially presented against such nostalgic backdrops as a 1920s grain elevator, a 1940s service station, and a 1950s drive-in theater. This is not a place where stationary artifacts from the past are revered in hushed silence. Instead, you can get behind the wheel of a Model T racer, take a place on a miniature moving assembly line in the car factory, or operate a "Gerber spout," a device that controls the distribution of grain into various bins in a grain elevator. Outdoors on the 156-acre grounds, the vintage machines come to life. Cars and bicycles cruise, farm equipment chugs, and aircraft fly overhead on a regular basis. Other items not to miss: The Aircraft Hall of Fame hangar and the Restoration/Conservation shop, where many of the vintage vehicles have been brought back to perfection. For snacks as well as lunch and dinner, the Galaxy Cafe offers meals and panoramic views. Be sure to ask about special events, live entertainment, and traveling displays.

Elk Island National Park is a nature preserve of unspoiled parkland located 28 miles east of Edmonton, just outside the town of Fort Saskatchewan, on Highway 16; (403) 992-6380. The park was created to save the area's elk from extinction. Today, within the park's fences, herds of elk, moose, and bison live undisturbed (along with hundreds of birds) and can be seen roaming free as you drive through the park. Yes, bison can be dangerous, but they should leave you alone unless provoked. Pick up a copy of *You Are in Bison Country* at the Park Information Centre, just off Highway 16, for safety tips. The center of "people activity" within the park is Lake Asotin, which has hiking trails, picnic areas, a nine-hole golf course, and cross-country skiing in the winter. Check the Asotin Interpretive Center (403-922-5790) for films and a schedule of daily activities.

About a half mile east on Highway 16 is the **Ukrainian Cultural Heritage Village,** Highway 16; (403) 662-3640. It tells the story of the Ukrainian immigrants and the development of their settlement in east central Alberta from 1892 to 1930. Costumed interpreters re-create a variety of historical characters. Tour farmsteads and the town site, whose historical buildings include a hardware store, and relax with a ride in a horsedrawn wagon.

Very young children love **Alberta Fairytale Grounds** (403-963-8161), 15 miles west on Highway 16, just west of the town of Stony Plain. The owner of this private park uses handcrafted puppets and fairytale scenes to delight the younger set as they follow a path through the woods. **Devonian Botanic Garden,** 3 miles north of Devon on Highway 60 (403-987-3055), is located within 190 acres of rolling sand dunes and large ponds. Nature trails and boardwalks make it possible to explore protected ecological areas and to bird-watch. Bring a picnic: Benches are located along the trails. There's also a Japanese garden, fragrant floral displays, and labeled native and introduced plants, as well as a pavilion of live butterflies.

FOR MORE INFORMATION

Edmonton Tourism has a **Visitor Information Centre,** open daily at Gateway Park (Highway 2), 2404 Calgary Trail Northbound S.W.; (403) 496-8400 or (800) 463-4667 to have a visitor's guide sent to you. An information center is located at City Hall and at the International Airport arrivals level; (403) 890-8382. Internet: http://www.ede.org.

DATS (Disabled Adult Transportation System) gives disabled visitors a temporary registration number. For further information or to register, call (403) 496-4570. To book transportation, call (403) 496-4567.

Emergency Numbers

Ambulance, fire, police: 911

Poison Center: (800) 332-1414

Children's hospital: Alberta Children's Hospital, 1820 Richmond Road, S.W. (403-229-7211), offers emergency services for children eighteen and younger.

Twenty-four-hour emergency room: Royal Alexandra Hospital, 10240 Kingsway Avenue; (403) 477-4111

Late-night pharmacy: Mid-Niter Drugs, 11408 Jasper Avenue; (403) 482-1171

INDEX

About the Author

Candyce H. Stapen is an expert on family travel. She appears on many television, cable, and radio shows, including *Good Morning America,* CBS *This Morning, Our Home,* WUSA-TV, D.C., and National Public Radio. A member of the Society of American Travel Writers as well as the Travel Journalists Guild, she writes several family travel columns on a regular basis, including columns for *FamilyFun, Vacations,* and the *Washington Times.* She is also the consulting travel editor for Family.Com.

Her articles about family travel appear in a variety of newspapers and magazines, including *Ladies' Home Journal, Family Circle, USA Weekend, Better Homes and Gardens, Family Travel Times,* the *New York Post,* the *Miami Herald, Caribbean Travel and Life, Florida Travel and Life,* and *Cruises and Tours.*

Other books by Stapen are *Great Family Vacations: Northeast* (Globe Pequot); *Great Family Vacations: South* (Globe Pequot); *Great Family Vacations: West* (Globe Pequot); *Family Adventure Guide: Virginia* (Globe Pequot); *Cruise Vacations with Kids* (Prima); and *Ski Vacations with Kids* (Prima).

Stapen lives in Washington, D.C., and travels whenever she can with her husband and two children.